# CPHIMS Review Guide

## Third Edition

Preparing for Success in Healthcare Information
and Management Systems

# CPHIMS Review Guide

## Third Edition

Preparing for Success in Healthcare Information and Management Systems

**CRC Press**
Taylor & Francis Group
Boca Raton   London   New York

CRC Press is an imprint of the
Taylor & Francis Group, an **informa** business

A PRODUCTIVITY PRESS BOOK

CRC Press
Taylor & Francis Group
6000 Broken Sound Parkway NW, Suite 300
Boca Raton, FL 33487-2742

© 2017 by the Healthcare Information and Management Systems Society.
CRC Press is an imprint of Taylor & Francis Group, an Informa business

No claim to original U.S. Government works

Printed on acid-free paper
Version Date: 20160603

International Standard Book Number-13: 978-1-4987-7245-7 (Paperback)

**Library of Congress Cataloging-in-Publication Data**

Names: Healthcare Information and Management Systems Society, issuing body.
Title: CPHIMS review guide : preparing for success in healthcare information
and management systems / HIMSS.
Other titles: Preparing for success in healthcare information and management
systems | Certified Professional in Healthcare Information and Management
Systems review guide | Preparing for success in healthcare information and
management systems
Description: Third edition. | Boca Raton : Taylor & Francis, 2017. | Preceded
by Preparing for success in healthcare information and management systems
: the CPHIMS review guide. 2nd ed. c2013. | Includes bibliographical
references and index.
Identifiers: LCCN 2016023661 | ISBN 9781498772457 (pbk. : alk. paper)
Subjects: | MESH: Management Information Systems | Systems Analysis | Health
Services Administration | Medical Informatics
Classification: LCC RA971.6 | NLM W 26.5 | DDC 610.285--dc23
LC record available at https://lccn.loc.gov/2016023661

**Visit the Taylor & Francis Web site at**
**http://www.taylorandfrancis.com**

**and the CRC Press Web site at**
**http://www.crcpress.com**

# Contents

**Acknowledgments** ................................................................................ xiii

**Preface**.................................................................................................... xv

**Editor**.................................................................................................... xix

**SECTION I  GENERAL**

**1  The Healthcare Environment**............................................................. 3
Learning Objectives ................................................................................. 3
Introduction.............................................................................................. 3
Healthcare Organizations ........................................................................ 4
   Hospitals ............................................................................................. 5
   Outpatient or Ambulatory Care ........................................................ 8
   Community Health Organizations ..................................................... 8
   Diagnostic and Pharmaceutical Services ......................................... 9
   Healthcare Payers .............................................................................. 9
Interrelations within and across Healthcare Organizations...................11
   Enabling Access to Comprehensive Care Services...........................11
   Assuring Effective Transfers of Care.................................................11
   Ensuring the General Portability of Care ........................................ 12
   Reporting Public and Population Health Information ..................... 12
   Obtaining Appropriate Reimbursement for Quality Care............... 13
   Supporting Particular Organizational Models of Care .................... 13
Roles and Responsibilities of Healthcare Information and Management
Systems Professions................................................................................14
Roles of Government, Regulatory, Professional, and Accreditation
Agencies in Healthcare ..........................................................................16
   Government........................................................................................16
   Healthcare Regulators .......................................................................17
   Professional Associations ..................................................................17
   Accreditation Organizations............................................................. 18
Summary ................................................................................................ 20
References .............................................................................................. 21

**2  The Technology Environment**........................................................ **25**
   Learning Objectives ........................................................... 25
   Introduction...................................................................... 25
   Hardware in Healthcare IT................................................ 26
      Technology Infrastructure.......................................... 26
      Servers...................................................................... 26
      Data Storage ............................................................. 27
      Mobile Devices.......................................................... 27
      Medical Devices ........................................................ 28
   Networks in Healthcare IT ................................................ 29
      Network Infrastructure .............................................. 29
      Communications........................................................ 30
   Software in Healthcare IT.................................................. 30
      Clinical Applications ................................................. 30
      Administrative Applications....................................... 32
      Financial Applications ............................................... 32
      Consumer Applications ............................................. 33
   Key Trends and Issues in Healthcare Technologies ........... 35
      Health Information Exchanges .................................. 35
      Interoperability and Standards ................................. 35
      Data Integration........................................................ 36
      Data Warehouses....................................................... 37
      Clinical and Business Intelligence (CBI).................... 37
      Telehealth and Telemedicine .................................... 37
      Privacy and Security................................................. 38
   Conclusion........................................................................ 39
   References ......................................................................... 39

**SECTION II  SYSTEMS**

**3  Systems Analysis**.......................................................................... **45**
   Learning Objectives ......................................................... 45
   Introduction...................................................................... 45
   Healthcare Problems and Opportunities for IT Implementation ................. 46
      Clinical Functions..................................................... 46
         Applications for Clinical Functions...................... 46
      Administrative and Financial Services....................... 47
         Applications for Administration and Finance......... 47
      Infrastructure............................................................ 48
         Security-Related Applications............................... 48
   Needs Analysis in Healthcare Facilities............................. 49
      Operational Needs .................................................... 49
      Staff Productivity and Satisfaction ........................... 50
      Increased Revenue and Cost Optimization............... 50

Patient Safety.................................................................................. 50
Quality of Care................................................................................ 50
Patient Access to Services............................................................ 50
Needs Summary..............................................................................51
Needs Prioritization.............................................................................51
Work Plan Development...................................................................... 52
Executive Summary........................................................................ 52
Introduction and Background........................................................ 52
Goals and Objectives..................................................................... 53
Resources........................................................................................ 53
Work Plan Accountability.............................................................. 54
Current Clinical Processes.................................................................. 54
Current Healthcare IT Integration Status......................................... 56
Deficiencies in Current IT Healthcare Practices ............................. 57
Patient Support and Satisfaction ................................................. 57
Reduction in Revenue Generation................................................ 57
Prescription Errors......................................................................... 58
Industry Standardization................................................................ 58
Alternative Approaches to Current Healthcare Processes ............. 58
Industry Standardization................................................................ 58
Alternative Ways to Reduce Prescription Errors......................... 58
Alternative Processes for Revenue Generation .......................... 59
Comparative Analysis of Alternatives............................................... 59
Proposal Evaluation ........................................................................... 60
Cost–Benefit Analysis..........................................................................61
Proposal Sensitivity Analysis.........................................................61
References ............................................................................................ 62

4  **Systems Design**.......................................................................... **65**
Learning Objectives ........................................................................... 65
Introduction......................................................................................... 65
Business Process Management........................................................... 66
Compatibility of System Components ...............................................67
Standards Compliance ........................................................................ 68
Process to Address Industry Trends................................................... 68
Structure of the System Design Team .............................................. 68
Detailed Technical Specifications...................................................... 69
Usability.......................................................................................... 70
Business Process Reengineering................................................... 71
Information Infrastructure ............................................................ 71
Data Management .......................................................................... 72
Creating a Request for Information (RFI)......................................... 73
Making a Buy versus Build Decision ................................................74
Process for a Build Decision ........................................................ 75

Buy Decision: Best-of-Breed versus Single-Vendor Solution .....................75
Creating a Request for Proposal (RFP) ...............................................75
Summary ....................................................................................................78
References ..................................................................................................78

**5  Systems Selection, Implementation, Support, and Maintenance ..... 81**
Learning Objectives ..................................................................................81
Introduction...............................................................................................82
Solution Selection Criteria .......................................................................83
Selecting Review Team Members .............................................................85
Solution Selection Activities .....................................................................86
Implementation Process............................................................................89
Organizational Change Management ........................................................90
Implementation Strategies.........................................................................90
Implementing Solutions ............................................................................91
System Integration to Support Business Requirements ...........................92
User and Operational Manuals and Training............................................93
Activation Planning and Immediate Postactivation Activities...................94
Managing Healthcare Information Systems...............................................95
Analyzing Data for Problems and Trends ................................................96
Ensuring Critical Functions Are Repaired, Maintained, or Enhanced ...........97
Business Continuity and Disaster Recovery Plans ...................................97
Bibliography ..............................................................................................98

**6  Systems Testing and Evaluation.......................................................99**
Learning Objectives ..................................................................................99
Introduction...............................................................................................99
Purpose of Systems Testing......................................................................99
Test Methodology .............................................................................100
Test Strategy ............................................................................................101
Test Tools.................................................................................................101
Test Execution .........................................................................................102
Test Controls............................................................................................104
Test Reporting .........................................................................................105
Final Evaluation.......................................................................................105
References ................................................................................................106

**7  Systems Privacy and Security .........................................................107**
Learning Objectives ................................................................................107
Introduction.............................................................................................107
Defining Requirements, Policies, and Procedures .................................108
Risk Assessment.......................................................................................109
Vulnerability Remediation ......................................................................110
User Access Controls...............................................................................110
Confidentiality, Integrity, and Availability .............................................111

Organizational Roles .................................................................................111

Data Management Controls .....................................................................112

Disaster Recovery and Business Continuity Plans ..............................113

Auditing ....................................................................................................113

Ongoing System Evaluation ...................................................................113

References ................................................................................................114

## SECTION III   ADMINISTRATION

**8   Administration Leadership** ...............................................................**117**

Learning Objectives ................................................................................117

Introduction .............................................................................................118

Participation in Organizational Strategic Planning ............................118

   Mission ..................................................................................................118

   Vision ....................................................................................................118

   Values ...................................................................................................119

   Goals .....................................................................................................119

Organizational Environment ..................................................................119

Forecasting Technical and Information Needs of an Organization ............ 120

Developing the IT Strategic Plan ..........................................................122

   Implementing the IT Strategic Plan ................................................124

Evaluating Performance ..........................................................................124

Evaluating Effectiveness and User Satisfaction ...................................125

Promoting Stakeholder Understanding of IT Opportunities and
Constraints ...............................................................................................127

Developing Policies and Procedures for Information and Systems
Management .............................................................................................. 128

Complying with Legal and Regulatory Standards ...............................129

Adhering to Ethical Business Principles ............................................... 130

Employing Comparative Analysis Strategies .......................................131

   Budgets .................................................................................................131

   Other Financial and Nonfinancial Indicators ...............................132

   Benchmarks ..........................................................................................132

   Quality Indicators ..............................................................................132

Preparing and Delivering Business Communications .........................133

Facilitating Group Discussions and Meetings .....................................137

Providing In-House Consulting Services ..............................................137

Developing Educational Strategies for IT Staff .................................. 138

Staying Current on IT Technologies and Trends ...............................139

Managing Risk .........................................................................................140

Quality Standards and Practices ............................................................141

References ................................................................................................141

**9   Administration Management** .........................................................**143**

Learning Objectives ................................................................................143

Introduction..................................................................................................143
Roles and Responsibilities for IT-Related Functions ..................................144
    Senior Management Roles and Responsibilities ....................................144
    General IT Roles and Responsibilities...................................................145
    Healthcare IT Roles and Responsibilities .............................................145
    Careers in Healthcare IT ......................................................................145
Achieving Staff Competency in Information and Management System
Skills ........................................................................................................146
    Employee Development........................................................................146
    Organizational Training and In-Service Programs.................................146
    Job-Related IT Certifications ................................................................146
    Miscellaneous Professional Development .............................................147
    Performance Evaluation .......................................................................148
Managing Projects and Project Portfolios...................................................149
Managing Vendor Relationships ................................................................151
Facilitating Steering Committee Meetings .................................................153
Adhering to Industry Best Practices ..........................................................154
Developing System, Operational, and Department Documentation............155
    System Documentation ........................................................................155
    Operational Documentation .................................................................155
    Department Documentation .................................................................155
Providing Customer Service.......................................................................156
    Service-Level Management....................................................................156
    Request Tracking..................................................................................157
    Problem Resolution ..............................................................................157
Managing Budget and Financial Risks .......................................................158
    Financial Risk Management ..................................................................158
    Budget Risk Management .....................................................................159
Managing Customer Relationships with Business Leaders ..........................160
Summary ...................................................................................................161
References .................................................................................................162

**10 Questions**.....................................................................................**165**
Chapter 1: The Healthcare Environment.....................................................165
Chapter 2: The Technology Environment ................................................... 167
Chapter 3: Systems Analysis ......................................................................168
Chapter 4: Systems Design ........................................................................170
Chapter 5: Systems Selection, Implementation, Support, and Maintenance....171
Chapter 6: Systems Testing and Evaluation................................................172
Chapter 7: Systems Privacy and Security ...................................................173
Chapter 8: Administration Leadership........................................................174
Chapter 9: Administration Management......................................................175

**11 Answer Key**...................................................................................**177**
Chapter 1: The Healthcare Environment.....................................................177

Chapter 2: The Technology Environment .................................................. 178
Chapter 3: Systems Analysis .................................................................. 179
Chapter 4: Systems Design .................................................................... 180
Chapter 5: Systems Selection, Implementation, Support, and Maintenance.... 180
Chapter 6: Systems Testing and Evaluation............................................ 181
Chapter 7: Systems Privacy and Security ............................................... 182
Chapter 8: Administration Leadership.................................................... 182
Chapter 9: Administration Management.................................................. 183

**12   Acronyms** .................................................................. **185**

**Appendix** .................................................................. **191**

**Index** .................................................................. **225**

# Acknowledgments

HIMSS wishes to express gratitude to the authors of the second edition (2013):

- Chris Arricale, MS, PMP, CPHIMS
- Melissa Barthold, MSN, RN-BC, CPHIMS, FHIMSS
- James W. Brady, PhD, M.Ed, CISM, CISSP, PMP, CPHIMS, FHIMSS
- Vic Eilenfield, MS, MHA, FACHE, CPHIMS
- Raymond A. Gensinger, Jr., MD, CPHIMS, FHIMSS
- Susan M. Houston, MBA, RN-BC, PMP, CPHIMS
- David H. Miller, CPHIMS
- John B. Salmon, CPHIMS
- Brando C. Sumayao, MSCIS, CPHIMS, FHIMSS

# Preface

Your purchase of this book is the first step in becoming a Certified Professional in Healthcare Information and Management Systems (CPHIMS) and being recognized for your specialized knowledge and skills. For more than a decade, CPHIMS certification has been the preeminent certification in healthcare information technology (IT) and is administered globally to healthcare IT professionals practicing in a variety of work settings.

The development and maintenance of the CPHIMS Exam is the responsibility of the CPHIMS Technical Committee within HIMSS. This committee is made up of experts from around the world who possess subject matter expertise in the areas tested on the exam.

This preface provides an overview of the eligibility requirements, testing procedures, and content of the CPHIMS Exam itself. Specific questions can also be addressed to certification@himss.org at any time.

The benefits of CPHIMS certification are broad and far reaching. Certification is a process that is embraced in many industries, including healthcare IT. CPHIMS is recognized as the "gold standard" in healthcare IT because it is developed by HIMSS, has a global focus, and is valued by clinicians and non-clinicians, management and staff positions, and technical and nontechnical individuals.

Certification, specifically CPHIMS certification, provides a means by which employers can evaluate potential new hires, analyze job performance, evaluate employees, market IT services, and motivate employees to enhance their skills and knowledge. Certification also provides employers with evidence that the certificate holders have demonstrated an established level of job-related knowledge, skills, and abilities and are competent practitioners of healthcare IT.

## Eligibility Requirements

To be eligible for the CPHIMS Exam, candidates must fulfill one of the following requirements for education **and** work experience:

Baccalaureate degree, or global equivalent, *and* five (5) years of associated information and management systems experience,* three of those years in a healthcare setting.†

Graduate degree, or global equivalent, *and* three (3) years of associated information and management systems experience,* two of those years in a healthcare setting.†

## Additional Resources

The CPHIMS Technical Committee recommends that review for the CPHIMS Exam focus on resources and programs that cover the tasks in the CPHIMS Content Outline. **It should not be inferred that questions on the CPHIMS Exam are selected from any single resource or set of resources, or that study from this or other resources listed, guarantees a passing score on the CPHIMS Exam.**

- *CPHIMS Candidate Handbook*: A must for all CPHIMS Exam candidates, the candidate handbook provides information that is helpful when applying for and scheduling the CPHIMS Exam. The handbook includes the CPHIMS Content Outline, directions on how to apply for the exam and schedule your exam appointment, and what to expect on the day of the exam as well as following the exam. It is recommended that all CPHIMS candidates download a copy of the handbook from www.CPHIMS.org.
- CPHIMS Self-Assessment Exam (SAE): The SAE, or practice test, is available for purchase from Applied Measurement Professionals, Inc.'s (AMP) LXRStore (http://store.lxr.com/). The SAE simulates the CPHIMS Exam in content, cognitive level, difficulty, and format. After taking the SAE, you will receive valuable, practical feedback in detailed score reports.
- *HIMSS Dictionary of Healthcare IT Terms, Acronyms and Organizations*: This dictionary was developed and extensively reviewed by industry experts. The resource includes
  - Definitions of terms for the IT and clinical, medical, and nursing informatics fields
  - Acronyms, with cross-references to current definitions
  - Academic and certification credentials commonly used in healthcare and IT

    For more information and to order a copy, visit the HIMSS store at www.himss.org/store.

---

* Information and management systems experience refers to work experience in systems analysis; design; selection, implementation, support, and maintenance; testing and evaluation; privacy and security; information systems; clinical informatics; and management engineering.

† A healthcare setting includes experience with a provider of health services or products to a healthcare facility (e.g., hospital; healthcare consulting firm; vendor; federal, state, or local government office; academic institution; payer; public health, etc.).

- The Learning Center, powered by HIMSS, offers three options to assist candidates in preparing for the CPHIMS Exam:
  - Option 1: Online course only
  - Option 2: Virtual instructor-led training only (four live webinars offered at various times throughout the year)
  - Option 3: Online course and virtual instructor-led training combo (available at various times throughout the year)

  For more information and the upcoming schedule, visit www.himsslearn.org.
- CPHIMS Review Course (face-to-face): The CPHIMS Review Course is a full-day course designed to review the skills and knowledge candidates have gained through previous education and work experience. Interact with an authorized CPHIMS Review Course instructor to get answers to your questions. The course features lecture, discussion, practice questions, and study materials available exclusively to CPHIMS Review Course participants. For more information on attending a course as a participant, or to schedule a course for employees at your facility, e-mail certification@himss.org.

## CPHIMS Exam Administration

The CPHIMS Exam is delivered by computer at AMP Assessment Centers throughout the world. Candidates who meet the eligibility requirements for the CPHIMS Exam may submit an application and fee at any time by visiting www.goAMP.com. The CPHIMS Exam is administered by appointment only Monday through Saturday (except major holidays). As a candidate, you may test where you wish and when you feel you are prepared to take the CPHIMS Exam.

Special group administrations of the CPHIMS Exam may be scheduled with HIMSS chapters, corporate members, organizational affiliate members, nonprofit partners, regional extension centers, or other groups through arrangement with HIMSS. For special group administration, mobile computer units (or paper and pencil, if desired) are sent to your facility, where the proctored CPHIMS Exam will occur. For more information on hosting an administration for your group, contact certification@himss.org.

The CPHIMS Exam is usually administered at national and international HIMSS events such as the Annual HIMSS Conference and Exhibition, World of Health IT, HIMSS AsiaPac, Middle East Health IT Leadership Summit & Conference, COACH eHealthAchieve, and COACH eHealth Conference. Special application and scheduling procedures may be in place for these events, so check with the event website to find out how to apply and schedule in conjunction with these events.

**JoAnn W. Klinedinst, MEd, CPHIMS, PMP, DES, FHIMSS**
*Vice President, Professional Development*
*HIMSS North America*

# Editor

**Susan Leonard, MA, CPHIMS,** has more than 25 years of experience in healthcare information technology (HIT), specializing in application support, training and program development, system implementations, and project management. Ms. Leonard has held several hands-on director and senior management–level positions overseeing all aspects of HIT industry conferences and education, clinical and billing healthcare information systems, and video conferencing technologies for use in providing telemedicine services. She has worked in various healthcare settings, including HIMSS, hospitals, HIT vendors, university-based physician practices, consulting firms, and nonprofit Health Center Controlled Networks. Susan holds a bachelor of science degree in management information systems and a master of arts degree in adult education. She also teaches as adjunct faculty for the National University online HIT master's and bachelor's programs.

# GENERAL

1

# Chapter 1

# The Healthcare Environment

## Learning Objectives

At the conclusion of this chapter, the reader will be able to

- Articulate the characteristics and services of different types of healthcare organizations (e.g., hospitals, clinics and ambulatory centers, community health organizations, healthcare payers, regulators, research, and academic)
- Recognize the various types of interrelationship models of care within and across healthcare organizations (e.g., health information exchange [HIE], population health, reimbursement, and continuity of care)
- Differentiate the roles and responsibilities of healthcare information and management system professionals within the organizational structures in which they work
- Describe the roles governmental, regulatory, professional, and accreditation agencies play related to healthcare and their impact on clinical outcomes and financial performance

## Introduction

In order to best understand the context of healthcare information and management systems, it is necessary to first understand the concept of health. The World Health Organization (WHO) asserts that "health is a state of complete physical, mental and social well-being and not merely the absence of disease or infirmity."[1] The WHO has not amended this definition since 1948.

Why is it important that we more fully understand this more holistic concept of health? If we do not present for care until we are in an advanced stage of disease or arrive with injuries from unsafe working or living practices, the cost of providing that care is likely to be high and the health outcomes often less than desired. The practice of healthcare, and thus the systems and management processes supporting it, is increasingly focused on those activities that have the greatest impact on the overall health of the community and patient populations. A state of health is not best achieved by limiting our engagement to patients' visits to the doctor's office and admissions to hospitals, but is increasingly extended to wellness encounters with nonphysician healthcare providers, virtual encounters through telehealth or mobile health technologies, and safety and preventive care outreach programs. The increasing strain of healthcare costs on national economies is forcing us to continually reevaluate our healthcare delivery paradigm to optimize health outcomes at an affordable cost. This is the macroeconomic context in which health information professionals and technologists will be performing their art.

The healthcare environment is an exceptionally complex one in which multiple players compete for placement on center stage. The four pillars of quality, access, cost, and value[2] require dynamic trade-offs in which healthcare professionals are under constant pressure to deliver the highest quality of care to the greatest portion of their supported population within tight cost constraints, while having to demonstrate the value of health information technology (IT). Placed upon this already complex four-legged stool are demands from multiple stakeholders, including governments, consumer groups, professional associations, regulatory organizations, payers/insurers, and suppliers.

The Organisation for Economic Cooperation and Development (OECD) provides a solid basis for comparing international approaches to organizing and resourcing national healthcare with several key indicators on health system performance across countries. Figure 1.1 illustrates the substantial variance in spending by country and the proportion of public to private contribution to overall national health expenditures.

These investments have seen great reductions in cardiovascular and infant mortality rates, but lifestyle and risk factors show that more than 20% of adults continue to smoke, while one in five children are now considered overweight or obese. Specific quality outcomes that nations are grappling with today are shown in Figures 1.2 and 1.3, with the examples of cervical cancer screening and survival rates, and hospital readmissions showing surprising variation across countries.

So it is not hard to develop a sense of the complexities of the healthcare environment in which we toil. The breadth of stakeholders, the balance of public versus private funding, and the active engagement to improve the health of populations one individual at a time produce a daunting task. This is the arena the health information professional and technologist enter to ensure that the best possible information management and systems support are available to improve the quality of life for the greatest number of our world's citizens.

## Healthcare Organizations

The number and types of organizations involved in the provision of care, supporting the provision of care, and paying for the care provided is large, complex, and constantly evolving. The simplest way to categorize these is

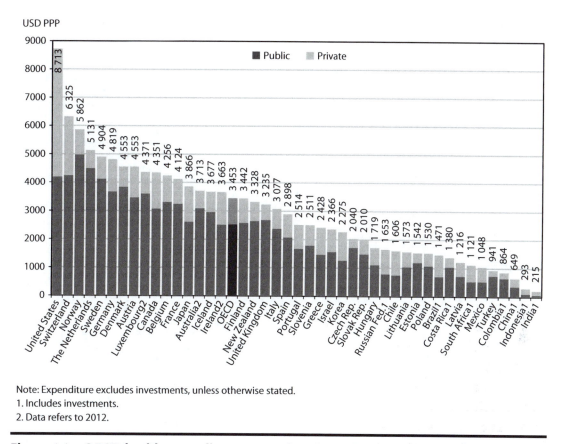

USD PPP

Note: Expenditure excludes investments, unless otherwise stated.
1. Includes investments.
2. Data refers to 2012.

**Figure 1.1    OECD health expenditure per capita: 2013. PPP, purchasing power parity. (From OECD, Health expenditure per capita, in *Health at a Glance 2015: OECD Indicators*, Paris: OECD Publishing, 2015. http://dx.doi.org/10.1787/health_glance-2015-59-en.[3])**

through the eyes of the patient. When speaking of accessing care, often a patient will say, "I went to see my doctor at her office" or "I was in the hospital last week to have my appendix out." So, in a broad sense, we have the constructs of hospital-based care—often referred to as inpatient care—and care from doctors' offices—referred to as outpatient or ambulatory care. Additionally, given the diverse types of diagnostic services and pharmaceuticals needed to support the healthcare process, providers of ancillary services are included as well. Lastly, regulators and payers of care are discussed. The interrelationships among these diverse players will be expanded upon in the next section. The following is an overview of many of these structures, which vary not only by country but also often by geographic location within countries.

## Hospitals

While hospitals may be categorized in any number of ways, a single hospital may also be classified in more than one way. For example, a hospital may be a private, not-for-profit, and specialty hospital, thus falling into three

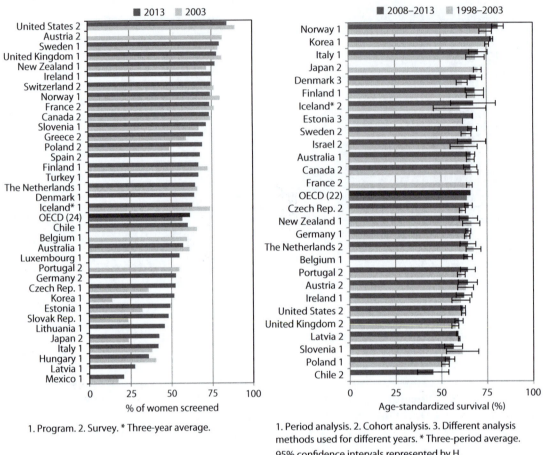

Cervical cancer screening in women aged 20–69, 2003–2013 (or nearest years)

■ 2013  ■ 2003

United States 2
Austria 2
Sweden 1
United Kingdom 1
New Zealand 1
Ireland 1
Switzerland 2
Norway 1
France 2
Canada 2
Slovenia 1
Greece 2
Poland 2
Spain 2
Finland 1
Turkey 1
The Netherlands 1
Denmark 1
Iceland* 1
OECD (24)
Chile 1
Belgium 1
Australia 1
Luxembourg 1
Portugal 2
Germany 2
Czech Rep. 1
Korea 1
Estonia 1
Slovak Rep. 1
Lithuania 1
Japan 2
Italy 1
Hungary 1
Latvia 1
Mexico 1

0    25    50    75    100
% of women screened

1. Program. 2. Survey. * Three-year average.

Cervical cancer five-year relative survival, 1998–2003 and 2008–2013 (or nearest periods)

■ 2008–2013  ■ 1998–2003

Norway 1
Korea 1
Italy 1
Japan 2
Denmark 3
Finland 1
Iceland* 2
Estonia 3
Sweden 2
Israel 2
Australia 1
Canada 2
France 2
OECD (22)
Czech Rep. 2
New Zealand 1
Germany 1
The Netherlands 2
Belgium 1
Portugal 2
Austria 2
Ireland 1
United States 2
United Kingdom 2
Latvia 2
Slovenia 1
Poland 1
Chile 2

0    25    50    75    100
Age-standardized survival (%)

1. Period analysis. 2. Cohort analysis. 3. Different analysis methods used for different years. * Three-period average. 95% confidence intervals represented by H.

**Figure 1.2   OECD screening and survival rates for cervical cancer. (From OECD, Screening, survival and mortality for cervical cancer, in *Health at a Glance 2015: OECD Indicators*, Paris: OECD Publishing, 2015. http://dx.doi.org/10.1787/health_glance-2015-53-en.[4])**

categories. Notable systems for classifying hospitals include classification by the following:

1. Ownership. Public (government-managed) versus private hospitals.
   a. In public hospitals, governments (at the national, provincial, state, or other level) own and are responsible for the operations. The healthcare providers in such hospitals are generally private practitioners, although in some countries the providers may be government employees as well (e.g., in the National Health Service [NHS] of the United Kingdom or the U.S. Veterans Health Administration hospitals).
   b. In private hospitals, staffing arrangements span a broad spectrum of private practitioners or groups of healthcare providers. Private hospitals in some countries are further classified as for profit versus nonprofit.

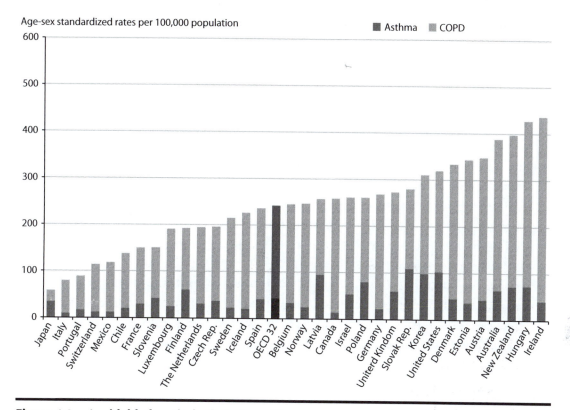

**Figure 1.3    Avoidable hospital admissions. Three-year average for Iceland and Luxembourg. (From OECD, Avoidable hospital admissions, in *Health at a Glance 2015: OECD Indicators*, Paris: OECD Publishing, 2015, http://dx.doi.org/10.1787/health_glance-2015-44-en.[5])**

   i. For-profit private hospitals, also referred to as investor-owned hospitals, often exist as part of a multihospital system with varying degrees of interrelationship among the system's hospitals. Examples of large, investor-owned hospital systems include the Hospital Corporation of America (http://hcahealthcare.com/) and BMI Healthcare in the United Kingdom (http://www.bmihealthcare.co.uk/).

   ii. Nonprofit private hospitals are not investor owned, but rather exist under laws at national and state levels allowing them to organize as nonprofit corporations, generally providing them the advantage of avoiding federal and property taxes. Canada's hospitals, although publicly financed, are almost exclusively private, nonprofit organizations,[6] albeit funded through the provincial/territorial governments. Just more than half of the hospitals in the United States operate as private, nonprofit organizations.[7]

2. Types of service provided. Hospitals are often classified by the types of service they provide. While the majority of hospitals will be general hospitals supporting the most common types of medical and surgical care requirements, hospitals specializing in more focused areas of care are becoming more prevalent. Such hospitals include psychiatric hospitals, which focus on

mental healthcare; rehabilitation hospitals, which generally focus on restoring neurological and musculoskeletal functions following treatment in an acute care facility; and children's hospitals, which focus on the care and treatment of children.

3. Teaching status. In addition to providing inpatient clinical services, teaching hospitals train future physicians and other healthcare providers. Often associated with academic institutions, teaching hospitals may be further classified as academic medical centers or university hospitals. Many such institutions also contribute substantially to medical research and publish much of the knowledge that advances the science of medicine.

4. Geographic location. Hospitals may be further classified as urban hospitals when located in large cities or as rural hospitals when substantially distant from major urban areas with greater resources. While such classifications appear mundane, the challenges of operating in urban and rural environments are different enough to require programs of specialization. Meeting government standards for classification as urban or rural may provide such hospitals access to special government funding programs.

## Outpatient or Ambulatory Care

When a patient's care does not require the intensive management of a hospital setting, that care is generally received in an outpatient or ambulatory care setting—most frequently in a doctor's office. Most primary care—the care practiced by primary care providers (PCPs) or general practitioners (GPs)—is provided in the ambulatory setting. Similarly, most PCP/GP referrals to clinical specialists for evaluation are completed in the ambulatory setting as well. There are multiple modes of accessing outpatient care, including single independent provider offices, larger multiprovider group practices in which a broader range of specialists may be available, and—while not a preferred approach from an expense perspective—hospital emergency departments. In the last few years, many less complicated surgical procedures not requiring an overnight hospital stay have been moved to the outpatient setting as well. The facilities providing such day surgeries are frequently called ambulatory surgery centers or surgicenters.

## Community Health Organizations

In the healthcare environment, a "community" generally refers to the specific geographic location in which healthcare is delivered. Thus, healthcare organizations serving the population of local areas tend to be broadly referred to as community health organizations. Community-centered hospitals and clinics in most nations provide most of the care available to their local populations. Some nations provide more formal designations of community healthcare organizations that impose both legally constrained definitions and operational characteristics. In Canada, a community health center (CHC) is a key provider of local health services and aspires to support access and comprehensive care, including health promotion and illness prevention, through a publicly administered process.[8] In the United States, CHCs are generally associated with medically underserved areas as defined by the Health Resources and Services Administration (HRSA). These health centers strive to provide comprehensive, culturally competent, quality primary healthcare services to medically underserved communities and vulnerable populations.[9] Small community hospitals located in rural areas of the United States may apply for designation as critical access hospitals (CAHs), allowing them to receive higher reimbursement rates.

## Diagnostic and Pharmaceutical Services

The most effective healthcare treatment quite frequently requires the aid of diagnostic services and pharmaceutical treatments, commonly referred to as ancillary services. While larger hospitals will generally have these capabilities, smaller hospitals and outpatient care centers will usually rely on external providers of such services to support comprehensive care to their patients. Key services provided in this area include laboratory and anatomic/anatomical pathology services, diagnostic imaging/radiology services, and pharmacies. Close associations with these service providers are formed with provider offices and hospitals to ensure effective and comprehensive healthcare delivery.

## Healthcare Payers

From the perspective of the healthcare delivery organization, payments generally come from three types of entities: government-financed and managed programs, insurance programs administered by private entities, and personal funds.

Government-financed and managed programs are generally funded through countries' general taxes. These programs may pay for the healthcare system directly, as does the single-payer system of the NHS of the United Kingdom, which finances hospitals and salaries of most NHS providers. Alternatively, government programs may provide funding for a national health insurance program, such as that in Canada, where the program is administered through provincial health plans. These plans fund hospitals through community trusts and pay providers through the government's insurance program. Multipayer systems, such as that of the United States, are more complex to administer. The U.S. system includes the federally managed program for Medicare, through which citizens 65 years of age and older have most of their healthcare needs provided for; the shared-cost federal/state program Medicaid, which supports care for low-income families; another federal/state program called the Children's Health Insurance Program (CHIP), which provides care to children of uninsured families that do not qualify for Medicaid; and several others for smaller groups of special populations. These three programs provide coverage for roughly one-third[10] of the U.S. population.

Insurance programs administered by private entities are generally funded by employers, citizens themselves, or a combination of both. Germany mandates shared health insurance contributions from employers and employees, but these funds are administered by about 1100 private, nonprofit sickness funds that cover more than 90% of the population by making payments to hospitals and providers. In the United States, roughly 55% of citizens have employer-based insurance and an additional 10% purchase insurance directly.[11] Even in the many countries that have universal healthcare programs, people who can afford to purchase private health insurance are usually allowed to do so. The purchase of private health insurance generally allows the purchaser to receive services that may not be covered under a national benefit structure and may also improve access to care. When healthcare organizations treat patients insured through a private entity, they bill the private health insurance entity rather than a government organization.

Healthcare services are often personally funded by individuals who have government or employer-supported health plans, as well as by the uninsured. While patient co-payments were not required by many universal coverage programs in years past, an increasing number of countries are adding this requirement to offset growing healthcare costs. In the United States, co-payments are required under most healthcare programs, whether government or privately managed. Persons with higher incomes may choose to avoid the constraints of insurance programs and, as they can tolerate the financial risk, are cash payers. Lastly, and perhaps most perversely, those who fail to qualify for government-supported programs such as Medicaid in the United States but still cannot afford to purchase health insurance find themselves at the mercy of a healthcare system that charges premium, nonnegotiated rates to those least able to afford such costs. A 2009 study on bankruptcies in the United States found that 62.1% of all bankruptcies in 2007 were medical; 92% of these medical debtors had medical debts of more than $5000, or 10% of pretax family income. The rest met criteria for medical bankruptcy because they had lost significant income due to illness or mortgaged a home to pay medical bills. Most medical debtors were well educated, owned homes, and had middle-class occupations. Three-quarters had health insurance.[12] Although politically divided, the Patient Protection and Affordable Care Act signed into law on March 23, 2010, was intended to help reduce some of these financial risks for patients in the United States and make healthcare more affordable and accessible.

In summary, from the perspective of the healthcare delivery organization, three basic types of payers are at play: government-financed and managed programs, insurance programs administered by private entities, and patients who pay with personal funds. Add to that the number of potential insurance companies in the market and the differences in payers' health benefits coverage, and the management of accounts receivable can become an incredibly complex task requiring sophisticated administration and automation support.

# Interrelations within and across Healthcare Organizations

The purposes of interrelationships among healthcare organizations are numerous. Some of the key requirements include enabling comprehensive care, assuring effective transfers of care, ensuring the general portability of information in support of care, reporting public and population health information, obtaining appropriate reimbursement for care, and supporting particular organizational models of care.

## Enabling Access to Comprehensive Care Services

As noted in the section above, healthcare organizations are reliant upon a number of partners within or outside of their organization to enable the delivery of comprehensive care. Providers in the outpatient setting often rely on external laboratory and radiology services to ensure accurate diagnoses and on the availability of pharmacies to provide prescribed medications to complete the provider's care plan for the patient. Absent effective communications—increasingly electronic today—the care process will break down and patient outcomes could suffer as a result.

## Assuring Effective Transfers of Care

When a provider determines that the scope of care required for a patient's treatment is outside of his or her capability, care is generally transferred to another provider or healthcare organization. Effectively communicating health information during the transfer of care is exceptionally important to the patient's welfare. When a complete set of information is transferred with the patient regarding the history of the present illness, along with subjective and objective findings that include the results of diagnostic tests performed and medications prescribed and administered, the receiving organization can advance the patient's treatment in a substantially more efficient and effective manner. When such information does not accompany a patient during transfer, precious time is often lost, as that information is re-created through repetitive evaluations and readministering diagnostic tests that are sometimes of an invasive nature. To facilitate the provision of essential health information during transfer of care between providers or facilities, an initiative in the United States encourages the use of Health Level Seven International's (HL7) Consolidated-Clinical Document Architecture (C-CDA), which is a standard for electronically transmitting continuity of care information.[13]

Both the loss of time in treating an acute patient and the need to repeat invasive tests can have adverse consequences for a patient. Not having a clear awareness of the pharmaceutical products a patient may be taking or has been administered in the present course of care can be life threatening and has led to attempts in some countries to ensure that medication reconciliation has taken place. In the United States, medication reconciliation is defined as the process of identifying the most accurate list of all medications that the patient is taking, including name, dosage, frequency, and route, by comparing the medical record to an external list of medications obtained from a patient, hospital, or other provider.[14]

## Ensuring the General Portability of Care

Even when patients are enrolled to a specific clinical organization or provider for care, there are times when they will need care from other providers. This occurs not only under the two scenarios covered above, but also when patients travel away from their routine places of care. If a patient who is several hundred miles away from home becomes ill or is injured in an automobile accident, having the correct health information available can have a powerful influence on the patient's health outcomes from the clinical intervention. The most common example is that of the new provider who does not know a patient's medication allergies. To overcome these challenges, some nations are implementing national health information exchanges (HIEs) that endeavor to provide virtual, real-time access to patients' health information. One such initiative is Canada's Health Infoway, a nonprofit organization made up of the 14 federal, provincial, and territorial deputy ministers of health. Infoway's mission is to "realize the vision of healthier Canadians through innovative digital health solutions."[15] In the United States, much work is under way to define standards to facilitate ease of sharing health information both through HIEs at the state level and nationally via the Nationwide Health Information Network (NHIN) and, more recently, through the Nationwide Interoperability Roadmap. The United Kingdom has also invested heavily in its Health and Social Care Information Centre (HSCIC) through its national health system, which connects England's healthcare organizations to facilitate the availability of clinical information that can be shared to support the continuity of care and safety of patients in the healthcare process.

## Reporting Public and Population Health Information

Improving health status at the local or national level requires more than ensuring information availability at the point of care. It requires a sort of information use that is often referred to as the secondary use of health information because the information is used outside of the direct healthcare delivery process, which is viewed as the primary use of health information. The United Kingdom's Secondary Use Services (SUS) through its HSCIC program leverages the SUS in support of public health, research, and management, among other activities. Similarly, the U.S. Centers for Disease Control and Prevention has been receiving health information from across the country for many years not only to support such public health activities as actively responding to disease outbreaks, but also to work proactively through education on prevention and healthy lifestyles through its Division of Population Health.

## Obtaining Appropriate Reimbursement for Quality Care

In most publicly funded healthcare systems, the hospitals and clinicians delivering the care are private entities, so a substantial amount of communication must occur to ensure reimbursement for the care provided. Whether a healthcare organization is a one-provider office, a multispecialty clinic, a hospital, or another entity, it must submit claims to be reimbursed for care provided. The exception to this rule, of course, is in those countries, such as the United Kingdom, that have a national health system with both government facilities and a largely government-paid healthcare staff. Claims may be submitted to state Medicaid offices, the Centers for Medicare & Medicaid Services (CMS) for Medicare, or private insurance companies in the United States or to provincial offices in Canada, but no healthcare organization will exist for long absent an ability to efficiently process—and be reimbursed for—claims for care. In multipayer systems, such as in the United States, this process can be exceptionally complex and require a surprising investment of administrative overhead and systems complexity. Both governments and major employers are increasingly concerned that improved health outcomes are associated with the cost of care. In the United States, the CMS Physician Quality Reporting System (PQRS) will provide incentive payments to "eligible professionals who satisfactorily report quality-measures data for services furnished during a PQRS reporting period."[16] Similarly, the Leapfrog Group supports healthcare purchasers and insurers by "mobilizing employer purchasing power to alert America's health industry that big leaps in health care safety, quality and customer value will be recognized and rewarded."[17]

## Supporting Particular Organizational Models of Care

While the number of models of care is too great to discuss at length here, a key trend we see in the industry today is the need to share increasing volumes of information among partners in the healthcare system. Such partners in care are often referred to as an integrated delivery system (IDS). Steven Shortell has defined the IDS as

> administrative entities that bring together a set of organizations that provide a coordinated continuum of services to a defined population and are willing to be held clinically and fiscally accountable for the outcomes and health status of the population served.[18]

While some IDSs are more integrated (from an ownership or a systems point of view) or more complete (providing a broader continuum of services) than others, the trend in the United States has been toward increasing integration. A type of IDS referred to as an accountable care organization (ACO) has been around for a few years and was recently codified in law by the Patient Protection and Affordable Care Act—often referred to as simply the Affordable Care Act.

In an ACO, inpatient and outpatient providers of care are administratively organized into a single organization, often including a health insurance company, to provide a full spectrum of healthcare services to large groups of Medicare patients. If the ACO is able to reduce costs to CMS for their enrolled population while improving the quality of care, the ACO gets to share in the cost savings. As might be imagined, proving improvements in quality concurrently with reduction in healthcare costs is an information-intensive process that requires close integration of the partners in an ACO. Many ACOs will likely be developed from existing IDSs, as the IDS model already has many of the components necessary to achieve the quality and cost objectives of CMS.

In summary, interrelations within and across healthcare organizations can be as simple as a GP requesting an x-ray for a patient or reporting a patient disease observation to a public health entity. On the other end of the spectrum, the relationship could be as complex as assembling an integrated network of care providers under an ACO with sophisticated cost and quality reporting requirements. Each of these constructs not only requires effective coordination, but is also increasingly supported by sophisticated automation capabilities that reduce the labor involved while ensuring more reliable process support.

## Roles and Responsibilities of Healthcare Information and Management Systems Professions

The number of position titles in the health information management (HIM) and health information technology (HIT or IT) space is quite large. In a single-provider office, the person who performs the broad range of HIM/IT tasks may work less than full-time or double as the office manager. In a large academic medical center or IDS, the IT department could include more than 100 personnel. The top IT position in healthcare organizations is usually referred to as the chief information officer (CIO). The CIO is generally accountable for a broad range of IT activities, including many that are not directly related to healthcare. Among these would be such things as maintaining organizational computing rooms, individual desktop computers, telephone communications (including an increasing variety of portable computing platforms), secure Internet access, local and wide area networks, and the organization's website.

In larger organizations, the complexity of HIM and IT functions leads to specialization. The chief security officer (CSO) endeavors to secure the healthcare organization's computing and communications assets from either intentional or unintentional security breaches from inside or outside the organization. Lead IT security personnel may carry the Certified Information Systems Security Professional (CISSP®) credential from the Information Systems Security Certification Consortium, Inc. (ISC2®).[19] Similarly, the privacy officer is responsible for ensuring that personally identifiable data, including protected health information, is accessed exclusively by those authorized to do so under a broad range of laws—in the United States, the Privacy Act and the Health Information Portability and Accountability Act (HIPAA), among others. A credential leveraged in supporting this role is that of Certified in Healthcare Privacy and Security (CHPS).[20]

The chief technology officer (CTO) is generally responsible for the technical architecture of the IT systems supporting the organization and often looks toward the developing market in HIM and IT to try and keep the organization competitive from a technology perspective. This could range across the full spectrum of such things as mobile computing platforms, cloud-based computing, and state-of-the-art clinical applications.

Health information managers have held roles in medical records departments for decades, but prior to the common availability of electronic health records (EHRs), there was not a strong relationship between HIM and IT departments. As medical records functions have become increasingly automated over the past few years, culminating in EHRs of advanced capabilities, HIM departments are finding themselves at the center of the IT activities in healthcare organizations. In the HIM area, you will find professionals with the Registered Health Information Administrator (RHIA) or Registered Health Information Technologist (RHIT)[21] credential in the United States or with the Certification in Health Information Management (CHIM) credential in Canada.[22] Healthcare organizations may also rely on the Certified Professional in Healthcare Information and Management Systems (CPHIMS)[23] credential to ensure that staff members in the IT department have a broad base of knowledge and experience in healthcare information and management systems.

The role of clinical informatics professionals is also expanding as the practice of medicine is increasingly supported by EHRs and other health information systems. The Stanford School of Medicine defines clinical informatics as

> the scientific discipline that seeks to enhance human health by implementing novel information technology, computer science and knowledge management methodologies to prevent disease, deliver more efficient and safer patient care, increase the effectiveness of translational research, and improve biomedical knowledge access.[24]

The American Medical Informatics Association (AMIA) advocates advanced training for clinicians to develop a clinical informatics subspecialty in the practice of medicine.[25] A frequently used title for staff with such backgrounds in the health information space is that of chief medical information officer (CMIO). Popular variants are chief medical informatics officer and chief health information officer (CHIO), and in the area of nursing, chief nursing informatics officer (CNIO). With the increasing use of IT in healthcare processes, effective integration of clinical insights into systems solutions is of great importance.

While the great variety of organizational structures in IT departments is driven by such factors as organization size, geographical distribution, and line of business, a sample organization structure a CIO may oversee could include

- Application development and support
- Data center operations
- Database administration
- Desktop support
- Information security
- Network operations

Similarly, the specific roles an IT organization may expect to fill would vary based on the functions the organization supports. These roles could be filled by staff, consultants, or contractors. Examples of the more common types of positions one might expect to see include

- Desktop support technician
- Database administrator
- Programmer/application developer
- Web developer
- Network engineer/analyst
- Systems analyst/administrator
- Project manager
- Security analyst

In summary, there is great variation in the size and structure of IT departments within healthcare organizations, which drives the number and specialization of jobs within the IT organization.

## Roles of Government, Regulatory, Professional, and Accreditation Agencies in Healthcare

Given the importance of healthcare in our lives—including our quality of life, our longevity, and even our ability to continue living following life-threatening encounters with disease or accidents—and the incredible expense of delivering high-quality healthcare to very large populations, it is not surprising that a tremendous amount of government oversight and a great number of regulatory bodies are involved in healthcare processes. An overview of these organizations and their associated activities is provided below.

### Government

The role of governments in healthcare is quite pronounced, as discussed in the section above on healthcare organizations. Because most countries continue to experience increases in the proportion of their gross domestic product (GDP) consumed by healthcare activities, they are concerned that these trends will weaken their national economies if not slowed—or even stopped and reversed. Stopping the growth in healthcare costs as a percentage of GDP requires exceptionally difficult decisions for governments in industrialized countries, as citizens have grown accustomed to the existing health benefits programs. While most OECD countries average under 11% of their GDPs consumed by healthcare expenditures, the United States is currently at more than 16% and Korea at just under 7%.[26] The growth in healthcare expenses annually has averaged 4%, while the growth in GDPs has averaged only 1.6%,[27] so it is easy to see that healthcare is consuming our national economies at an unsustainable rate, making governmental engagement in these factors essential.

To address the growth in healthcare costs, many nations' governments are considering changes to their health programs. Among these are enhancements to the primary care delivery system to manage chronic diseases more effectively in Australia, experimentation with privatization in Canada, global budgeting and competition among sickness funds in Germany, requiring long-term care residents to pay for room and board in Japan, and consideration of pro-market reforms in the United Kingdom.[28] Similarly, the development of ACOs in the United States is being encouraged with a goal of producing better health outcomes at lower cost. Such trends will continue as we collectively grapple with the best ways to balance quality, access, cost, and safety for the greatest proportion of our populations.

## Healthcare Regulators

Healthcare regulatory agencies serve a broad range of functions in the healthcare environment, generally by implementing the provisions of a nation's health laws through a more explicit system of regulations. In the United Kingdom, the Health and Care Professions Council (HCPC) is the statutory regulator for more than 300,000 health and care professionals in the country. The HCPC maintains standards of proficiency and conduct for the professions it regulates. In the United States, the dominating regulatory entity is the CMS. CMS drafts the rules and finalizes the regulations for the management of multiple federally subsidized healthcare programs for the nation through a complex process of rule making involving public engagement. The Food and Drug Administration (FDA) in the United States evaluates and approves medical devices and new drugs used in the treatment of patients. Similarly, medical devices in Canada are regulated by Health Canada's Therapeutic Products Directorate.

While it may be a common belief that regulatory organizations are always government entities, it is not uncommon to find that private-sector organizations, commissions, and associations may perform in a regulatory capacity as well. These are addressed in the following sections.

## Professional Associations

According to the *Merriam-Webster Dictionary*, a profession is "a calling requiring specialized knowledge and often long and intensive academic preparation."[29] Professional associations in the healthcare environment have proliferated greatly, many serving in a semiregulatory role. Total Professions of the United Kingdom provides a good description of the roles and functions of professional bodies, stating that they may

- Set and assess professional examinations
- Provide support of continuing professional development through learning opportunities and tools for recording and planning
- Publish professional journals or magazines
- Provide networks for professionals to meet and discuss their field of expertise
- Issue a code of conduct to guide professional behavior
- Deal with complaints against professionals and implement disciplinary procedures[30]

Total Professions further distinguishes between professional and regulatory bodies by stating that "a regulatory body is like a professional body but it is not a membership organisation and its primary activity is to protect the public. Unlike professional bodies, it is established on the basis of legal mandate."[31]

Professional associations exist for nearly every medical specialty, nursing and allied health profession, health administration, and IT profession. A sampling of professional associations related to healthcare and healthcare IT in the United States is shown in Table 1.1.

## *Accreditation Organizations*

Accreditation organizations (AOs) have substantial interactions with healthcare organizations and generally play a semiregulatory role in that they often serve on behalf of federal organizations to ensure specific standards or conditions

**Table 1.1  Professional Associations Related to Healthcare and Health IT in the United States**

| Clinical | Administrative and IT |
|---|---|
| American College of Surgeons | American College of Healthcare Executives |
| American Congress of Obstetricians and Gynecologists | American College of Physician Executives |
| American Gastroenterological Association | American Academy of Medical Administrators |
| American Academy of Physician Assistants | Information Systems Security Certification Consortium, Inc. (ISC²) |
| American Academy of Family Physicians | Healthcare Information and Management Systems Society |
| American Academy of Pediatrics | American Health Information Management Association |
| American Nursing Association | Project Management Institute |

of participation (CoP) are met. The Joint Commission and Joint Commission International (JCI)[32] are perhaps the most recognized AOs utilized for certification of hospitals in the United States and internationally. JCI currently operates in more than 90 countries around the globe. In the United States, the AOs under CMS are very visible examples of accreditation agencies. CMS AOs determine compliance with Medicare CoP. When a healthcare organization is certified by a CMS AO for compliance with CMS requirements, the organization is deemed to have met the requirements and may then bill CMS for covered services. For participation in Medicare programs, a number of other organizations are authorized to act as AOs, as shown in the Table 1.2.

The interrelationships among government agencies, regulators, professional associations, and AOs can be surprisingly complex, especially in the United

**Table 1.2   CMS-Approved Accreditation Organizations**

| Organization | Program Type |
|---|---|
| Accreditation Association for Ambulatory Health Care (AAAHC) | Ambulatory surgical centers (ASCs) |
| Accreditation Commission for Health Care, Inc. (ACHC) | Home health agencies (HHAs) |
| | Hospices |
| American Association for Accreditation of Ambulatory Surgery Facilities (AAAASF) | ASCs |
| | Outpatient physical therapy (OPT) providers |
| | Rural health clinics (RHCs) |
| American Osteopathic Association/ Healthcare Facilities Accreditation Program (AOA/HFAP) | ASCs |
| | Critical access hospitals (CAHs) |
| | Hospitals |
| Community Health Accreditation Program (CHAP) | HHAs |
| | Hospice |
| DNV Healthcare (DNVHC) | Hospitals |
| | CAHs |
| Joint Commission | ASCs |
| | CAHs |
| | HHAs |
| | Hospices |
| | Hospitals |
| | Psychiatric hospitals |

*Source:* Centers for Medicare & Medicaid Services, http://www.cms.gov/Medicare/Provider-Enrollment-and-Certification/SurveyCertificationGenInfo/Downloads/AOContactInformation.pdf.[33]

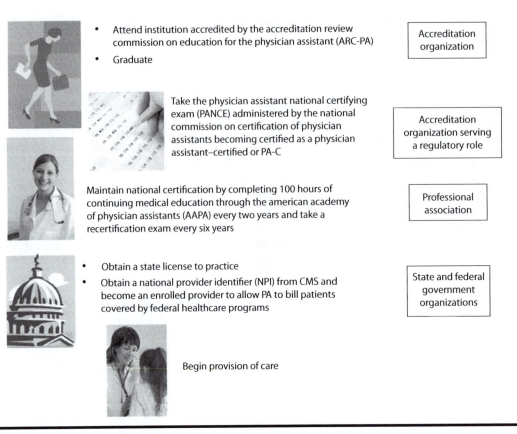

**Figure 1.4 Steps and organizations involved in becoming a practicing physician assistant. (Adapted from AAPA, Becoming a PA, Alexandria, VA: AAPA, http://www.aapa.org/ your_pa_career/becoming_a_pa.aspx.[34])**

States. Figure 1.4 shows the many organizations that play a role in the life of a physician assistant moving through training and into medical practice.

## Summary

At the beginning of our discussion, we determined that it was important to be able to

■ Articulate the characteristics and services of different types of healthcare organizations (e.g., hospitals, clinics and ambulatory centers, community health organizations, and healthcare payers)
■ Recognize the various types of interrelationship models of care within and across healthcare organizations (e.g., HIE, population health, reimbursement, and continuity of care)
■ Differentiate the roles and responsibilities of healthcare information and management system professions within the organizational structures in which they work

■ Describe the roles government, regulatory, professional, and accreditation agencies play related to healthcare and their impact on clinical outcomes and financial performance

We have covered the breadth of organizational structures in the public and private domains, defined the nature of their interactions, identified roles of healthcare information and management systems professionals, and described the great number of government, regulatory, professional, and accreditation organizations affecting our healthcare delivery systems today. The complexity of the processes can be overwhelming. Fortunately, advances in automation, including inexpensive data storage, increasing network capacities, and simplified software programming tools, will allow professionals in healthcare information and management systems to make life simpler for those who deliver care by transferring much of the information processing requirements to automated tools. This chapter provides a high-level framework for the environment in which you will employ these tools.

# References

1. Preamble to the Constitution of the World Health Organization. Adopted by the International Health Conference, New York, June 19–22, 1946.
2. HIMSS (Healthcare Information and Management Systems Society). http://www.himss.org/ASP/aboutHimssHome.asp (accessed December 1, 2015).
3. OECD (Organisation for Economic Cooperation and Development). Health expenditure per capita. In *Health at a Glance 2015: OECD Indicators*. Paris: OECD Publishing, 2015. http://dx.doi.org/10.1787/health_glance-2015-59-en (accessed April 22, 2016).
4. OECD (Organisation for Economic Cooperation and Development). Screening, survival and mortality for cervical cancer. In *Health at a Glance 2015: OECD Indicators*. Paris: OECD Publishing, 2015. http://dx.doi.org/10.1787/health_glance-2015-53-en (accessed April 22, 2016).
5. OECD (Organisation for Economic Cooperation and Development). Avoidable hospital admissions. In *Health at a Glance 2015: OECD Indicators*. Paris: OECD Publishing, 2015. http://dx.doi.org/10.1787/health_glance-2015-44-en (accessed April 22, 2016).
6. Makarenko J. Canada's health care system: An overview of public and private participation. *Mapleleafweb*, October 22, 2010. http://www.mapleleafweb.com/features/canada-s-health-care-system-overview-public-and-private-participation#public (accessed December 1, 2015).
7. U.S. Census Bureau. Hospitals—Summary characteristics: 1990 to 2009. In *Statistical Abstract of the United States*. Suitland, MD: U.S. Census Bureau, Table 172. http://www.census.gov/prod/2011pubs/12statab/health.pdf (accessed December 1, 2015).
8. Canadian Association of Community Health Centres. http://www.cachc.ca/?page_id=7. (accessed December 1, 2015).
9. U.S. Department of Health and Human Services, Health Resources and Services Administration. http://bphc.hrsa.gov/about/ (accessed December 1, 2015).
10. U.S. Census Bureau. Health and nutrition. In *Statistical Abstract of the United States*. Suitland, MD: U.S. Census Bureau. http://www.census.gov/prod/2011pubs/12statab/health.pdf (accessed December 1, 2015).

11. U.S. Census Bureau, U.S. Department of Commerce. Income, poverty, and health insurance coverage in the United States: 2010. Suitland, MD: U.S. Census Bureau, 2011, p. 29. http://www.census.gov/prod/2011pubs/p60-239.pdf (accessed December 1, 2015).

12. Himmelstein DU, Thorne D, Warren E, Woolhandler S. Medical bankruptcy in the United States, 2007: Results of a national study. *Am J Med* 122(8): 741–746, 2009. http://www.pnhp.org/new_bankruptcy_study/Bankruptcy-2009.pdf (accessed December 1, 2015).

13. Health Level Seven International. *HL7/ASTM Implementation Guide for CDA Release 2—Continuity of Care Document (CCD®) Release 1*. Ann Arbor, MI: Health Level Seven International. http://www.hl7.org/implement/standards/product_brief. cfm?product_id=6 (accessed December 1, 2015).

14. Centers for Medicare & Medicaid Services. Eligible hospital and critical access hospital: Meaningful use menu set measures, measure 6, stage 1. Woodlawn, MD: Centers for Medicare & Medicaid Services, November 7, 2010. http://www.cms. gov/Regulations-and-Guidance/Legislation/EHRIncentivePrograms/downloads/6_ Medication_Reconciliation.pdf.(accessed December 1, 2015).

15. Canada Health Infoway. https://www.infoway-inforoute.ca/en/about-us (accessed December 1, 2015).

16. Centers for Medicare & Medicaid Services. Physician quality reporting system: Analysis and payment. Woodlawn, MD: Centers for Medicare & Medicaid Services. https://www.cms.gov/Medicare/Quality-Initiatives-Patient-Assessment-Instruments/ PQRS/index.html (accessed December 1, 2015).

17. Leapfrog Group. http://www.leapfroggroup.org/about_leapfrog (accessed December 1, 2015).

18. Shortell SM, Casalino LP, Fisher ES. Achieving the vision. In Crosson FJ, Tollen LA, eds., *Partners in Health: How Physicians and Hospitals Can Be Accountable Together*. San Francisco: Jossey-Bass, 2010, pp. 53–54.

19. Information Systems Security Certification Consortium (ISC2®). https://www.isc2. org/cissp/default.aspx (accessed December 1, 2015).

20. American Health Information Management Association. http://ahima.org/certification/chps (accessed December 1, 2015).

21. American Health Information Management Association. http://ahima.org/certification (accessed December 1, 2015).

22. Canadian Health Information Management Association. https://www.echima.ca/ cchim/certification (accessed December 1, 2015).

23. Healthcare Information and Management Systems Society. http://www.himss.org/ ASP/certification_cphims.asp (accessed December 1, 2015).

24. Stanford School of Medicine. https://clinicalinformatics.stanford.edu/background. html (accessed December 1, 2015).

25. American Medical Informatics Association. https://www.amia.org/education (accessed December 1, 2015).

26. OECD (Organisation for Economic Cooperation and Development). Health expenditure as a share of GDP, 2013 (or nearest year). In *Health at a Glance 2015*. Paris: OECD Publishing, 2015. http://dx.doi.org/10.1787/health_glance-2015-graph151-en (accessed April 22, 2016).

27. OECD (Organisation for Economic Cooperation and Development). Health expenditure per capita. In OECD, H*ealth at a Glance 2015: OECD Indicators*. Paris: OECD Publishing, 2015. http://dx.doi.org/10.1787/health_glance-2015-59-en (accessed April 22, 2016).

28. Shi L, Singh DA. *Delivering Health Care in America: A Systems Approach*. 5th ed. Burlington, MA: Jones & Bartlett Learning, 2012, pp. 20–27.

29. Merriam-Webster. Profession. http://www.merriam-webster.com/dictionary/profession (accessed December 1, 2015).

30. Total Professions. Role of professional bodies. Berkhamsted, UK: Total Professions. http://www.totalprofessions.com/more-about-professions/role-of-professional-bodies (accessed December 1, 2015).

31. Total Professions. Regulatory bodies. Berkhamsted, UK: Total Professions. http://www.totalprofessions.com/more-about-professions/regulatory-bodies (accessed December 1, 2015).

32. Joint Commission International. http://www.jointcommissioninternational.org/About-JCI/ (accessed December 1, 2015).

33. Centers for Medicare & Medicaid Services. http://www.cms.gov/Medicare/Provider-Enrollment-and-Certification/SurveyCertificationGenInfo/Downloads/AOContactInformation.pdf (accessed December 1, 2015).

34. AAPA (American Academy of Physician Assistants). Becoming a PA. Alexandria, VA: AAPA. http://www.aapa.org/your_pa_career/becoming_a_pa.aspx (accessed September 14, 2012).

# Chapter 2

# The Technology Environment

## Learning Objectives

At the conclusion of this chapter, the reader will be able to

- Describe various technologies that support the healthcare environment (e.g., network, communications, hardware, mobile, and medical devices)
- Articulate the characteristics of applications commonly used in healthcare organizations (e.g., clinical, administrative, financial, and consumer)
- Identify future trends and key issues in healthcare technologies (e.g., health information exchange [HIE], interoperability and standards, telehealth, privacy, and security)

## Introduction

The world now is steered by technology and computers—from Twitter to the National Oceanic and Atmospheric Administration, everything we do and touch and that touches us has a computer in the process. Healthcare may have been a little bit slower than other industries to adopt information technology (IT), but now the electronic health record (EHR) is an essential part of every facility that provides care to patients—from home health to the intensive care unit. Patients are no longer surprised when the provider pulls out a computer instead of a paper chart and pen.

Most hospitals and outpatient sites provide wireless networks for staff to use in caring for patients and a different network for family and visitors to access. It is common to see patients updating their status on Facebook or Twitter from their hospital beds or outpatient center during their visits. Where hospitals used to have policies forbidding employees from accessing social networks during working hours, many institutions now have instructions on how to friend the hospital. Many patients have separate personal health records (PHRs) they manage on an Internet site, as well as access to a patient portal through the facility's

EHR system. Healthcare IT is changing the way that healthcare does business, as well as the way that clinicians care for patients. An understanding of the attributes of healthcare IT, as well as knowledge of the applications and hardware required for their use, is essential in helping to improve the care and the safety of the care provided to patients.

There are three components of the technology environment:

1. Hardware: The actual servers (virtual and physical), network connections, and devices used to access information
2. Applications: The software used by administrative, clinical, and support staff to process and store data, manage patients' records, and provide information
3. Networks: The wired or wireless connections that link the infrastructure together and enable accessibility of the applications and patient data

A healthcare facility requires these three components to function. While this may seem a very simplistic listing, these are essential to providing IT to a healthcare institution. And, while essential, with the rapid changes in technology and improvements in software, the sections of these components change frequently. A central processing unit (CPU) that was fast just a few years ago has been replaced by a new model—which is significantly faster. A storage server of 4 gigabytes (GB) was considered large only a few years ago; now, that is a small hard drive. Mobile devices used to be large and cumbersome; now they fit in the palm of the hand. The decreased access time—and increased speed—for a hard drive enables the application to return data to the requesting clinician much more quickly. The technology changes are supporting—and changing—the applications and the functions of the applications. The illustrations here are not intended to be a complete listing but to provide an overview.

## Hardware in Healthcare IT

### Technology Infrastructure

The basis of any technology has to be the hardware systems that store data, run applications, and connect those applications and tools together. The physical routers, switches, and virtual and physical servers are some of the integral parts needed to connect clinicians, administrators, providers, and patients to necessary clinical systems, information, and support. Firewalls, both physical and software based, protect the network from unauthorized access as well as maintain security of the information in the system.

### Servers

While the vision that many people have of IT is a room full of servers, that is no longer completely accurate. Most healthcare IT departments have virtual as well as physical servers. What application is installed on which type of server is determined by the vendors' recommendations, as well as the capabilities of the organization to support this technology. Virtual servers can serve as test servers as well as production servers. The servers are part of the most expensive equipment in a healthcare IT shop and must be managed well and appropriately. Application Service Providers (ASPs) and cloud computing provide alternative options for those organizations that may not have the appropriate space or resources to house and maintain their data in-house.

## Data Storage

Most healthcare IT departments have used magnetic tape storage, optical disc storage, and even hard drive storage for patient information, bills, and financial accounts—all the thousands of data elements generated by each patient's care. There are, depending on the type of patient, regulations on how long patient data must be maintained. For example, in the United States, information about a baby's birth must be maintained for 23 years, or 2 years after the baby reaches majority. Many healthcare organizations are simply resigned to keeping charts forever.

With paper records, that translates to a large amount of money to store stacks of paper that will probably never be looked at again. Health information management departments have looked for a less expensive and more reliable storage method. Historically, most organizations were forced to store paper charts off-site and have to order them when or if they are needed, thus adding transportation costs to and from the storage area to the record-keeping costs. Some health systems have a practice of scanning paper charts, and then appropriately disposing the paper chart. EHRs have reduced or eliminated the need for paper chart storage. Current practice, where data is stored, backed up and archived, is changing—often to the cloud. The cloud can provide room for storage, even when those storage needs may double every few years.

## Mobile Devices

Hardware needs to be designed to support clinical workflow, and increasingly that means portable devices and wireless connectivity. Healthcare institutions are using mobile wheeled carts with wireless access, as well as smaller handheld devices. Carts can be configured to meet end users' needs, from drawers for storage to holders for bar code medication scanners and locked drawers for security of medications. Carts that carry only some version of computers (carts can support thin and fat clients) can be designed for outpatient clinics and other clinical areas that have no need for drawers or scanners, and other carts can have medical devices mounted on them. It is important to remember that while standardization may be a goal, one documentation device will not meet every area's or end user's needs.

The popularity of smartphones, and their increased functionality, is prompting end users to ask for similar devices for use in the healthcare units. The tablet is one of the most popular handheld devices. Most EHR vendors have updated their applications for use on handheld devices. Devices with touchscreens are being configured for healthcare, with attention to the concern about maintaining good infection control practices while using equipment that is touched by gloved hands. Several devices, such as Magnetic Resonance Imaging (MRI) scanners, employ touchscreens to program the examinations and review the images.

A major concern with any handheld device that connects to the institution's network is security, especially when end users actually bring their own devices (BYOD) to work. Prior to permitting staff's use of their personal devices in the clinical areas, it is important to establish a policy to ensure that Protected Health Information (PHI) is safe, that the institution can wipe a device clean if it is compromised, and that passwords are required to access the device. The decision to permit data storage on a personal device must be dependent on maintenance of the data's security.[1,2]

## *Medical Devices*

Many physiologic devices, such cardiac monitors, ventilators, some IV fluid pumps, medication pumps, and vital sign monitors, have the ability to send out the data they obtain, often in HL7 format. This integration with the EHR helps staff by decreasing data entry and transcription errors, as well as saving time. Depending on the EHR, this data could be sent directly to preconfigured fields, or a third-party device can be used to translate the data into EHR-acceptable format. It is important to require validation of the information by the clinician prior to permanently storing that data in the EHR.

Laboratory devices can conduct tests and export the information to the EHR. Typically, radiologic images are stored in a picture archiving and communication system (PACS) and viewed via a link from the EHR to the image in PACS or enterprise imaging system. Both areas have specific regulatory agencies that supervise the use of those devices and regulate them. As an example, in the United States, the Food and Drug Administration (FDA) regulates medical devices. Since so many of those devices have incorporated advanced technology, IT must be aware of the laws and regulations from the FDA that apply to hardware and software that is IT supported. In addition to radiologic images, any display of physiologic data, such as heart rhythms, fetal monitor tracings, and ventilator or heart waveforms, and any implantable device, such as an automatic cardiac defibrillator, are covered by the FDA. In addition, the FDA is looking at mobile medical apps. Examples of these are applications that display fetal heart tracings or cardiac waveforms on physicians' cell phones.[3] The institution's biomedical engineering department must work closely with IT to maintain these important systems.

In Europe, the Parliament and the Council of the European Union have developed directives for medical devices and *in vitro* diagnostics. Canada has medical device regulations, as does Japan.[4] In Russia, the Ministry of Public Health and Social Development of the Russian Federation controls medical devices.[5] The World Health Organization (WHO) has published a large amount of information about medical device requirements on its web page.[6] According to the WHO, "65% of 145 countries have an authority responsible for implementing and enforcing medical device specific product information."[7] There is discussion that the European Commission's regulations for devices are not strong enough to really protect patients.[8]

## Networks in Healthcare IT

### *Network Infrastructure*

The network, while still dependent on network cables, is increasingly connected using wireless points. Putting the information for clinicians at the point of care requires wireless access points, not hard or physical wires. Clinicians want data at their fingertips and do not accept the model of going to the patient's room and then back to the nurses' station to log in to the clinical system and retrieve results. Providers can now take the electronic chart with them to the patient's room, where they can review lab results, x-ray reports, and other tests with the patient. Wireless access points can support this workflow, permitting clinicians to work with the information they need when and where they need it. This wireless and cabled access supports more than just documentation stations. Virtual private networks (VPNs), voice over Internet protocol (VoIP) using fiber-optic cables and coaxial cables, and supporting protocols govern the connection of routers and switches. Local area networks (LANs) using Ethernet and token ring, and wide area networks (WANs) using multiprotocol label switching (MPLS) or asynchronous transfer mode (ATM) are all in use, supporting the hardwired and wireless networks. VPN technology is a safer, more secure method of providing remote access to an organization's network and servers. VPNs, using tunneling protocols and encryption, require authentication to block out unauthorized users.

There are guidelines and rules from regulatory bodies and professional organizations, and standards that require documentation about patients and the care given to those patients, as well as documentation of procedures. One of the major requirements of an EHR is that it must be able to support the documentation, order entry, and lab results reporting required by regulations, professional standards, and patient need. Ideally, that care is documented when and where it is provided, thereby reducing errors.[9]

There are many areas in an organization that have cabled access to the organization's intranet (internal) and Internet (external). Cabled access is more reliable and faster. Many institutions already have cable that was installed before wireless was within the price range and speed requirements of most IT departments. Clinical departments, as well as administrative and support services, usually have hardwired desktop computers. Some healthcare providers, especially in outpatient settings, have installed a desktop or fixed device in each patient exam room. Specific clinical areas, such as radiology examination rooms, need special hardware, such as larger, high-resolution monitors and high-speed graphic cards that will support detailed images. In addition, hardware devices in patient care areas have to be cleaned with harsh cleansing agents. To make this possible, some hospitals have installed microstatic keyboards and mice, as well as silicone covers for monitors.[10,11]

## *Communications*

There are many different types of data communication protocols and media available in healthcare IT today, from the standard telephone landline with conferencing and video capabilities to various devices that use VoIP to broadband access. Data communication protocols allow information to transmit from one point or media to another. One of the most common examples would be the telephone. Some of the devices look like the same cell phones that are used outside the hospital, while some are clip-on, hands-free phones worn by staff members. As with other devices in use in the clinical areas, such as tablets and medical devices, infection control is a major concern. Materials for these devices need to be antibacterial and cleanable. While some of these devices can send and receive text messages, there are concerns about the legality and safety of using text messages for patient orders. Other examples of communication protocols would include broadband access, T1 lines, and Wi-Fi for transmitting data across computer networks or accessing the Internet.

# Software in Healthcare IT

Software provides the face of healthcare IT. Hardware is not typically visible to the end users, but the applications that sit on that hardware are. Use of the various software applications, along with changes in workflow and processes, can benefit the organization. The software is what the end user works with, using a human–computer interface. There are a large number of applications, so we will discuss the major groups of applications and examine some of the newer ideas that are in the pipeline.

## *Clinical Applications*

As with most specialties, healthcare IT has developed its own terminology and acronyms. Some of the terms seem interchangeable when, in fact, they do have different meanings. The electronic health record (EHR), the electronic medical record (EMR), and the personal health record (PHR) are examples of this. The EMR is the continuous, longitudinal electronic record in one specific setting—a provider's office, a hospital, or a home healthcare service. The EHR is a longitudinal record covering multiple settings over time.[12–14] The PHR is a medical record often created, edited, maintained, and controlled by the patient and possibly includes importation of clinical data from other sources. Often created on a website, it is accessible by providers when the patient invites providers to review information in the PHR using secure access.

Clinical applications support patient care wherever it is being delivered. The most apparent clinical application is the EHR. In some institutions, this is a one-vendor application; in others, it is a best of breed, with many different vendor applications performing different functions. The EHR is used by clinicians to document patient care, from medication administration to order entry, as well as to retrieve patient data from the lab or from radiology. The provider's office can send electronic prescriptions to the patient's pharmacy, as well as import data from an inpatient stay or outpatient testing.

The EHR interfaces with specialized systems in different departments. As an example, in the United States, radiology and pathology labs have specific requirements, with formatting and data display governed by different accrediting agencies, such as Clinical Laboratory Improvement Amendments (CLIA), the College of American Pathologists (CAP), and the American College of Radiology.[15,16] In Europe, the European Cooperation for Accreditation[17] covers laboratory certifications. Professional dietitians, case managers, and social workers all have specific needs in software functionality, often dictated by professional or regulatory standards.

Some clinical areas, such as the perinatal areas (labor and delivery, nursery, neonatal intensive care, and postpartum), the perioperative areas (preop unit, operating rooms, and postanesthesia care unit), the critical care units, the outpatient centers for primary care, and special functions like renal dialysis, have specialized documentation and information needs. The PACS stores and displays images from ultrasounds to computed tomography (CT) scans and MRIs. These systems require fine-resolution monitors, large storage drives, and large amounts of RAM for image display. Some of the major EHR vendors are able to support all the specialty areas; others do not and require the purchase and interface of a niche system specific to each specialty. The goal of all these systems is to communicate and exchange this patient health information, also known as interoperability. Interoperability is one of the most important attributes of clinical systems, since data should not be entered into systems more than one time. It is essential that these systems communicate with each other. Table 2.1 presents examples of specialized systems and their related clinical areas and users.

The availability of clinical data at the point of care has transformed how clinicians care for patients. They no longer need to go to the radiology department to look at MRIs or CT scans; those images can now be made available in the EHR application, saving time for clinicians, as well as money for the institution, since there are no films to create, store, or retrieve. Perinatal systems archive the fetal monitor strips electronically, saving thousands of dollars in charges for storage of paper fetal strips.

**Table 2.1  Sample Specialized Systems and Their Clinical Areas and Users**

| System | Clinical Area | Users |
|---|---|---|
| PACS | Radiology | Radiologists |
| | | Nurses |
| | | Technologists |
| | | Physicians providing direct care |
| Fetal monitor archiving | Labor and delivery | Physicians |
| | | Nurses |
| Perioperative system | Preoperative area | Physicians |
| | Postoperative area | Nurses |
| | Operating room | Schedulers |
| | | Billers and coders |
| Intensive care | Intensive care units | Physicians |
| | | Nurses |

## Administrative Applications

Administrative applications provide support for clinicians, as well as the administrative staff in an institution. These applications run the gamut from electronic time cards, payroll, staff competency record keeping, and educational applications, to scheduling both staff for work shifts and patients for procedures and office visits. Bed management systems, which include staff from housekeeping and patient transportation, as well as clinicians, are very helpful in getting patients into a room as soon as possible. Popular applications in the last few years include equipment-tracking applications that use radio frequency identification (RFID) technology, thus saving staff time spent in hunting for needed equipment. Web-based applications that permit staff to bid for understaffed shifts are being implemented, reducing overtime labor costs and increasing staff satisfaction, as do systems that permit self-scheduling.

## Financial Applications

Financial applications in healthcare IT cover all the features of any organization's financial needs, but possibly with more variables than most businesses have to entertain. From the solo provider's office to the multihospital, multiprovider health system, there is a need for financial systems. Multiple regulations govern how billing can be done, how bills are submitted, and the details that have to be included with a bill, such as diagnosis codes and providers' licenses and billing numbers—the list is incredibly long. Systems have to handle charge posting via both orders and manual charge entry, payment posting, and billing based on the providers. Insurance, coinsurance, and deductibles have to be part of the calculations, as do revenue codes, supplies, tests, and medications. Items that require a provider's order and cannot be billed to patients without an order must be distinguished from items that do not require an order and can be billed to patients. Statements need to be provided to patients and claims to insurance companies. These billing systems are commonly referred to as practice management systems.

A general ledger must accurately track charges, bills, and payments. Payroll systems need to accept data from the electronic time card system and convert it to salary costs, correctly matching hours worked, both regular and overtime, and calculate any overtime pay, holiday bonuses, shift differentials, or additional wages earned from professional certifications. It also has to track earnings for paid time off, usually based on the number of hours worked by the employee. The accounts payable portion of the software must also be in sync with all the other systems; financial systems have to communicate in real time. The supply chain mission and support has to include all methods of supply purchasing, as well as invoice payment, and ensure that they are linked correctly.

## Consumer Applications

Consumers are becoming more and more involved in electronic records and their patient health information. Not infrequently, patients request electronic versions of their charts from providers. The importance of the consumer's relationship to the record and the information in that record is more apparent. While there used to be discussions about who owned the medical record, that seems to have been decided in the patient's favor. Most EHRs have a patient portal that permits the patient to view test results (after provider review and release to the patient), ask for prescription refills, and send the provider or the office staff a secure e-mail, as well as schedule an appointment. Some portals permit patients to add comments to their EHR.[18,19]

Some PHRs are stand-alone and are not connected with an institution's EHR. These applications may be web based, such as HealthVault from Microsoft[20] or an application installed on the user's computer or mobile device. In the United States, the Centers for Medicare & Medicaid Services (CMS) encourages the use of PHRs[21,22] and provides a link to Blue Button, a PHR initiative which originated through the Veteran's Administration and is now being offered through other healthcare organization patient portals. MyPHR is a website that assists the user in determining what type of PHR—web based or software, free or fee required—is best. The website is sponsored by the American Health Information Management Association (AHIMA) and also provides information on the value of a PHR for seniors, parents, and caregivers.[23] The National Committee on Vital and Health Statistics also provides detailed information on the advantages of a PHR.[24] AHIMA provides a questionnaire for consumers interested in setting up a PHR. Convenient guides are helpful to patients around the world.[25] Web-based PHRs give the patient full control of the record's contents, and often offer the opportunity to import prescription medication history from national drugstore chains or results from laboratories. According to Gherardi et al.,[26] PHRs are becoming very popular in Europe, the United Kingdom, and Scandinavia. The publication *IT and People* issued a call for articles on PHRs for their August 2012 edition to encourage discussion of the implementation, design, forms, security, and use of PHRs by patients and care providers.[26] Vendors are increasing their promotion about the PHR across Europe, the United Kingdom, and China.[27]

Some healthcare organizations have partnered with web-based PHR vendors and upload records into patients' PHR applications from those healthcare institutions. Some healthcare insurers also provide the ability to create a PHR from their websites.[28] In the United States, a national survey conducted by the California HealthCare Foundation (CHCF) provides evidence that PHRs actually support patients in improving their own health.[29] In the survey, caregivers did note that PHRs were almost a necessity in maintaining knowledge and continuity of care for family members with multiple chronic conditions.

The numbers of patients using PHRs is growing rapidly, with the CHCF survey reporting that most patients want to use PHRs that their physician or insurer provides. The survey also identified security as the major stumbling block to PHR adoption, with patients looking for evidence that any information they enter into the PHR is completely secure. Most websites clearly provide information on how security and privacy of the patients' records is maintained. Most allow the patients to decide who can view their information, often by providing a secure URL or separate login/password for the healthcare provider. Patients have found that after establishing a PHR through their insurance company or other third-party vendor, information could not be easily transferred to a different PHR, resulting in the patients having to reenter the data in their new systems. PHR use may increase with the medical home and accountable care platforms, as they provide incentives for keeping patients healthy.[30] In addition, the use of in-home health monitoring systems and wearable devices has also intensified the need for PHRs. In the United Kingdom, the National Health Service's Summary Care Record project is under way. The Summary Care Record also includes HealthSpace, a PHR.[31] Patients are encouraged to participate in HealthSpace by adding medications that they take or appointments with providers they have scheduled.

Patients are also very interested in communicating electronically with their providers. According to the *Wall Street Journal*,[32] doctors are far behind the rest of the world in using electronic communications, and either patient portals or secure messaging applications can provide security for this increasingly popular communication. Most patient issues can actually be addressed in e-mail by office staff, leaving only a few e-mails that the physician or nurse practitioner needs to address. Patients want the convenience of electronic communication with their providers, but at the same time, both sides of the communication have to be secure. While providers may not have the skill to set up secure communications, there are web-based and application-driven tools that will provide both security and convenience.

The requirement to be able to provide "human-readable" medical records in electronic format is something very new to healthcare. In the past, patients had to go to the health information management department, complete paperwork to request their own records, and often pay a per-page fee for a copy of the paper record. As an example, in the United States, Stage 1 of the CMS Meaningful Use requires that a copy of the medical record be available to the patient within 24 hours of the request.[33] While it is not always easy to retrieve data from EHR systems, this requirement has to be fulfilled. Ensuring the EHR can provide this information, whether on a portable drive, DVD or CD, or pushed out through an existing patient portal, is essential. And regardless of the regulations, the smarter patients want copies of their records. Patients want to see their records, as determined by a group of researchers in the United States and Canada.[34]

## Key Trends and Issues in Healthcare Technologies

### *Health Information Exchanges*

Health information exchanges (HIEs) and regional health information organizations (RHIOs) are essential to supporting a longitudinal health record for Americans. The primary stone in building a RHIO is ensuring that the HIE accurately links each patient's data across the different venues, from an inpatient visit to office visits to an emergency department in a different state, and transmits that data. Ensuring this transmission of data to connect varying types of information from various systems is a work in progress,[35,36] and is essential to the creation of any countrywide—or hopefully, worldwide—health information network. In Europe, the eHealth organization is sponsoring the Digital Agenda for Europe, which includes proposing broadband connections for healthcare.[37] The European Commission provides the Health-EU portal, a website that presents eHealth work in progress, from projects to reduce air pollution to the EuroNeoStat II, a neonatal European information system.[38] At completion, in the United States, RHIOs will connect inpatient records, records from providers' offices, home health services, and patients' PHRs into true, comprehensive EMRs. Privacy and security standards are strict to ensure privacy and confidentiality of every patient's information. The vision is that the HIEs will connect around the world, supporting patient care wherever the patient is.

### *Interoperability and Standards*

An important facet of all healthcare IT applications is the use of standards. Interoperability is essential to smooth functioning of healthcare IT, and systems that support standards ensure that functionality. Health Level Seven (HL7) is an international standard interface language used in healthcare;[39] Digital Imaging and Communications in Medicine (DICOM) is used as a standard for images,[40] and the Systematized Nomenclature of Medicine - Clinical Terms (SNOMED CT) is the most comprehensive multilingual clinical healthcare terminology in the world,[41] while the International Statistical Classification of Diseases and Related

Health Problems (ICD) provides diagnosis codes for most disease conditions.[42,43] In the United States, these codes, along with current procedural terminology (CPT) codes, classify patients' diagnoses and the procedures they had, and provide a link between each procedure and the diagnosis that required it.[44] In France, the International Society for Pharmacoeconomics and Outcomes Research (ISPOR) has developed charge codes for providers, including the correct prices that can be charged for a specific procedure.[45] These codes can be entered into the system by clerical staff as well as providers, and in most cases, these codes have a large part in determining if an institution or provider will receive the maximum amount of reimbursement for performing a procedure or the minimum amount.

Interoperability is "the extent to which systems and devices can exchange data and interpret that shared data"[46] and the "uniform movement of healthcare data from one system to another such that the clinical or operational purpose and meaning of the data is preserved and unaltered."[12] With the current movement to exchanging patient data, regardless of the physical location of the patient and the patient's home data, those standards, especially for data formats and programming languages, have become increasingly important and necessary.

Without standards, interoperability is impossible; without standards, healthcare IT would most resemble the Tower of Babel, with no system or device speaking the same language and resulting in duplicative effort and work from clinical and administrative staff. In the United States, governing standards are included in the Final Rule, published by CMS in August 2012, as well as the Advisory Board for Health Standards in Europe.[47]

Included in the discussion of standards are nursing and other disciplines' terminologies. These terms can be used by nurses as well as other providers, including physicians, to document patient care. The need to standardize terms affects all parts of healthcare and especially impacts quality reporting. The use of standard words for documentation improves data and research, since it is clear what the standardized terms mean.

There are challenges to EHR interoperability throughout the world. The integration effort currently in place in Europe is improving the chances of adoption. This integration needs to move quickly, as the number of specialty systems is increasing. The specialty systems are often intended for use by only one discipline, moving away from an integrated EHR.[48]

## *Data Integration*

Data integration and the use of interface engines are essential in healthcare IT. Interface engines permit systems to be connected correctly. It is not enough to simply send data from one application to another—there are many rules that must be followed. If data does not go to the right patient's chart, errors in the patient's care, bill, and final report could result. Interface engines in a healthcare IT environment really drive the systems, matching data and patients correctly.

Without data integration and interface engines, a national health information network in either the United States or the rest of the world will never exist.

## Data Warehouses

Data warehouses are being developed and used much more frequently in today's healthcare. The value of being able to store data from multiple sources, such as the EHR and ancillary systems, is clearly recognized. Storing data in one place—the warehouse—from multiple sources allows it to be queried at the same time. Healthcare institutions have multiple requirements for submission of their data to different organizations, from the Bureau of Vital Statistics to the American Heart Association in the United States or the European Society of Cardiology. Often, these organizations require submission of the same quality improvement data elements, but just want it in a different format. The warehouse can support this type of quality reporting, as well as clinical research. Data mining can be used to identify populations at risk, search for patterns of illness, and identify potential study candidates or those patient populations that are doing well.[49] Defining a data model, deciding if a data mart would be more helpful than a warehouse, and determining how to search the warehouse are all decisions that should be made by an experienced database manager.

## Clinical and Business Intelligence (CBI)

According to the HIMSS Clinical and Business Intelligence Committee, CBI consists of "technologies, applications and practices for the collection, integration, analysis, and presentation of clinical information, for the purpose of better clinical decision-making. In recent times, quality in healthcare is being shaped by evidence-based medicine and the proper utilization of data."[50] Tools of clinical and business intelligence can provide support to clinicians to improve patient safety and patient care, as well as analyzing operating room use and staff overtime patterns. Collecting—and reporting in a meaningful way—supports not only direct patient care, but also all aspects of healthcare, including predictive analytics. Hospitals want to show that they are providing high-quality, low-cost care for their patients; providers want to show that they are doing the same. Data and data analysis are the only keys to providing that information. More and more organizations around the world are clinical and business intelligence, whether by using specific applications or by constructing data warehouses, to document the care they provide, as well as to show trends in patients' conditions and document improvements in patients' status and population health outcomes based on the care that they were given.

## Telehealth and Telemedicine

One of the fastest-growing healthcare fields that requires IT support is telehealth and telemedicine. According to the American Telemedicine Association (ATA), there were 38,000 telehealth visits for Medicare patients in 2009.[51] Telehealth can be simply two professionals communicating at a distance or a consultation from an academic medical center to a rural hospital with a severely injured trauma victim.

This type of telehealth consult requires broadband accessibility for both sides of the telehealth visit; video cameras with detailed resolution capabilities; audio/microphone equipment; equipment that will directly transmit data through the computer, such as blood pressure cuff and pulse oximeter; and the ability to send radiologic images, lab results, and any other reports needed for the visit to the physician being consulted.

Telehealth can increase access to specialized care to those living in underserved areas. Patients like telehealth, as they can often see a specialist faster than in a face-to-face appointment; their physician is included and they do not have to drive to the visit. The Veterans Administration did a large study that demonstrated the effectiveness of home health monitoring for patients with chronic diseases—both cost-effectiveness and patient outcomes—which showed decreased readmission of these patients within 30 days of discharge.[52] School children, working with the school nurse, can have a telehealth consultation and get appropriate medication and treatment while their parents stay at work and the children stay at school. Academic medical centers offer emergent consults for emergency department patients and new babies with medical issues, as well as interpretation of cardiac rhythms, reading of radiologic studies, and scheduled telehealth office visits. Equipment selection and configuration, transmission of data and image files, and real-time video/audio during a consultation all must be supported by the IT department to make telehealth as easy and seamless as a face-to-face office visit.[53]

Mobile technologies and applications (mHealth) are another growing aspect of telehealth. The WHO has a large mHealth project for tobacco control in progress.[54] There are mHealth programs in place or being developed to support maternal health, assist with the global health survey of communicable and infectious diseases and diabetes/obesity, and develop an mHealth global strategy.[7] Mobile health, with more than one-half of the population of rural areas having a cellular phone, is quickly becoming increasingly important in worldwide healthcare, education, and provision.

## *Privacy and Security*

Maintaining patients' information, ensuring that it is kept private and secure, is the first charge for EHR administration. As an example, while patients' data has to be shared through HIEs and RHIOs, it must remain confidential. Increasingly, data regulations are including strong language about privacy and security, emphasizing that the EHR can and must be developed without compromising a patient's privacy. Systems, as part of their design, have to be able to provide the patient an accounting of disclosures. The system must be able to maintain levels of confidentiality. For example, a nurse or physician must be able to see the patient's laboratory results, but a nurse's aide using that same EHR should not be able to see that information.

While disclosures of information can be made to appropriate agencies, such as the patient's insurance provider, those agencies cannot be given complete access to the patient's record, but must be given the minimum amount of information necessary.

Ethically, healthcare providers have an obligation to keep any patient's information private and confidential. The healthcare professions have codes of ethics that clearly detail the nurse's and physician's obligation to protect the patient's information.[55]

## Conclusion

Understanding the basic foundation of healthcare technologies, applications, and other tools used in connecting them together provides healthcare professionals and others allied to the field the ability to create, support, and maintain healthcare information. Knowledge of these fundamental areas, as well as key issues and trends, is the basis of building healthcare IT and supporting healthcare providers in their work of caring for patients in a safe, accurate, and timely manner.

## References

1. Seymour D. Mobile security toolkit considerations for employee-owned mobile computing devices. 2012. http://www.himss.org/ResourceLibrary/ResourceDetail. aspx?ItemNumber=10545 (accessed April 22, 2016).
2. Wireless, smartphones and applications. 2012. http://www.csoonline.com/article/2134942/data-protection/useful-settings-alert--how-to-secure-iphones--ipads.html (accessed April 22, 2016).
3. Food and Drug Administration. Draft guidance for industry and Food and Drug Administration staff—Mobile medical apps. Silver Spring, MD: Food and Drug Administration, 2011. http://www.fda.gov/MedicalDevices/ (accessed April 22, 2016).
4. Process Quality Associates. ISO 13485. London: Process Quality Associates, 2006. http://www.pqa.net/ProdServices/ISO/ISO13485.html (accessed April 22, 2016).
5. Emergo Group. Medical device approval process in Russia. Austin, TX: Emergo Group, 2012. http://www.emergogroup.com/resources/articles/russia-medical-device-approval-process (accessed April 22, 2016).
6. World Health Organization. Medical devices. Geneva: World Health Organization, 2012. http://www.who.int/medical_devices/en/ (accessed April 22, 2016).
7. World Health Organization. 2012. http://www.who.int/en/ (accessed April 22, 2016).
8. Fiore K. New device rules criticized at EASD meeting. MedPage Today, October 3, 2012. http://www.medpagetoday.com/MeetingCoverage/EASD/35119?utm_content=&utm_medium=email&utm_campaign=DailyHeadlines&utm_source=WC&xid=NL_DHE_2012-10-04&eun=g440157d0r&userid=440157&email=mbarthold@umc.edu&mu_id=5537079 (accessed April 22, 2016).

9. Kohle-Ersher A, Chatterjee P, Osmangeyoglu HU, Hochheiser H, Bartos C. Evaluating the barriers to point-of-care documentation for nursing staff. *Comput Inform Nurs* 30(3): 126–133, 2012.

10. Hedge A, James T, Pavlovic-Veselinovic S. Ergonomics concerns and the impact of healthcare information technology. *Int J Ind Ergon* 41: 345–351, 2011.

11. Man & Machine. Requirements for a medical grade keyboard. Landover, MD: Man & Machine, 2012. http://www.man-machine.com/applications/medical-grade/7-Requirements-for-a-medical-grade-keyboard.htm (accessed April 22, 2016).

12. HIMSS (Healthcare Information and Management Systems Society). *HIMSS Dictionary of Healthcare Information Technology Terms, Acronyms and Organizations.* 3rd ed. Chicago: HIMSS, 2013.

13. Office of the National Coordinator, Department of Health and Human Services. *Benefits of EHRs* [Issue brief]. Washington, DC: Office of the National Coordinator, 2012. http://www.healthit.gov/providers-professionals/electronic-medical-records-emr (accessed April 22, 2016).

14. European Commission/Information Society. 2012. http://ec.europa.eu/information_society/activities/health/index_en.htm (accessed April 22, 2016).

15. American College of Radiology. *ACR-AAPM-SIM technical standard for electronic practice of medical imaging* [Resolution ACR-Resolution 35]. Reston, VA: American College of Radiology, 2012. http://www.acr.org/~/media/ACR/Documents/PGTS/standards/ElectronicPracticeMedImg.pdf (accessed April 22, 2016).

16. Centers for Disease Control and Prevention. Certifications, licenses and accreditations. Atlanta, GA: Centers for Disease Control and Prevention. www.cdc.gov/clia (accessed April 22, 2016).

17. European Cooperation for Accreditation. 2012. hhttp://www.european-accreditation.org/home (accessed April 22, 2016).

18. Mayo Clinic Staff. Personal health record: A tool for managing your health. Scottsdale, AZ: Mayo Clinic, 2011. http://www.mayoclinic.org/healthy-lifestyle/consumer-health/in-depth/personal-health-record/art-20047273 (accessed April 22, 2016).

19. HIMSS (Healthcare Information and Management Systems Society). eConnecting with consumers. Chicago: HIMSS, 2012. http://www.himss.org/ResourceLibrary/ResourceDetail.aspx?ItemNumber=10527 (accessed April 22, 2016).

20. Microsoft HealthVault. 2012. http://www.microsoft.com/en-us/healthvault/ (accessed April 22, 2016).

21. CMS (Centers for Medicare & Medicaid Services). Personal health records. Baltimore: CMS, 2012. http://www.cms.gov/Medicare/E-Health/PerHealthRecords/index.html (accessed April 22, 2016).

22. Personal health records (PHR). 2011. http://www.medicare.gov/manage-your-health/personal-health-records/personal-health-records.html (accessed April 22, 2016).

23. American Health Information Management Association. 2012. http://myphr.com/ (accessed April 22, 2016).

24. National Committee on Vital and Health Statistics. *Personal health records and personal health record systems: A report and recommendations from the National Committee on Vital and Health Statistics.* Hyattsville, MD: National Committee on Vital and Health Statistics, 2006. http://www.ncvhs.hhs.gov/ (accessed April 22, 2016).

25. AHIMA Personal Health Record Practice Council. Helping consumers select PHRs: Questions and considerations for navigating an emerging market. Chicago: American Health Information Management Association, 2006. http://library.ahima.org/xpedio/groups/public/documents/ahima/bok1_032260.hcsp?dDocName=bok1_032260 (accessed April 22, 2016).

26. Gherardi S, Kensing F, Osterlund C. Personal health records: Empowering patients through information systems? *IT and People*, 2012. https://ec.europa.eu/digital-single-market/en/news/personal-health-records-empowering-patients-through-information-systems-manuscript-submission (accessed April 22, 2016).

27. MMRGlobal moving into Europe with MMRPro and MyMedicalRecords. Los Angeles: MMRGlobal, 2012. http://phx.corporate-ir.net/phoenix.zhtml?c=178404&p=irol-newsArticle&ID=1704074&highlight= (accessed April 22, 2016).

28. Aetna. Aetna's personal health record. Hartford, CT: Aetna, 2008. http://www.aetna.com/employer-plans/document-library/corporate-wellness-program/aetna-personal-health-record.pdf (accessed April 22, 2016).

29. California HealthCare Foundation. New national survey finds personal health records motivate consumers to improve their health. Oakland: California HealthCare Foundation, 2010. http://www.chcf.org/media/press-releases/2010/new-national-survey-finds-personal-health-records-motivate-consumers-to-improve-their-health (accessed April 22, 2016).

30. Lewis N. Consumers slow to adopt electronic personal health records. *Information Week*, April 8, 2011. http://www.informationweek.com/healthcare/electronic-medical-records/consumers-slow-to-adopt-electronic-perso/229401249# (accessed April 22, 2016).

31. NHS (National Health Service). Introduction to summary care records. London: NHS, 2012. http://www.nhs.uk/NHSEngland/thenhs/records/healthrecords/Pages/servicedescription.aspx (accessed April 22, 2016).

32. Should physicians use email to communicate with patients? *Wall Street Journal*, January 23, 2012. http://online.wsj.com/article/SB10001424052970204124204577152860059245028.html (accessed April 22, 2016).

33. Department of Health and Human Services. *Health information technology: Initial set of standards, implementation specifications, and certification criteria for electronic health record technology; Final Rule* (45 CFR Part 170). Washington, DC: Government Printing Office, 2010.

34. Wiljer D, Urowitz S, Apatu E, DeLenardo C, Eysenbach G, Harth T, Leonard KJ. Patient accessible electronic health records: Exploring recommendations for successful implementation strategies. *J Med Internet Res* 10(4), 2008. http://dx.doi.org/10.2196/jmir.1061 (accessed April 22, 2016).

35. E-HIM Work Group on Patient Identification in RHIOs. Surveying the RHIO landscape: A description of current RHIO models, with a focus on patient identification. 2006. http://library.ahima.org/xpedio/groups/public/documents/ahima/bok1_028980.hcsp?dDocName=bok1_028980 (accessed April 22, 2016).

36. TechTarget. Regional health information network. Newton, MA: TechTarget, 2010. http://searchhealthit.techtarget.com/definition/Regional-Health-Information-Organization-RHIO (accessed April 22, 2016).

37. European Commission. Commission proposes over 9 billion for broadband. Brussels: European Commission, 2011. https://ec.europa.eu/digital-single-market/ (accessed April 22, 2016).

38. European Commission Health-EU. Your gateway to trustworthy information on public health. Brussels: European Commission, 2012. http://ec.europa.eu/index_en.htm (accessed April 22, 2016).

39. Health Level Seven International. 2012. http://www.hl7.org/ (accessed April 22, 2016).

40. DICOM (Digital Imaging and Communications in Medicine). http://dicom.nema.org/ (accessed April 22, 2016).

41. SNOMED CT (SNOMED Clinical Terms). http://www.ihtsdo.org/snomed-ct/ (accessed April 22, 2016).

42. HIMSS (Healthcare Information and Management Systems Society). ICD-10 playbook. Chicago, HIMSS, 2012. http://himss.org/ASP/topics_icd10playbook.asp (accessed April 22, 2016).

43. CDC (Centers for Disease Control and Prevention). Classification of diseases, functioning and disability. Atlanta, GA: CDC, 2011. http://www.cdc.gov/nchs/icd/icd10cm.htm (accessed April 22, 2016).

44. American Medical Association. 2012. http://www.ama-assn.org/ama/pub/physician-resources/solutions-managing-your-practice/coding-billing-insurance/cpt.page (accessed April 22, 2016).

45. Meyer F, Denis C. France—Medical devices. Lawrenceville, NJ: International Society for Pharmacoeconomics and Outcomes Research, 2011. http://www.ispor.org/htaroadmaps/francemd.asp (accessed April 22, 2016).

46. HIMSS (Healthcare Information and Management Systems Society). Interoperability & standards. Chicago: HIMSS, 2012. http://www.himss.org/asp/topics_interoperability.asp (accessed April 22, 2016).

47. CEN-CENELEC Advisory Board for Healthcare Standards. 2009. http://www.cen.eu/cen/Sectors/Sectors/Healthcare/Forum/Pages/currentissues.aspx (accessed April 22, 2016).

48. Lakovidis I. Towards personal health record: Current situation, obstacles and trends in implementation of electronic healthcare record in Europe. *Int J Med Inform* 52(1–3): 105–115, 1998. http://www.ijmijournal.com/article/S1386-5056(98)00129-4/abstract?showall=true= (accessed April 22, 2016).

49. Wickramasinghe N, Calman RA, Schaffer JL. *Defining the landscape: Data warehouse and mining: Intelligence continuum* [HIMSS white paper]. Chicago: Healthcare Information and Management Systems Society, 2007. http://www.himss.org/content/files/Intel_Continuum06052007.pdf http://www.himss.org/ResourceLibrary/ResourceDetail.aspx?ItemNumber=11002 (accessed April 22, 2016).

50. Clinical business intelligence committee. 2012. http://www.himss.org/get-involved/committees/clinical-business-intelligence (accessed April 22, 2016).

51. Medicare—Telehealth coverage. In Medicare—ATA Wiki. http://atawiki.org.s161633.gridserver.com/wiki/index.php?title=Main_Page (accessed April 22, 2016).

52. Darkins A, Ryan P, Kobb R, Foster L, Edmonson E, Wakefield B, Lancaster AE. Care coordination/home telehealth: The systematic implementation of health information, home telehealth and disease management to support the care of veteran patients with chronic conditions. *Telemed e-Health* 14(10): 1118–1126, 2008. http://dx.doi.org/10.1089/tmj.2008.0021 (accessed April 22, 2016).

53. HIMSS (Healthcare Information and Management Systems Society). Telehealth. Chicago: HIMSS, 2012. http://www.himss.org/News/NewsDetail.aspx?ItemNumber=47466 (accessed April 22, 2016).

54. World Health Organization. Mobile health (mHealth for tobacco control). Geneva: World Health Organization, 2012. http://www.who.int/tobacco/mhealth/en/ (accessed April 22, 2016).

55. Erickson JI, Millar S. Caring for patients while respecting their privacy: Renewing our commitment. *Online J Issues Nurs* 10(2), 2005. http://nursingworld.org/MainMenuCategories/ANAMarketplace/ANAPeriodicals/OJIN/TableofContents/Volume102005/No2May05/tpc27_116017.html (accessed April 22, 2016).

# SYSTEMS

**II**

# Chapter 3

## Systems Analysis

## Learning Objectives

At the conclusion of this chapter, the reader will be able to

- Describe the major components of the systems analysis process with regard to IT implementation in healthcare
- Articulate the problem that can be resolved through proper policies based on IT
- Explain the current and developing trends in IT systems analysis
- Perform a cost–benefit analysis of a proposed initiative
- Identify the project management stages that are most important to the systems analysis phase

## Introduction

Over the last two decades, different industries have adopted the use of information technology (IT) in their various operations in order to enhance growth, conform to emerging standards, attract new customers, maximize profitability, and acquire business intelligence. Different sectors, however, have adopted IT use in different capacities. The health sector, like all others, is striving to enhance the acceptance of better and easier techniques available through an IT implementation. However, the average use of IT in healthcare has lagged behind other industry sectors for the better part of the last decade. Healthcare has many potential benefits from IT implementation in both managerial operations and patient-related operations. This chapter focuses on systems analysis with regard to IT implementation in healthcare facilities, and it identifies problems that could be solved through proper policies based on IT and links those problems with possible opportunities presented by current and developing IT trends. In addition, this chapter presents an example of a working proposal to aid in the implementation of profitable IT practices, as well as in performing a cost–benefit analysis of a sample proposed initiative.

## Healthcare Problems and Opportunities for IT Implementation

The healthcare situation in the global platform is experiencing dynamic changes in several ways. The major avenues of the change involve the following.

### Clinical Functions

A significant percentage of modern healthcare facilities are using IT systems in clinical operations. However, the majority of units are still dependent on traditionally used systems, such as physical patients' document keeping, lab reports, drug administration history, and other functions. Historically, they have lacked computerized order information and histories for drugs and other substances, medical supplies catalogs, and lab test results. In addition, they lacked an integrated, interoperable electronic health record (EHR); image and film archiving and associated communications systems; the result analysis mechanism for ordinary patient processes such as lab tests and drug prescriptions; decision support facilities in clinical systems; prescription error alert systems; and electronic monitoring of high-care patients, especially in intensive care units (ICUs). While much progress has been made in these areas over the past decade, we still have a long way to go before we achieve a global, interoperable healthcare system in all types of healthcare settings.

### Applications for Clinical Functions

EHRs involve standardizing the way in which patients' records are entered, stored, and retrieved, not just within an organization, but across different hospitals, caregivers, government-controlled organizations, and other interested parties. The biggest challenge regarding EHRs has been the establishment of an industry standard to use so that an efficient workflow can be realized that would allow for seamless retrieval and use of records for patients, even when patients are moved to units other than where they were initially treated.

This kind of data pool would imply a dedicated system with necessary checks and balances to prevent unauthorized access to and manipulation of patient records, while at the same time enabling data entry by different care units when patients make additional visits to any facility. This concept is delicate in view of the possibility of malicious addition or manipulation of patient data by different staff in different facilities. Moreover, a lack of universal standards in proper coding and categorization of prescriptions and procedures has hindered the implementation of interoperable EHR systems in the last two decades. This problem can now be sufficiently handled by high-end software applications that are being developed by individual and corporate research entities.[1]

One such authority, the Health Information Technology for Economic and Clinical Health Act (HITECH Act), is a U.S. government initiative to enable EHR availability in a secure and safe manner that allows EHR use across the health-care spectrum. Presently, other systems that are being pursued include computerized practitioner order entry (CPOE), which may replace conventional order cataloging and fulfillment in a manner that will enhance tracking, logistic synchronization, and cost-effectiveness, and the clinical decision support system (CDSS), which, in its basic form, will give informative guidelines to practitioners regarding medication and procedures, including warning systems relating to high-risk medications and processes.

In addition, the picture archiving and communication system (PACS) will integrate inputs from multiple radiological and diagnostic tools to allow easy, consistent, and accurate treatment of different conditions, while radio frequency identification (RFID) may help to track patients within a medical unit without the need to restrict them to a particular location or allocate a nurse to them. The vital signs collectable from this system may include pulse rate, temperature level, blood pressure, and other metabolic/respiratory signals. Benefits of such a system, if properly collected, stored, and secured, when integrated with other dedicated software applications, may shorten treatment time, allow more freedom, and lead to cost efficiency and better resource utilization within a hospital or other healthcare facility. Automated dispensing machines (ADMs) will aid in drug dispensing, while electronic materials management (EMM) systems will operate like the resource planning systems used in other sectors to manage information processing regarding pharmaceuticals, new drug development, and coding, among other functions. Such a system would reduce medication errors, which, as of the year 2000, were responsible for more than 98,000 deaths in the United States alone.[2]

## *Administrative and Financial Services*

Functions that could be enhanced through investment in IT in the administrative category include general ledger operations, such as revenue and cash flow, expenses, purchases, and other day-to-day transactions. Other functions are billing, cost accounting systems, payroll, personnel management and integrated human resource functions, patient registration and booking, and electronic management of materials, among others.

### *Applications for Administration and Finance*

IT may find many basic as well as advanced applications in administrative and financial services. Human resource management has experienced radical changes in operational methods as a result of IT implementations. Systems for employee management, role definition, reward and recognition support, and performance development have been successfully automated thanks to dedicated software such as enterprise relational database management systems (RDBMSs). Such systems allow easy, timely, and accurate workflow management in human resource mobilization and development, saving time and costs that would otherwise be allocated for additional staff. Other functions, such as payroll, budgeting, internal audits, and strategic planning, have also been made easier, more precise, and tailor-made for specific analytical objectives without incurring additional monthly or yearly charges due to the use of IT systems. Patient registration and tracking can become more enhanced and efficient, and access to the online statistics of every facility within an area may be useful in referrals and in discharge notification, enabling time saving and better emergency handling.

## Infrastructure

Infrastructure is a broad category that incorporates various equipment with diverse applications, both general and specific. Current security standards have shifted toward biometric sensors for movement and access control in many major private and public buildings and premises. These security standards enhance accountability in system access and support user logging, which enhances safety and responsibility among authorized personnel. The healthcare sector could, perhaps, benefit the most from such systems, given the delicate nature of confidentiality requirements involved in patient records access and dissemination. Biometric sensors typically used include fingerprint or palm scanners, voice recognition systems, and eye scanners, among others. Other more dedicated systems include bar coding systems for medication grouping, ordering, cataloging, and stock control. Security infrastructure may also include closed-circuit TV cameras and night infrared cameras.

### Security-Related Applications

Since IT relates to healthcare security, it may find many uses, some of which may not be achieved in other ways. Patient information access logging is important in ensuring confidentiality and professionalism in the way patients are treated. It increases patients' confidence in their practitioners and boosts their trust levels. In addition, the use of biometric systems will eliminate to a large extent ambiguity in accountability in delicate cases due to their high precision levels and extremely low chances of identity theft or manipulation, unlike conventional security protocols when any person with forced access to pass codes may steal information. In addition, healthcare research facilities may hold expensive machinery that, if it falls into wrong hands, may be used in ways detrimental to society. For instance, ultra-modern DNA synthesis machines, if used by experts, may find applications in the terrorist underworld. Other chemicals and drugs in healthcare facilities may also be abused or sold to unsuspecting people as legitimate prescriptions and lead to catastrophic consequences. Such security measures cannot be overlooked, and government control is restricting the use of certain machinery and equipment to high-security facilities, limiting the range of services that healthcare units with lower security may offer.

Another broad category of infrastructure has to do with network development and all associated controls. Medicare processes large amounts of information internally, not to mention the external linkage requirements associated with referrals and national accountability reports that must be processed and sent to government control and data collection agencies and other industry regulatory bodies. The baseline network infrastructure includes servers, end-user computer stations, switches, network access points, all associated cabling, and external access infrastructure. While very elaborate high-level applications have been incorporated into network infrastructures in a significant number of healthcare facilities, the majority of care units are using their network support equipment for only slightly more than baseline uses, such as record keeping and document sharing.

## Needs Analysis in Healthcare Facilities

In order to develop a proper proposal for sustainable IT supplementation in the core processes of the healthcare sector, it is important to identify the main challenges in the sector and specifically those needs that can be sufficiently met by the implementation of sustainable, secure, and cost-efficient IT practices. This section will give a detailed needs analysis to lay the foundation for the chapter. The analysis focuses on requirements that may be categorized as operational, administrative, or industry related.

### *Operational Needs*

Healthcare facilities need to streamline their core administrative and financial operations with the current global standards in order to foster interoperability in record keeping and analysis with other stakeholders, investors, and business partners. Currently, healthcare as an industry is behind average industry standards in IT acceptance. Such processes as payment processing, e-bill systems, human resource systems, stock intake, auditing, and other similar functions can be sufficiently integrated with the use of developing software.[3] In order for a system to be sustainable and standard, it is necessary to select a universally accepted platform for data storage and analysis in which organizations may pool data relating to logistics and facilities. Financial as well as private human resource information does not need to be pooled in a central storage facility, but adopting software dedicated to easing these functions on a private level is necessary in order to reduce costs, enhance operational efficiency, and increase profitability. Operational needs may be broken down into several areas.

## Staff Productivity and Satisfaction

The use of IT may reduce time wasted by operational staff performing administrative work and enhance patient attendance time, which is the key need for patients. It will also reduce unnecessary routines in patient care and reduce work of clinical staff due to rigorous, non-work-related duties. Additionally, it will improve employee satisfaction and reduce fatigue due to extensive overtime schedules. Better productivity will invariably lead to increased patient volumes.

## Increased Revenue and Cost Optimization

Increased visitor capacity per unit may boost revenues for a care unit due to a larger number of admissions and discharges per month following shortened lengths of stay, reduced unit costs for bulk purchases, and improved capability to meet overhead expenses. Cost optimization needs to be realized through bulk purchases, efficient stock control, and reduced cost per day for each patient. In this regard, IT practices will save costs for the unit as well as daily treatment and accommodation charges to the customer.

## Patient Safety

A significant number of deaths and serious medical malpractice cases are reported each year due to errors in treatment, procedures, or prescriptions. The major cases involve adverse drug events (ADEs) due to wrong prescriptions that affect patients negatively, admissions following adverse drug events, errors in surgical procedures and blood transfusions, and malpractice expenses such as corrective procedures, court litigations, and compensations. There is an urgent need to reduce such occurrences, many of which can be satisfactorily handled by the application of proper IT processes.

## Quality of Care

Patient quality of care deals with the satisfaction that patients get from care providers' efforts to resolve their problems. It may involve time of delay, time of treatment, appropriateness of procedures used and drugs administered, and the levels of professionalism, confidentiality, and courtesy of the staff. Moreover, it may involve specific professional services, such as recognition and accreditations, complication management, physician or nurse time with patients, and reduced length of stay.[3]

## Patient Access to Services

Apart from the length of stay, patients are concerned with delay time for such processes as lab reports, billing, online services such as viewing and scheduling, preventive care management, and outpatient care appointment bookings.

There is a need to upgrade systems that can be automated to handle most of the routine work not requiring case-specific diagnosis, such as remote patient appointment bookings and all associated alerts on scheduling, integrated lab linkage with other hospital systems that eliminates the need for extended physical queues at facilities, and electronic procedures for alternative bill settlement by customers. If proper systems are established to meet the outlined objectives, other needs relating to healthcare that cannot be quantified but lie at the core of healthcare provision will also be realized. This will lead to nonmonetary benefits such as good patient–physician relationships and improved community health.[3]

## Needs Summary

The foregoing discussion highlights the need for all-around IT supplementation to help healthcare catch up with other sectors in terms of modernization and integration. In essence, what is required is sufficient planning to implement safe, sustainable, and cost-effective IT practices to help healthcare in (1) administrative, (2) operational, (3) patient-related, and (4) industry-related functions. There is a need for a seamless backbone IT platform that integrates these four needs, as well as sustainable controls for the IT implementation to ensure it remains secure, serves the maximum purpose possible, and is practical for universal adaptability in order to satisfy the core concern within various healthcare institutions, which is the integration of policy implementation.

# Needs Prioritization

While all the needs listed above are urgent and important, there are certain ones that must be prioritized in order for IT acceptance in healthcare to stand. These processes are the backbone of healthcare, and all other requirements are built on them. For instance, patient security and safety are core driving factors for any practitioner, and they surpass the need for good bookkeeping or profit optimization. Without proper observance of fundamental safety concerns, healthcare units are likely to face legal implications that could cause them to lose their license, rendering futile any advancement they may have in their other operations. This section will therefore seek to address the need for prioritization of IT acceptance in healthcare facilities based on the hierarchy of the needs model. The primary priority from an individual facility's perspective is patient safety, followed by profitability, then ease of processes, and lastly, industry standardization. From the healthcare industry's perspective, the priorities are likely to be patient safety and security, professionalism, standardization, profitability, and ease of processes. Obviously, the ease of processes is in most cases tied with profitability.[4] The project must therefore address IT implementation issues from both perspectives and attempt to strike a balance. Figure 3.1 illustrates the differing priorities of individual facilities and the healthcare industry.

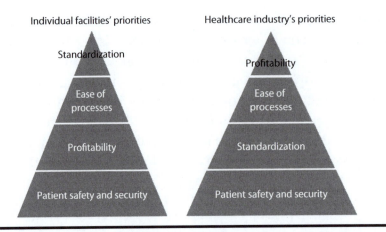

**Figure 3.1    Differing priorities of individual facilities and the healthcare industry.**

# Work Plan Development

A work plan is aimed at establishing a step-by-step implementation setup for a project, including materials and equipment layout, intended workflow processes, managing the time, analyzing processes, and evaluating outcomes. In the healthcare IT implementation plan, a proper work plan involves putting in place procedures to realize the needs for IT acceptance by healthcare facilities, starting with the primary priorities and proceeding to other priorities.[5] Sample elements of a work plan are presented below.

## Executive Summary

This project is aimed at analyzing the efficiency of the current systems in healthcare and assessing the situation with the purpose of providing a working alternative that is IT enhanced and will lead to the realization of target objectives of the sector. The plan will provide the project implementation phases as well as define specific operations to be carried out during each phase.

## Introduction and Background

The implementation of IT policies in healthcare has been faced with many challenges, rendering the process complex and nonstandardized.[6] Establishing a comprehensive industry standardization process has been impossible due to various individual interests among care providers, drug and device manufacturers, pharmaceutical companies, and regulating bodies. Thus, there has been a diverse range of new drugs and other medication practices localized in small market segments without proper administration and regulation. In addition, a wide network of healthcare facilities operating in different geographical, economic, technological, and cultural settings has made it difficult for the various stakeholders to come together and develop an enhanced global EHR system that will ensure standardization of procedures, leading to a net lag in technology acceptance in the healthcare sector. The IT sector, however, has advanced and infiltrated all major sectors on the global platform, forcing all industries to confirm or become outdated. This is the case in the healthcare sector as well, prompting stakeholders to start seeking urgent and sustainable methods in preparation for standardization and alignment with emerging trends on the global IT platform.

## *Goals and Objectives*

The goal of this work is to find a structure for IT integration in the healthcare sector's main processes, which includes cost-effectiveness, patient safety and care, ease of processes, and industry standardization. To this end, specific objectives must be identified initially that include the following:

- Evaluation of the current operational situation in each healthcare facility. This step will include analysis of current clinical processes such as process mapping. It will also document the current trends that can be found in healthcare procedures, including administrative and operational trends and integration of workflows.
- Identification of the major problems in these processes with respect to the optimization of the IT use. This stage will involve comparing the efficiency of the current processes with the efficiency typically achievable in a similar setting with IT implementation.
- Identification of alternative solutions to these problems through the implementation of IT policies. This process will involve providing alternative solutions to the current processes and will include software and hardware recommendations, as well as a proposal for a working interface with existing resources.
- Carrying out a comparative analysis of the alternative processes and the original routines. Flow charts, tables, process flows, and other analytic tools will show relationships and deviations between the systems, thereby guiding the policy implementation decisions.
- Evaluation of alternative solutions in alignment with the specific objectives set out in the plan. This stage will involve rethinking the project intentions and comparing them with realized outcomes to assess efficiency.
- Evaluation of the ethical, legal, social, and economic implications of the alternatives through a comprehensive cost–benefit analysis.
- Developing a proposal for implementing recommendations and following up after the project to enable quality improvement.

## *Resources*

The plan will usually involve the purchase of additional materials, as well as the hiring of support staff. The major resources should be assigned as follows:

- Personnel—The category will involve all people contracted in the rollout process, including software support teams, simulation teams, project evaluation teams, engineers in various capacities, technical teams, and other necessary personnel.
- Partners—These may be governments, government-sponsored partners, nongovernment organizations, and private investment agencies, among other stakeholders.
- Equipment—This includes facilities and computers, software, and related capital purchases.
- Legal and regulatory infrastructure intended for the implementation of IT.

### Work Plan Accountability

The resources available for the implementation of a proposal will be regulated and governed by a project management or steering committee that will be responsible for budgetary allocations, expenditure monitoring, and accounts reconciliation. In addition, time management will be essential in order to complete the phases of the project implementation within the specified time frame.

## Current Clinical Processes

Operations and processes in the healthcare sector can be analyzed in four broad categories: administrative and financial, operational, process flow, and standardization. Generally, the healthcare industry scores below average in terms of IT adoption. According to research conducted by the Lewin Group in North America in 2007, only about 2.5% of revenues were spent on IT in the hospitals sector. In addition, physicians invested even less in IT (1.5%).[7] In the year 2012, however, most healthcare institutions reported IT implementation of some form.

Figures 3.2 and 3.3 present typical process flow diagrams that aid in identifying areas of two healthcare processes that are manageable using IT.[8]

Figure 3.2 shows the process flow for a typical client briefing about lab reports. A nurse will usually try to reach a patient more than four times in stated durations, usually from a few hours to a day. This process takes time, delays other functions, and consequently, leads to fewer patients served per day. The proper IT implementation, even on the internal level, may allow convenient patient briefing and follow-up using trusted e-mail services, among other channels. Patients can usually be given the option to choose their preferred channel of communication before leaving the hospital or other care facility.

A typical referral process involves even more delay. The referral-patient booking process is diagrammed in Figure 3.3.[9] The figure clearly demonstrates delays introduced in current healthcare systems due to lack of integration between the communication and decision-making systems involving care providers, referral

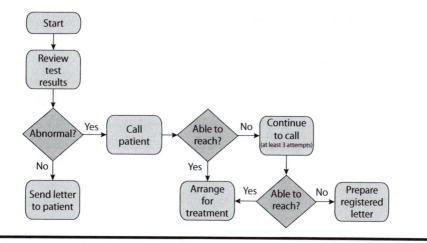

**Figure 3.2   Process 1: Laboratory results patient information process.**

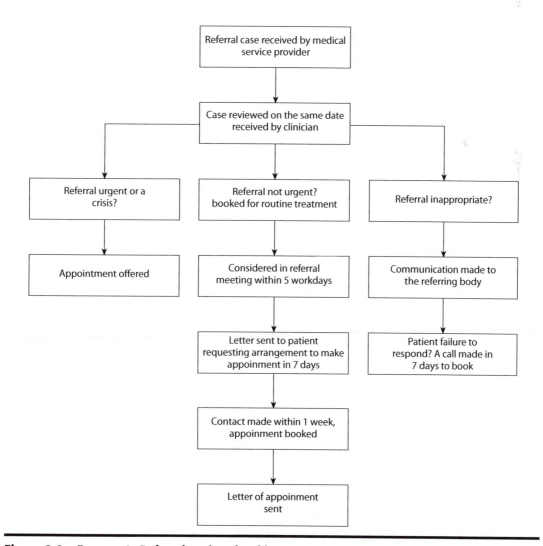

**Figure 3.3   Process 2: Referral-patient booking process.**

centers, and patients. In the workflow diagram, it may be noted that a referral patient may wait up to two weeks between the date of referral and the date of appointment booking solely due to communication and work arrangement delays. Referrals may not appear urgent on the reported data sheet, but patients' situations may become aggravated during the waiting period when they are unable to obtain help. As a result, patient services may be greatly compromised due to the systems' inefficiency. In addition, the lengthy waiting period can be greatly reduced if proper IT policies that incorporate remote meetings, such as video and audio conferencing, are implemented. The time spent between contacting a patient and receiving a response constitutes service degradation for the patient and revenue loss for the care provider.

A reduced number of patients are seen per day; therefore, customer satisfaction levels may also decline. While authentication issues may be cited as the reason for insistence on the use of official letters by care providers, the bulk of the processes requiring care provider–client correspondence involve non-vital documents, such as requests for bookings. A possible method of bypassing this hindrance through the IT-based communication implementation is to develop a web-based communication and client support system that would allow secure communication between the customer and the care provider. In this platform, customers would be able to receive e-mails and respond to booking notifications.

In addition, digital signing is a standard that is progressively being adopted by many industry sectors and is a concept that may be beneficial to healthcare providers when they send documents requiring authorization or authentication. As an alternative, the use of registered mailing services may greatly reduce the feedback duration for sensitive medical cases. Apart from the operational perspective, billing systems and other workflow routines in most facilities are also very inefficient. The entire process, which includes a medical history review, booking to be attended by the physician, physician duration, prescription, queuing at the pharmacy, and bill settlement, involves avoidable delays. These work stages can be sufficiently improved by computer-aided work management and decision making.

## Current Healthcare IT Integration Status

The Healthcare Information Technology Standards Panel (HITSP) is the body in charge of seeking a way forward in healthcare IT standards integration. It enlists organizations, research facilities, vendors, and healthcare providers to become actively involved in sponsoring and establishing a common standard for IT in healthcare. The organization was created in 2005 by the Office of the National Coordinator for Health Information Technology (ONC) and has standardized various protocols for EHRs and other clinical processes. One of its main priorities has been empowering consumers by allowing them access to their clinical information, such as medication history and lab results. It also seeks to integrate EHRs with laboratory systems and to streamline biosurveillance by defining standards for the exchange of information among healthcare providers and public health authorities.

In 2007, its main case uses included consumer access to information such as personal records transfer and access permissions grant. It also included emergency response services, medication management, and a care facilities quality survey. In its last major release on January 20, 2010, HITSP laid out an interoperability program for North American healthcare institutions.[9] This work continues through the ONC Health IT Standards Committee and remains a top priority at the federal level.

# Deficiencies in Current IT Healthcare Practices

From the discussion provided above regarding process flows in the healthcare sector's IT policies and practices, it can be seen that there are still some obstacles to customer satisfaction, healthcare business profitability, and industry integration. These obstacles, which are restricting the sector's potential growth, will be analyzed in this section based on the industry's key performance indicators (KPIs). Client satisfaction through good services and support, business growth through revenue generation, efficient service process arrangement, and proper implementation integration can be attained through the corporate initiative.

## *Patient Support and Satisfaction*

Unnecessarily high numbers of patients leave healthcare units without treatment due to long waits for service. Physicians see fewer patients per day when lengthy delays are caused by lack of proper equipment. Such slow systems also lead to extra work for the available personnel, which causes degradation in service quality. Proper patient support and safety also have a correlation with employee retention and employee satisfaction. When healthcare workers are overwhelmed, they tend to perform more poorly and have higher exit rates than workers in places where IT supports workflow management.

## *Reduction in Revenue Generation*

Many healthcare systems are not efficient in revenue generation, and there is a possibility for improvement through IT innovation. Delays in customer service lead to low numbers of attended patients per day, which results in revenue losses. In addition, many patients leave unattended, which leads to business loss. On top of this, healthcare facilities lose potential clients who might have been referred by existing customers if they had not been annoyed by long wait times. In addition to losing business, healthcare units incur extra expenses due to overtime work by doctors and nurses when workloads are heavy. These increased operational expenses and reduced business revenue contribute to overall reduction in business profitability. Inefficient facilities also require a significantly higher number of workers to cope with the physical workflow and lack of integration, which results in extra costs.[10]

## Prescription Errors

The current healthcare system does not fully utilize software-supported decision making for medication orders, even though it would greatly enhance the checking of prescriptions to ensure proper diagnosis support, drug type, and dosage. This has resulted in numerous prescription errors, which may lead to adverse patient reactions and deaths. Improper prescriptions have also led to an increase in drug-related claims, legal penalties, license withdrawals, and other challenges that could be avoided by proper IT support.

## Industry Standardization

Continued lack of healthcare IT standards has led to the loss of tremendous opportunities to improve interoperability, data sharing, and transitions of care. This situation will be significantly changed when sustainable policy frameworks can be agreed upon and implemented by IT experts and enforced by government to expand the implementation of IT integration.

# Alternative Approaches to Current Healthcare Processes

To increase revenue, provide a seamless link between facilities and regions, and improve the patient experience in healthcare workflows, certain IT-based procedures can be implemented. The following section explores these alternatives according to the deficiency area.

## Industry Standardization

HITSP and ONC have made a lot of positive achievements in IT integration over the last decade. While there are numerous challenges in such an attempt and many success stories, we continue to work toward this accomplishment through different avenues.[11] Future initiatives might include a new integrated architecture that would meet a cross section of market needs. This platform would be such as to link with all major existing software and hardware configurations in the market, such as EHRs, DMSs, and imaging programs, among others.

## Alternative Ways to Reduce Prescription Errors

Unlike the global integration challenge, prescription errors can be handled from a local perspective while awaiting the market integration standards. Many software applications are dedicated to prescription information and decision support systems. Avoidance of ADEs is one major KPI that can be addressed by IT implementation in the healthcare sector. One such software category is called the clinical decision support system, which provides updated information regarding recommendations for prescriptions to nurses, physicians, and other qualified healthcare workers. This system is typically integrated with the EHR and CPOE systems in order to perform a proper scenario analysis with appropriate patient backup before a provider writes a prescription. Many commercially available software options offer this functionality.

## *Alternative Processes for Revenue Generation*

Financial processes are, perhaps, the easiest to simulate in IT process integration due to their general nature and resemblance to other industries' financial processes. Revenue generation draws primarily from workflow optimization, which mainly seeks to reduce query time and thus queue time, reduce waiting time through the implementation of fast patient data retrieval and diagnostic support, and reduce laboratory scheduling and patient briefing time by enhancing fast decision-relay procedures and online client information alternatives. Online support may be an easy way for patients to obtain their lab results electronically signed by their care providers without having to wait in queue. Such a system is not out of reach and may be developed by most modern web applications. In addition to saving time and encouraging more customers, an IT-based process would lead to higher levels of perceived efficiency, productivity, better customer experiences and satisfaction, and therefore more referrals.

This chain of flow would, in turn, generate more revenue and lead to higher growth rates. Many software applications have support for workflow management, and most of them do not require very high initial investments in comparison to the average capital requirements of a modern healthcare facility.

## Comparative Analysis of Alternatives

This section summarizes the current versus expected status of various aspects of a healthcare IT implementation.

Intended achievements attributable to the new system implementation are presented in Table 3.1 and supported by various research into IT-related healthcare practices. While the extent to which key industry players may benefit from the implementation of these new IT practices may vary, it is likely that the net results will be beneficial.[6] In addition, the capital implications of implementing IT-based healthcare support systems are within investment range. Long-term investment costs should be recoverable from the benefits obtained from healthcare interoperability.

**Table 3.1  Comparative Analysis of Core Processes in Healthcare**

| Variables | Current Status | IT-Enhanced Status |
|---|---|---|
| Patient service | Lengthy queue times, typically 20 minutes | Queue times reduced by up to 5 times |
| | Long durations for record retrieval | Instant record retrieval |
| | Long wait times for lab reports, prescriptions, and correspondence | Shortened lab report delays, instant prescription information, and instant messaging |
| Service processes | Manually coordinated | Computer simulated and optimized |
| | Delays and inefficiency in processes | Very efficient monitoring |
| | Duplicated work and delayed completion | Proper process scheduling |
| | Lack of feedback, rigid decision making | Decisions based on feedback with continuous dynamic optimization |
| Erroneous prescriptions | Prevalent errors, with numerous legal and financial implications | Greatly reduced number of prescription errors and minimal revenue loss |
| | High admission rates for ADEs | Greatly reduced admissions due to ADEs |
| | Capacity limited by number of prescription-related admissions | More capacity for new cases due to reduction of ADEs |
| Industry standardization | Highly localized | Universally available |
| | Business losses due to lack of interoperability | Enhanced business due to interoperability |
| | Limited data access | Optimized data access and improved quality of care |

# Proposal Evaluation

The organizational business plan for most healthcare facilities has four major objectives: patient satisfaction, revenue generation, efficient processes that cut costs and increase profits, and conformity to industry standards. The proposed solution model should meet all those requirements. First, customer satisfaction is achieved through efficient processes that reduce delay time, enhance the customer experience, and offer good follow-up on patient issues. Second, revenue generation is enhanced through shortened staff time spent per patient, which leads to increased daily patient attendance figures. Third, efficiency in the process flows reduces work duplication and improves service quality, both of which increase revenue generation through cost cutting. Fourth, the proposal expressly seeks to establish a platform for standardization of healthcare IT processes. In summary, the proposed solution enhances the general business requirements and objectives for the average healthcare provider and ultimately the patient.

## Cost–Benefit Analysis

The stakeholders who stand to gain or lose due to this policy implementation are healthcare facilities, patients, medical practitioners' representative bodies, drug and medical equipment manufacturers, state and federal governments and related authorities, and computer equipment and software manufacturers and vendors. The expected cost–benefit elements include finance, service quality, control, and time, among others. The important variables to be considered in the analysis are the time of implementation, cost of implementation, alternatives to the proposal, impact on stakeholders, impact on external parties, sustainability versus ongoing operating costs per year, and value of time to be used in the implementation. The HIMSS Health IT Value Suite is another model that provides both a structure and vocabulary with which the enterprise can organize its value proposition strategy. The suite highlights hundreds of examples of hospitals, physician practices, communities, and accountable care organizations that have realized the full value of Health IT.[12]

Table 3.2 provides a sample of a cost–benefit analysis for the enhanced IT project.

The anticipated outcome of the cost–benefit analysis predicts a continuous reduction in investment costs and a net increment in revenue generation for manufacturers of products that support or can be adapted to the new standard, healthcare facilities, and drug and medical equipment manufacturers. Similarly, the net long-term outcome for the patient is better service, improved quality of care, and greater satisfaction.

### *Proposal Sensitivity Analysis*

Any proposed IT implementation may exhibit various levels of sensitivity to different stakeholders at different times and also to all stakeholders over the course of time. The project's sensitivity to these challenges or changes in the environment will rely on the establishment of a support team to ensure conformity of a project's various elements and initiatives.

**Table 3.2   Cost–Benefit Analysis of Proposed Healthcare IT Implementation**

| Variables | Costs | Benefits |
|---|---|---|
| Financial implications | • Internal equipment and software upgrade | • Increased revenues of up to 50% per year |
| | • Licensing fees | • Access to the global interoperability platform |
| | • Loss of investment for users of nonstandard applications | |
| Customers | • Possible compromise of privacy and safety due to malicious information access and manipulation | • Improved services, care, and access to records |
| | | • Reduction of prescription errors and resources wasted due to ADEs |
| Drug and medical equipment manufacturers and related bodies | • Possible losses in equipment standardization, but generally minimal negative effects | • Better policy implementation due to globalization of standards |
| | | • Less counterfeiting and associated losses |
| | | • Possibility of forming stronger representative bodies |
| Governments | • Reduced control of medical and healthcare practices for member states | • Increased diplomatic ties |
| | | • Better availability of globally competitive healthcare standards for citizens |
| Interoperability and standards | • Possible realignment of the structure to include international representation | • Achievement of core objective of standardization of healthcare |
| Hardware and software developers and manufacturers | • Possible loss of business for companies whose products fail to support the new standards | • Numerous opportunities for new developments and increase in sales |

# References

1. Morrissey J. Capital crunch eats away at IT. *Mod Healthc* 34(8): 32–62, 2004.
2. Institute of Medicine. *Preventing Medication Errors.* Washington, DC: National Academies Press, 2006.
3. Armoni A. *Effective Healthcare Information Systems.* Hershey, PA: IRM Press, 2002.
4. Spekowius G, Wendler T. *Advances in Healthcare Technology Shaping the Future of Medical Care.* Dordrecht, Netherlands: Springer, 2006.

5. HandsOn Network. Developing a work plan. Atlanta: HandsOn Network. http://www.handsonnetwork.org/developing-work-plan (accessed April 22, 2014).

6. Tyrrell S. *Using Information and Communication Technology in Healthcare.* Abingdon, UK: Radcliffe Medical, 2002.

7. Shoniregun C, Dube K, Mtenzi F. *Electronic Healthcare Information Security.* New York: Springer, 2010.

8. National Council of State Boards of Nursing. New nurse toolkit. Chicago: National Council of State Boards of Nursing. https://ncsbn.org/QI-FlowChar.pdf (accessed April 22, 2016).

9. Hertfordshire Partnership NHS Foundation Trust. Schedule 4—Patient booking. Hertfordshire, UK: Hertfordshire Partnership NHS Foundation Trust.

10. Duplaga M, Zielinski K, Ingram D. *Transformation of Healthcare with Information Technologies.* Amsterdam: IOS Press, 2004.

11. Bates D, Gawande A. Improving safety with information technology. *N Engl J Med* 348(25): 2526–2534, 2003.

12. Healthcare Information and Management Systems Society (HIMSS). http://www.himss.org/ValueSuite.

# Chapter 4

## Systems Design

## Learning Objectives

At the conclusion of this chapter, the reader will be able to

- Identify system designs to accommodate business processes
- Develop requests for information and requests for proposals
- Ensure compatibility of software, hardware, network components, and medical devices
- Ensure compliance with applicable industry, regulatory, and organizational standards
- Ensure a process exists to incorporate industry, technology, infrastructure, legal, and regulatory environment trends
- Design an information infrastructure that supports current and anticipated business needs (e.g., business continuity and disaster recovery)
- Evaluate existing and emerging technologies to support the organization's future growth and strategies
- Employ effective data management practices

## Introduction

The *Dictionary of Computing* defines *system design* as "the activity of proceeding from an identified set of requirements for a system to a design that meets those requirements."[1] System design depends upon the definition of *system*, which, according to the *Oxford English Dictionary*, means "a set or assemblage of things connected, associated, or interdependent, so as to form a complex unity."[2] Healthcare information technology (IT) systems today take that complexity to a new level in function and interoperability. These systems must support advanced clinical functionality, patient accounting, and financial accounting and have been doing this for years. But now, the systems must also support functionality demanded by new healthcare regulations, medical devices, mergers, and acquisitions, as well as address changes and advances in the IT industry. One author suggests that the complexity of an IT system, with thousands or millions of lines of code, and the personalities of the people using it, the organizational dynamics, and the processes involved converge to make system design extremely difficult.[3] A key relationship exists between people, processes, and the organization.

Every organization conducts its business in different ways, depending on its vision, mission, history, government regulations, corporate culture, and other factors. An organization's way of doing business becomes its business process, which may be well defined or more loosely defined. New methods of defining and improving business processes, such as Lean and Six Sigma, appeared and have gained adoption over the past 10–20 years. Business process management (BPM) represents a method to understand an organization's processes and then apply this understanding to the design of a system.

The system design team drives the deliverables. They take the system requirements from systems analysis and translate them into detailed technical specifications for the system. Some design teams benefit greatly by focusing on usability. The emergence of business process reengineering (BPR), BPM, or management engineering and process improvement (ME-PI)[4] in healthcare offers a new approach to system design.

The system being designed may be internally developed or purchased from a vendor, and the process for system design varies with these two options. Dealing with a vendor requires more formal processes, including requests for information (RFIs) and requests for proposals (RFPs). The RFI assists the design team in deciding whether to solicit an RFP for a commercial off-the-shelf (COTS) solution or develop the system internally (not as common), known as a buy versus build decision. When selecting a COTS solution, the decision will often include discussions of selecting a best-of-breed system that requires more integration between vendors, or a single-vendor solution. The RFP represents the key deliverable of the system design team once a buy decision has been made.

## Business Process Management

In order to design successful systems, organizations must define their business objectives, create a business case, and then use workflow analysis and mapping to align their business processes to support those objectives. For a hospital, an example could be that they would like to improve their admission intake time from two hours to one hour within the next year to improve patient satisfaction.

Creating a business case to support the objectives involves defining a comprehensive view of the project, as well as the financial justification and return on investment (ROI). The key elements of the business case include[5]

■ Executive summary
■ Situational analysis and problem statement

- Project description
- Solution overview
- Solution detail
- Solution alternatives
- Costs
- Benefits
- Implementation timeline
- Critical assumptions and risk assessment
- Strengths, weaknesses, opportunities, threats (SWOT) analysis
- Conclusions and recommendations

One solution alternative is to utilize workflow mapping and analysis. Workflow mapping involves developing a diagram for a current process from start to finish in the correct order, including all inputs and outputs to the process. This is typically known as the "as-is process." At this point, the workflow may be analyzed to look for improvements and a gap analysis conducted.

## Compatibility of System Components

Any healthcare enterprise today owns and continually purchases a plethora of hardware, software, network components, and medical devices. The hardware may include laptop computers, servers, and tablets, each running its own operating system that is not necessarily compatible with other operating systems. The application software that runs on these devices serves a variety of purposes from patient accounting to payroll, laboratory, pharmacy, radiology, dietetics, and so on. Network components include routers (wired and wireless), firewalls, and Internet connectivity. Networks today must support connectivity of devices within the enterprise, but patients and visitors may also demand Wi-Fi access. Medical devices such as ultrasounds, MRIs, critical care devices, and even blood pressure cuffs all provide information digitally and must connect to the network as well. For more information on hardware, software, and networks, refer to Chapter 2, "The Technology Environment."

Organizations should define a process by which purchases of any of these components should be reviewed by the IT department for compatibility. Remember that compatibility does not mean that devices or software will work out of the box. There may be system integration involved to incorporate the device onto the network. For example, a new radiology information system may connect to the existing network from a physical standpoint, but may need to have a Health Level Seven (HL7) interface customized in order to talk to the existing electronic health record system. This process dictates close cooperation between the IT department and the procurement/purchasing department so IT has a chance to review purchases, thus avoiding such hidden costs of integration and causing potential delays.

## Standards Compliance

Healthcare providers face a huge number of external standards from government and industry, in addition to their own internal standards. Some of these affect the entire organization, and others affect just one department. Some countries even dictate which vendor IT system the organization must purchase. ASTM International, HL7, Digital Imaging and Communications in Medicine (DICOM), and other international organizations publish many standards related to healthcare IT. The Institute of Electrical and Electronics Engineers (IEEE) publishes standards for wired and wireless networking used by most countries in the world. Just as an enterprise must have a process to address compatibility of system components, it must also develop a process to address standards compliance. Given the number of standards, this is not a simple effort. There must be an overlap between business process and compliance management. System design should attempt to address standards by the clear definition of technical specifications.

## Process to Address Industry Trends

With the extensive changes occurring in healthcare and technology, a process must exist or be created to evaluate and incorporate industry, technology, infrastructure, legal, and regulatory trends. This process must address areas that in the past were governed by departments other than IT. The digitization of telephone systems means that these systems generally share the same networks as IT and have become a part of the IT organization. Medical devices such as electrocardiographs, ultrasound, and magnetic resonance imaging devices now generate millions of bytes of medically relevant data and must be integrated into the electronic patient record. The purchase of such devices must include IT participation to ensure they can be integrated without an additional large purchase of professional services.

## Structure of the System Design Team

The members of the system design team may vary based on the complexity and scope of the project. A project sponsor, one of the team's key members, should kick off the project with the team and help determine the business goals and how those goals should be measured. Once the team has been established and the goals clearly defined, the sponsor may not need to be involved in more detail-oriented design meetings. Below is a list of potential team members:

■ Project sponsor
■ Project manager/leader

- Business analyst(s)
- Data/process modeler
- Technical lead/architect
- Biomedical engineers
- Application developers
- Quality assurance analysts
- Information security officer
- Stakeholders/users
- Legal counsel
- Procurement expert

## Detailed Technical Specifications

The design team must create comprehensive, detailed, technical specifications that not only cover the function of the system or applications, but also address nonfunctional issues, such as information infrastructure. Some of the key areas of technical specifications that should be addressed are

- System and network architecture—Does the system have to fit into the organization's existing architectures or may it vary?
- Security and data encryption—Does the system integrate into the organization's security standards?
- Disaster recovery—What is the recovery time objective (RTO), or the time it will take to recover the system in a disaster? What is the recovery point objective (RPO), or to what point in time must the system be restored?
- Data conversion—What are the data conversion options if converting from one system to another with different data models?
- Response times—What are the expected response times and how will they be measured?
- System backups—What are the backup options? How long will backups run?
- System monitoring—How will the system be monitored? Will it fit into the organization's existing monitoring infrastructure?
- Change management—How does the vendor of a newly purchased system handle changes? Is there a regular schedule, or is it done at customer convenience?
- Availability—What are the availability requirements? What is the downtime associated with system upgrades?
- Time zone and daylight savings time support—Does the system support multiple time zones, especially if the organization has facilities in different time zones? Are system outages required for spring or fall clock changing?
- Standards—Does the system support integration standards such as HL7, International Statistical Classification of Diseases and Related Health Problems, 10th Revision (ICD10), or DICOM?

■ Government regulations—Does the system meet current government regulations? What is the vendor commitment for turnaround of new regulations?

■ System integration—Will the system automatically integrate with the other healthcare systems and medical devices in the enterprise, or will it cost more to integrate it?

■ Usability—Much focus is being placed on usability today, and that topic will be discussed in more detail below. Usability should include accessibility for persons with disabilities as well as the use of mobile devices.

■ Workflow definitions—The definition of desired workflows is another key area of the design that will be discussed in more detail later in the chapter.

■ Data management—Does the system fit the organization's data management policies and procedures for such functions as backup, recovery, and archiving?

## *Usability*

As previously mentioned, interest in usability has grown significantly over the past decade due to increased EHR adoption. HIMSS created the EHR User Experience (UX) Community to help clinicians and health IT professionals overcome some of the more common challenges with usability. The community has created several useful tools, including the Usability Maturity Model (UMM).[6] IT examines three nonhealthcare usability models and uses common themes from those models to create a healthcare model with five phases:

■ Phase 1: Unrecognized—lack of awareness of usability
■ Phase 2: Preliminary—sporadic inclusion of usability
■ Phase 3: Implemented—recognized value of usability and small teams using it
■ Phase 4: Integrated—benchmarks implemented and have dedicated user experience team
■ Phase 5: Strategic—business benefit well understood, mandated, budgeted, and results used strategically in the organization

The report documents how an organization can take itself from one phase to another and recommends the following tactics to expand usability within the organization:

■ Include usability in contracts
■ Create feedback loops from users to vendors
■ Talk about tasks and workflows
■ Educate about ROI related to usability
■ Engage organizational leaders in usability
■ Include usability metrics on one project
■ Interview users to determine key usability issues

- Compile evidence from usability assessments
- Look for and document usability wake-up calls
- Find a business/organization driver supporting need for usability

## Business Process Reengineering

Reengineering is the fundamental rethinking and radical redesign of business processes and workflow to achieve dramatic improvements in critical, contemporary measures of performance, such as cost, quality, service, and speed.[7] Many organizations today employ Lean or Six Sigma to reengineer their processes. Lean focuses on creating more value for customers with fewer resources.[8] Lean emphasizes the transformation of the entire organization by looking at the business issues of purpose, process, and people. Denver Health generated more than $135 million in financial benefit over a six-year period through the use of Lean processes and has even started marketing its own Lean training program to parties outside the organization.[9] Six Sigma strives to eliminate defects in processes to a level of 3.4 defects per million opportunities.[10] Six Sigma utilizes an acronym to improve processes known as DMAIC: define, measure, analyze, improve, control. Valley Baptist Health System in Harlingen, Texas, won numerous awards for its use of Six Sigma and lists almost 100 quality initiatives in progress on its website: http://www.valleybaptist.net/connect-with-us/about-valley-baptist/quality-initiatives.

Many vendors offer BPR tools today, and some of the process modeling tools are available for free downloading. BPR has matured to the extent that there are industry standards for process modeling called Business Process Model Notation (BPMN) and even for transferring models from one vendor to another called XML Process Definition Language (XPDL). Some healthcare IT systems today include BPR software that can allow organizations to design their own processes. In 2010, the Chester County Hospital in West Chester, Pennsylvania, received a CMIO IT Innovators Award for a workflow that decreased catheter-associated urinary tract infections by 50%.[11]

## Information Infrastructure

The information infrastructure must be able to support today's business requirements and anticipate emerging or future business requirements. A current trend, known as bring your own device (BYOD), is one example of an emerging requirement prompted by doctors, nurses, and other employees who want to use their own notebook computers, tablets, or smartphones on the enterprise network. Most healthcare organizations today probably do not have the proper security and network infrastructure in place to support a BYOD strategy. A good example of a future business requirement is Internet Protocol version 6 (IPv6). Most healthcare organizations today utilize Internet Protocol version 4 (IPv4). While today's applications do not support IPv6 yet, new infrastructure purchases, including new operating systems and network hardware, now support both, and

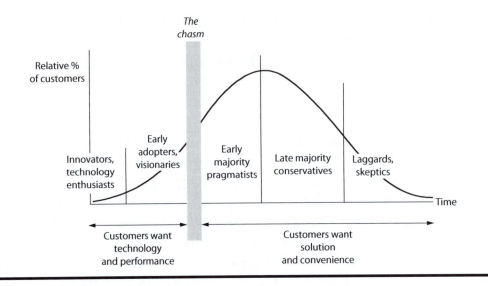

**Figure 4.1 Technology adoption curve.**

organizations that make sure their new purchases have that capability will be well positioned for the future. Overall, an organization should have a process in place to examine or evaluate emerging trends and technologies. This evaluation should be done on a regular basis as new technologies emerge or existing technologies begin to be adopted. As part of the process, the organization should decide where it wants to be on the technology adoption curve (Figure 4.1).

As more and more healthcare records are electronic, business continuity emerges as a key part of the IT infrastructure. Organizations must plan for various types of disasters, whether natural or man-made. Off-site storage of data becomes a minimal requirement. Many sites negotiate contracts with disaster recovery vendors to retain not only copies of data, but also the capability to restore entire systems. Larger organizations may own multiple data centers in which they may mirror their data. Networks must be in place to access these remote sites. The business continuity plan must not only ensure that the remote sites are in place, but also test the plan at frequent intervals to make certain that it can be executed.

## Data Management

Healthcare organizations must address a wide variety of issues related to their data. Data Management International (DAMA®) created a framework for data governance that defines 10 data management functions within the organization:[12]

1. Data governance—Planning, supervision, and control over data management and use
2. Data architecture management—As an integral part of the enterprise architecture
3. Data development—Analysis, design, building, testing, deployment, and maintenance
4. Database operations management—Support for structured physical data assets

5. Data security management—Ensuring privacy, confidentiality, and appropriate access
6. Reference and master data management—Managing golden versions and replicas
7. Data warehousing and business intelligence management—Enabling access to decision support data for reporting and analysis
8. Document and content management—Storing, protecting, indexing, and enabling access to data found in unstructured sources (electronic files and physical records)
9. Metadata management—Integrating, controlling, and delivering metadata
10. Data quality management—Defining, monitoring, and improving data quality

The organization must define a process for addressing those data management functions. Then, the system design team must ensure that the system fits into that process.

Once the technical specifications have been completed, the system design team can proceed to the buy versus build decision. If the team is unsure whether a commercial product exists to meet the specifications, the next step should be to produce an RFI.

## Creating a Request for Information (RFI)

An RFI solicits background information on companies and their capabilities. It may be used to help decide whether vendors offer a solution to the healthcare IT need being addressed versus developing the solution in-house. A typical RFI includes the following sections, which were abstracted from an actual RFI released by the Veterans Health Administration:[13]

1. Introduction
   a. This section notes that the RFI is for information and planning purposes only and that no contracts will be offered.
2. Background
   a. This section describes the current environment.
3. Requirements
   a. This section clearly describes what the responding vendor must address. The specific RFI used in this example included requirements in the areas of
      i. Project management support
      ii. Reporting
      iii. Development, integration, implementation, maintenance
      iv. Training and education
      v. Adoption reporting
      vi User acceptance and field testing support

4. Submittal information
   a. Length of response requirements, such as maximum number of pages, font size, and paragraph spacing (single vs. double)
   b. Responding company name, experience, and qualifications
   c. Where, when, and how to submit the proposal

## Making a Buy versus Build Decision

Once the vendor RFI responses are received and evaluated, the design team should now have the information it needs to make the decision whether to build the system internally or proceed to the creation of an RFP for a buy decision. It is important to note that very few systems are developed in-house, although, historically, this was a popular option.

The factors that influence the buy versus build decision include[14]

- IT strategy—What is the overall strategy for IT? Are most systems internally developed or purchased?
- Core versus noncore systems—Is the system key to the success of the organization or ancillary?
- Commodity versus competitive advantage—Is the system a commodity, such as payroll or word processing, or specific to a healthcare line of business, such as a surgicenter?
- Maturity—Is the internal IT department mature enough for internal development? Is the market mature enough to have a wide choice?
- Requirements fit—Does the product meet the critical requirements?
- Cost and value—Does a product meet the cost requirements, including implementation, support, maintenance, and upgrades? What are the ongoing maintenance costs of internally built solutions, including retaining the knowledge of the developers?
- Time and timing—How long will it take to develop versus acquire? How long will it take to implement? How long will it take to get updates from the vendor versus make changes in-house?
- Political factors—Does a particular vendor influence the decision? Does the project sponsor have a bias?
- Regulatory support—What is the track record of the vendor in providing regulatory support versus the experience meeting those requirements in-house?
- Platform—Does the vendor support the organization's preferred platforms, including hardware, network, security, and infrastructure?
- Integration—How well will the vendor product integrate with other products in the organization's portfolio?
- Life cycle cost estimate—What are the overall costs over 5–10 years to deploy, implement, and support the system?

After studying the above factors carefully, the design team can make the decision to build or buy.

## *Process for a Build Decision*

Once a decision has been made to build the system, there must be changes to the membership of the design team to include more technical members, such as data modelers, technical architects, and application developers. The State of New York Office of Information Technology Resources developed a guidebook that provides a good outline of the system design processes, techniques, and deliverables when the system is developed in-house (Table 4.1).[15]

## *Buy Decision: Best-of-Breed versus Single-Vendor Solution*

For decades, design teams lingered over the tough decision of selecting best-of-breed or single-vendor, tightly integrated solutions. Generally, smaller niche vendors develop best-of-breed systems because they can focus their resources on a small set of requirements for a specialized system to be used in, for example, a lab, radiology, or emergency department. Larger vendors usually market tightly integrated systems since they have more resources to develop enterprise solutions that can meet a wide range of requirements, if not all. Among decision makers, preferences seem to have moved back and forth across the decades. Single-vendor decisions ruled the 1980s, while the pendulum swung back toward best-of-breed applications in the 1990s. Even though standards such as HL7 and DICOM matured during the 1990s to assist in integrating best of breeds, individual vendors had their own interpretations of those standards, which did not necessarily align. Healthcare IT departments had to hire integration analysts and purchase interface engines to enable such systems to talk to each other. Industry organizations such as Integrating the Healthcare Enterprise (IHE) evolved to promote integration between vendors, and IHE demonstrations at HIMSS national meetings still draw a crowd. Today, patient safety and other initiatives seem to have pushed the industry back toward single-vendor solutions that tightly integrate computerized practitioner order entry (CPOE), pharmacy, and electronic medication administration records (eMARs).[16] The final decision should come from the systems design team after the RFP process.

## *Creating a Request for Proposal (RFP)*

If the decision is made to buy, then an RFP should be created to find an appropriate system on the market to meet the specified requirements. Unlike the RFI, the RFP is seeking vendor responses with the intent to purchase one of their products. The RFP is typically much lengthier and involved than the RFI.

**Table 4.1  System Design Processes, Techniques, and Deliverables When a System Is Developed In-House**

| Processes | Techniques | Process Deliverables (Outcomes) |
|---|---|---|
| Prepare for system design | Interviews | Established team and environment for system design |
| | Site walk-throughs | |
| Define technical architecture | Interviews | Technical architecture |
| | Document gathering and reviews | |
| | Role/authorization analysis | |
| Define system standards | Interviews | System standards |
| | Brainstorming | |
| | Policy and standards reviews | |
| Create physical database | Formal walk-throughs | Databases and system files |
| | Standard data definition languages | |
| | Data administration techniques (data normalization, de-normalization) | |
| Prototype system components | Iterative prototypes/reviews | Prototype and proof-of-concept results |
| | Presentations | |
| | Graphical user interface (GUI)/ report development tools | |
| Produce technical specifications | Function decomposition | Technical specifications |
| | Expressing logic: pseudocode, structured English, object-oriented logic | |
| | Operational requirements assessment | |

*Source:* Adapted from New York State Office of Technology, *New York State Project Management Guidebook*, Albany: New York State Office of Technology, 2003, http://www.cio.ny.gov/pmmp/guidebook2/index.htm.

Below is an outline of a sample RFP that can be found on the HIMSS website:[17]

1. Request for proposal
   a. General contact information—Who should get the response?
   b. Background—What is the purpose of this RFP?
   c. Services requested—What are the application and services being requested?
   d. Technical questions—What are the hardware platform, operating system, and so forth?
   e. Prebid conference call—For interested vendors, what are the date, time, and details for a prebid conference call?
   f. Evaluation criteria—What are the criteria by which the proposal will be judged, such as proposer experience, reputation, financial stability, quality of submission, and references?
   g. Selection process—What are the process and dates for reviewing proposals and responding to proposers?
   h. Addendums—Any other information that will be provided.
   i. Notable dates—What are dates for prebid call, close of questions, RFP submission, and notice of award?
   j Submission process—How can the proposal be submitted, including by e-mail, in person, or by carrier, and who should receive it?
   k. Federal contractor—Insert this section if the requestor is a federal contractor.
2. Requested services/functions
   a Detail of desired features
3. Deployment and development schedule
   a. What are the dates required to meet the requestor's requirements?
4. Training/warranty
   a. What training and support are offered during the warranty period?
   b. What are the details of the warranty?
5. Professional services fees
   a. What are the fees for professional services during implementation?
   b. What are the fees after implementation?
6. References
   a. What references are available to contact who have done similar projects with the proposer?

The technical requirements represent the most important part of the RFP. The *Mars Climate Orbiter* spacecraft crashed because its software used metric units while the mission control software used English units. In the face of unclear requirements, some vendors may submit high bids to mitigate risks or to cause other vendors not to bid at all. When requirements are unclear, vendors make their own assumptions about what is being asked and submit vastly different bids based on those assumptions. Once a contract is signed, the differing assumptions of the vendor and the customer may lead to project delays, inability of the vendor to deliver, or even litigation. If a contract ever escalates to the point of litigation, unclear requirements make it much harder to plead a case.[18]

## Summary

Successful system design centers on the design team, which must include the proper members. The design team should create clear, documented technical specifications. Two ways in which the design team can produce such requirements are by examining usability and focusing on business process improvement. From the technical specifications, the team may generate an RFI to solicit industry input. This input can facilitate the buy versus build decision. If a build decision is made, the RFI can also assist the team to decide on a best-of-breed versus a tightly integrated product. The team then focuses on the creation of the RFP, which will in turn lead to system selection and implementation as discussed in Chapter 5.

## References

1. Daintith J. System design. In *A Dictionary of Computing*. Oxford: Oxford University Press, 2004. http://www.encyclopedia.com/doc/1O11-systemdesign.html (accessed December 2, 2015).
2. System. In OED Online. Oxford: Oxford University Press, 2012. http://www.oed.com/ (accessed August 11, 2012).
3. Berg M. Implementing information systems in health care organizations: Myths and challenges. *Int J Med Inform* 64(2–3): 143–156, 2001. http://www.ijmijournal.com/article/S1386-5056(01)00200-3/fulltext (accessed December 2, 2015).
4. HIMSS (Healthcare Information and Management Systems Society). Management engineering and process improvement. Chicago: HIMSS. http://www.himss.org/library/management-engineering-process-improvement-healthcare (accessed December 2, 2015).
5. Prosci. Business case. BPR Online Learning Center. Fort Collins, CO: Prosci. https://www.prosci.com/change-management/thought-leadership-library/making-a-business-case-for-change-management (accessed April 22, 2016).
6. HIMSS (Healthcare Information and Management Systems Society). HIMSS Usability Maturity Model (UMM). Chicago: HIMSS. http://www.himss.org/ResourceLibrary/ContentTabsDetail.aspx?ItemNumber=39016 (accessed December 2, 2015).
7. Hammer M, Champy J. *Reengineering the Corporation: A Manifesto for Business Revolution*. New York: Harper, 1993.
8. Lean Enterprise Institute. What is Lean? Cambridge, MA: Lean Enterprise Institute. http://www.lean.org/WhatsLean/ (accessed December 2, 2015).
9. Denver Health Lean Academy. http://www.denverhealth.org/LEANAcademy/AboutLEANAcademy/CaseStudies.aspx (accessed December 2, 2015).

10. What is Six Sigma? iSix Sigma. http://www.isixsigma.com/new-to-six-sigma/getting-started/what-six-sigma/ (accessed December 2, 2015).
11. Stevens M. Health IT Innovation Awards: 5 health IT projects that improved care. *CMIO Magazine*, August 30, 2010. http://www.cmio.net/index.php?option=com_art icles&view=article&id=23893:health-it-innovation-awards-5-health-it-projects-that-improved-care (accessed December 2, 2015).
12. Data Management International. DAMA-DMBOK functional framework. Data Management International, 2008. http://www.dama.org/ (accessed December 2, 2015).
13. My recovery plan, MyHealtheVet Office of Informatics and Analytics sources sought notice. 2012. https://www.fbo.gov/?s=opportunity&mode= form&id=e7e03227fd31bf 8d61a296a560f7cc6a&tab=core&_cview=0 (accessed December 2, 2015).
14. Low G. Factors affecting the buy vs build decision in large Australian organizations. *J Inf Technol* 23(3): 118–131, 2008. http://www.palgrave-journals.com/jit/journal/v23/n2/full/2000098a.html (accessed December 2, 2015).
15. New York State Office of Technology. *New York State Project Management Guidebook*. Albany: New York State Office of Technology, 2003. http://www.cio.ny.gov/pmmp/guidebook2/index.htm (accessed December 2, 2015).
16. Hoehn BJ. What is the best clinical information strategy? *J Healthc Inf Manag* 24(4): 10–12, 2010. http://s3.amazonaws.com/rdcms-himss/files/production/public/HIMSSorg/Content/files/Code%2093_What%20is%20the%20best%20clinical%20information%20system.pdf (accessed December 2, 2015).
17. HIMSS (Healthcare Information and Management Systems Society). mHealth app RFP template. Chicago: HIMSS, 2010. http://www.himss.org/ResourceLibrary/ResourceDetail.aspx?ItemNumber=10493 (accessed December 2, 2015).
18. Perkins B. RFPs: The costs of being unclear. *Computerworld*, June 11, 2007. http://www.computerworld.com/s/article/293860/RFPs_The_Costs_of_Being_Unclear (accessed December 2, 2015).

# Chapter 5

# Systems Selection, Implementation, Support, and Maintenance

## Learning Objectives

At the conclusion of this chapter, the reader will be able to

- Facilitate solution selection criteria
- Select and review team members
- Conduct solution selection activities (e.g., demonstrations, site visits, and reference checks)
- Employ organizational change management techniques in support of solution implementation
- Provide knowledge transfer through user and operational manuals and training
- Execute the implementation of solutions
- Integrate systems to support business requirements
- Manage healthcare information systems (e.g., operate and upgrade)
- Analyze data for problems and trends (e.g., error reports, help desk logs, surveys, performance metrics, and network monitoring)
- Prioritize issues to ensure critical functions are repaired, maintained, or enhanced
- Incorporate solutions into organizational disaster recovery and business continuity plans
- Develop system and personnel downtime procedures

## Introduction

The selection process begins with the identification of a need and subsequent approval of a project proposal. The successful implementation and adoption of a new application or system is dependent on an organized system selection process, followed by a well-planned and executed implementation strategy. Once a need has been identified within an organization, an effective governance committee evaluates it against the organizational mission, goals, objectives, information technology (IT) strategic plan, budget, and available resources.

Once the decision is made to move forward, objectives, goals, and measures of success should be clearly defined. Once the high-level strategy is defined, the team is assembled to analyze and further define the requirements. It is important to have the appropriate team members to ensure the analysis includes all parts of the organization affected by the new solution. Through this analysis, opportunities for process improvement and workflow efficiencies are identified.

Chapter 4 discussed in detail the items that should be included in a request for information (RFI) or request for proposal (RFP). To summarize,

An RFI
- Is an informal request for information that does not require commitment from either party
- Is a collection of documents designed to collect information regarding prospective vendors and their ability to meet the defined need or high-level requirements
- May or may not include budget or cost information

An RFP
- Is a formal request that leads to a contract between the organization and the selected vendor(s)
- Is a collection of documents that outline the detailed requirements and how each responding vendor will be compared for a final decision
- Always includes timelines and budget or cost information

Evaluating the vendors that respond to the RFP includes on-site visits, reference checks, and even demonstrations. After the list of possible vendors is narrowed down to a few, contract negotiations allow the organization to get the best possible deal based on price, payment plan, support levels, and ongoing support. It is important to include a step to verify any federal, state, and local government regulations as part of any standard selection practice.

After the application and vendor have been selected, it is time to begin implementation. Understanding the different implementation strategies will help the organization choose the one that best fits its culture, objectives, and available resources. Proper planning and a defined methodology will help decrease project risk and lead to a successful activation. For a smooth transition to support, the implementation project should include planning for postlive activities, such as configuration management, user communication, user support, and new employee training, along with operations and maintenance, to ensure continuous performance of the system.

## Solution Selection Criteria

As mentioned earlier, system selection begins with a defined need based on the organization's strategic objectives or a solution to a problem that blocks achievement of an organizational or departmental objective. The selection and implementation processes are built around fulfilling the need and realizing the solution that will meet the organization's expected outcomes. The process defined below should be used as a template and modified as needed to fit the specific situation and satisfy the current regulatory requirements.

The need and justification for a project are often described in a formal business case, project proposal, or a needs assessment. This document outlines the goal and objectives of the request, along with the high-level resources required to meet them. The needed resources may be financial, human, software, hardware, or capital. Most organizations request a business case prior to approving the proposed system selection process. If the organization does not require a business case, it is imperative that the IT governance committee request one. The challenge comes from defining the required resources this early in the process. Most often they are defined through scientific guesses. If time allows, market research can provide more accurate estimates. Market research starts with high-level requirements, not the detailed ones identified later in the process, and may be conducted formally or informally. Formal market research is completed through a process similar to the RFI process. With market research, however, it is clearly stated that the RFI is for research only, with no intent to purchase at this time. The informal process is completed through vendor exhibitions, Internet searches, and contact with other similar organizations.

The business case or project proposal should present the need and requirements, not necessarily the solution. The different options to meet the needs, with associated resources, should be defined. This document should avoid the identification of a single solution, but rather several solutions or recommendations. The governance committee reviews the business case and decides whether to move forward based on the system's fit within the organization's strategic plan or operational goals and the availability of resources to complete.

Once approval to move forward is received, the selection criteria are built on the defined need and high-level requirements that the business case identified as necessary for the solution. Whether the need is to improve office scheduling processes through automation or to create a paperless environment in an acute care setting, the requirements go beyond end-user functionality to include non-functional necessities also.

A list of requirements could include the following

Functional requirements
- Application with organization-specific functionality
- Security and privacy requirements
- Regulatory requirements
- Reporting capability, including standard and custom reporting
- Integration with other applications or devices
- Access from multiple locations (acute care, long-term care, clinics, etc.)
- Access from mobile devices
- Redesigned workflow
- Decision support functionality

Nonfunctional requirements
- Facility IT infrastructure space, cooling, and power
- Hardware for production, development, testing, and training environments
- Hardware for disaster recovery or high availability
- Hardware for reporting
- Backup and recovery plans and procedures
- Workstation and printer requirements and hardware
- Wired and wireless networks
- System installation, configuration, and maintenance documentation
- Supplemental staffing for implementation, training, and postlive support
- Independent verification and validation to reduce risk by providing impartial reviews of business and technical aspects of the project
- Processes for issue resolution and requests for enhancement
- Maintenance and support process and procedures
- Expected procurement and implementation timeline, along with any constraints that would affect the timeline
- Expected availability, reliability, and scalability

A gap analysis might be the first step in defining these requirements. What is the status of your current application(s)? Are you planning to replace or enhance those systems? What manual processes can and must be improved through automation? Throughout this process, it is important to focus the analysis on the identified need. Requirement creep can occur very quickly if the team is not focused. The governance committee and executive sponsors are there to help with ensuring the requirements fit within the defined goals and objectives.

Once the requirements are defined, they should be ranked to show which are required, preferred, or optional. It is rare for vendors to be able to meet every requirement, so clarity about which ones are absolutely necessary helps during the evaluation of responses. The rankings should be agreed upon by all committee members and used consistently for all vendors. The requirements and rankings feed into the RFI or RFP documentation as defined earlier in this chapter.

Through this process a decision to build versus buy should be made. There are many factors that influence this decision. Does the organization have the skill set to build and support the new solution? Is there room in the budget to buy? What is the expected timeline? Which option fits with the organizational IT strategy? Is there a vendor who can meet the need and defined requirements? Based on these factors, the decision to build or buy may occur early in the process, after reviewing the RFI/RFP responses, or anytime in between.

Having the appropriate people involved in the selection process is key to being successful. The governance committee and executive sponsors have already been introduced. A facilitator should be identified early on to ensure that the activity progresses as expected, the defined process is followed, and the right people are involved in the review team.

## Selecting Review Team Members

The selection of the review team should be completed as early as possible. It is possible that the entire team might not be needed at the very early stages of the process or that some members may not be as actively involved as others. Team members should be identified early so they will be ready to participate when needed. Decisions about team membership should balance the importance of including the right people with the need to keep the size manageable.

The exact members will depend on what is being selected and should include representatives from clinical, organizational operations, IT, and the business department to ensure all affected areas are involved. Below is a list of who might be involved in the selection team:

- Facilitator—Provides overall leadership and coordination of the system selection process.
- Executive sponsors—Provide support, clarify mission, facilitate necessary resources, and act as champions within the organization.
- Technical representatives—Provide technical expertise, such as IT, biomedical, and telecommunications.
- Business representatives—Provide business or clinical end-user expertise. These individuals are highly knowledgeable about the current business and workflows and represent the end users.
- Program/project manager—Provides implementation and methodology expertise.
- Contracting representative—Provides contracting, negotiation, and process expertise.
- Financial representative—Provides budgetary expertise.
- Organizational change leader—Provides expertise related to facilitating change within the organization.

■ Governance committee—Provides oversight but is often not directly involved in the team. The selection team reports back to this group. Once implementation begins, this group will remain intact to monitor and ensure the project's success. In some organizations, this group is called a steering committee.

The role of team members is to represent their specific area within the organization. It is very difficult to include everyone who will be affected by the new system on the team. Members should be expected to gather information from their peers to bring back to the team. This process helps to ensure that the right information will be reviewed and included where needed throughout the selection process. All requirements should be reviewed and approved by the team.

## Solution Selection Activities

Once the requirements have been approved and the decision to buy has been made, it is time to look for vendors that are able to meet them. It is important to consult with your contracting or legal representative to understand the organizational rules and regulations about contacting vendors prior to a signed contract. Some regulations are in place to avoid giving any one vendor an advantage. The contract representative will be able to guide you through the selection activities. The following elements may be involved in solution selection:

■ RFI. The request for information provides a format for gathering information about which vendors are able to meet the high-level requirements. The responses are compared to the documented requirements, which may be modified prior to posting the RFP if it is clear some required items are not available or require more definition.
■ RFP. The request for proposal provides the official request for vendors to submit how they will meet the requirements, which are more defined and include timelines and budget details.
■ Evaluation of RFP responses. Responses should be reviewed and scored based on ability to meet required, preferred, and optional requirements. This step is accomplished with the entire team doing independent scoring of each response, followed by team discussion and consensus on a final score. This process helps identify which vendors can meet the organizational need and provides the first opportunity to eliminate any vendor that cannot.
■ Comparison to IT strategic plan. When evaluating the responses, it is important to understand how a vendor's solution or planned implementation will fit with the organization's IT strategic plan. Is the IT road map leading in the direction of virtualization, to simplification of technologies, or to a decreased number of vendors? How does the offered solution fit with this road map?

It might be OK if the solution does not fit, but that fact should be considered during selection.

- Compliance with regulatory requirements. Pertinent regulations should be part of your requirements and listed as essential. All vendors should be evaluated against any government, regulatory, or security requirements.

- Background checks. Once the list of possible vendors is decreased, some research should be done. This would include evaluation of their financial stability, market share, and customer satisfaction. How long a product has been on the market and how many other customers are using it should be matched to your organization's risk tolerance level. Are you an early adopter who can tolerate some issues with the application if you are able to work with the vendor on new features and functionality? Or would you prefer a solid, reliable application that the vendor has had time to refine? The outcome of this activity should be included in the scoring of each vendor.

- Demonstrations. Requesting a demonstration allows vendors to show how they can meet the request. This provides a visual that is very beneficial, but it is often done with a generic version of the product. This does not reflect how it can be customized to fit the organization's workflows or processes. Prior to the demonstration, it is suggested that a list of scenarios be provided to the vendors so they will show how their product can meet your needs, rather than highlight only the features that they choose. All vendors should be guided to demonstrate the same scenarios to ensure they can be compared to each other. Whenever possible, the same people should be invited to all scheduled demonstrations. Having each vendor demonstrate how their product fits within the same scenarios and having the same people attending each meeting make it easier to properly compare and score each option prior to final selection. It is important to control the agenda very tightly, making sure all scenarios are covered and, if you choose, allowing vendors to demonstrate additional functionality at the end. Demonstrations should be scheduled closely together, if possible, so the information is fresh when they are scored.

- Site visits. Visiting a site that has already worked with a vendor and implemented their solution provides an opportunity to speak with people directly, ask specific questions, and see how the solution works within their workflows and processes. This helps to demonstrate how the system can be customized during the implementation to fit defined workflows and processes. Questions to ask during site visits would range from what it is like to work with the vendor, how they respond to requests for support during the implementation or after live, and how easy it is to customize the application or to integrate it with other systems. The number of site visits is often dependent on the number of vendors remaining at this point in the process. The decision on who should participate often depends on who will be affected by the implementation and the distance to be traveled for the visit. It is optimal if the organization, and not the vendor, chooses what sites to visit, but this is not always an option.

- Client references. If a site visit is not possible, a call with the reference site would still provide the ability to ask questions. While the selection team will not be able to actually view the system live, the same questions can be asked. Through use of remote web meeting technologies, it is possible to have a demonstration of how a client is using the system without the travel. This provides the ability to understand the implementation process, so remember to ask about any lessons learned from their experience. Just like a demo, there should be predefined questions to be asked for each reference site. Simple web searches and informal contacts with peers can also provide some good reference information.

- Selection meetings. Throughout this process, the team is meeting regularly to continuously evaluate and score the remaining vendors against the new information obtained through the research, demonstrations, site visits, and original proposal scores. Through this process, the number of vendors should be decreased to two or three. The team's comments and final evaluations of each of the remaining options are provided to the contracting representative for negotiations.

- Negotiation. The contract representative negotiates with the remaining vendors to obtain the best solution for the organization. This would include cost, software, hardware, implementation services, support, and maintenance. The selection committee, as well as a legal representative, should carefully review all documents sent to the organization from the vendors because once the papers are signed, they are a binding contract. During negotiation, there may be multiple requested modifications to the documents that require back and forth communication. This process can take a while since each modification needs to be properly reviewed by the other party before they come back with their modifications, and so on. The cost tables should include costs for items such as software licenses, integration, data conversions, training, implementation services, hardware, and third-party software licenses.

- Selection. Based on the negotiations and the final offer from each of the remaining vendors, the team makes a selection. Each step of this process, along with the justification of the selection, should be documented in case any vendor chooses to contest the award. The final agreements often include items such as payment schedule, vendor and client responsibilities, delivery schedule, system installation and configuration documentation, specific deliverables, standard project plan, penalties for not meeting deadlines, termination process, assignment of licenses, and process for upgrades or updates.

- Budget development. During the negotiations, the budget is developed based on the costs defined during negotiation and selection. The budget often needs to include costs beyond the system vendor. Other items that might be included in the project budget are contractors to supplement the organization's staff; business change management requirements; hardware not purchased through the software vendor, such as new workstations or printers; costs from other vendors for integration services; training; travel; and standard fixed or variable costs, such as space and staffing. The budget is typically finalized within 30 days after the final contract is awarded.

The formality, steps included, and length of this process can vary greatly. There are various reasons for this beyond the organizational contracting process. The contract size, a time constraint, or the desire to stay with a single vendor might shorten this process. With each step, a document or process that is cut brings some level of risk. The organization needs to balance the risk versus the benefit of shortening the process.

## Implementation Process

Now that a system has been selected, it is important to define how it will be implemented. While the phases of an implementation are fairly standard, there are a variety of defined methodologies that differ only in the terminology they use or the number of phases. The basic phases implementation projects go through include plan, design, build, test, train, go live, and closeout. It is important to remember that they all start with gathering information and planning what work is required, along with when and how it will be done. Most projects fail due to lack of planning, poor planning, or not following the plan. If the organization does not have a defined project management strategy, it would be important to take the time to decide what processes will be followed throughout the project. This includes defining the project team's roles, the project manager's authority, the documentation and deliverables expected throughout the project, and the role of the governance or steering committee.

The initial activity is to plan how the project will be accomplished. This includes defining what is within and outside the scope of the project. The project sponsors will approve the scope prior to any other plans being finalized. Also to be prepared are the risk management plan, the change management plan, the training plan, the testing plan, the issue management plan, the work breakdown structure, and the communication plan. All of these documents make up the project management plan and define the tasks scheduled to successfully complete the project. When preparations begin for the activation (go-live), the activation plan is developed and approved.

At the end of the planning phase, after the sponsors approve the project management plan, a kickoff meeting is conducted to communicate the project to all stakeholders. The agenda often includes the following:

- The project scope
- The project management methodology, or how the project will be managed

- The change management process, or how changes are requested, analyzed, and approved
- Identified risks and their mitigation strategies
- Introduction of the project team and their roles
- High-level milestones and schedule
- The communication plan

## Organizational Change Management

Any new system will have an impact on the organization, and some change will need to occur. It is not good enough to just automate a process; the process should be improved through automation. Changes affect everyone from top management to end users. Planning for these changes and evaluating the different options for managing them should begin during the procurement process. It is important to have top-level support, as well as a member of senior leadership on the change management team, to show commitment and provide strong leadership. The team should also include members from all affected areas, so they have a sense of ownership and commitment to the project's success.

The team should define a strategic plan similar to the project plan used for implementing the software. The strategic plan should take into consideration the organizational culture and politics related to how staff handle change. The types of resistance that might occur should be identified, along with the strategy to break down the resistance and move on to acceptance. A clear communication plan will ensure the information is properly disseminated throughout the organization.

Adoption often is affected by users' perceptions of how the system fits with their workflow. Does it provide efficiencies or appear to be extra work? Does the system functionality cause a perceived negative change in processes, or can the system be made to fit within the processes and even improve them? Often the adoption is based on perceived benefit by the end users. The staff has to be ready for the change, which is why stakeholder involvement in the workflow redesign is critical. Having end users involved in hardware selection, such as workstations on wheels or mobile devices, provides feedback to the project team about the usability of the devices being evaluated.

## Implementation Strategies

There are multiple strategies for implementing a new system. Early in the project, they should be evaluated to determine which one is the right fit for the organization.

- Big bang—Going live with all functionality to be implemented in all locations at the same time. If there is a legacy system being replaced, this might be the only option. This strategy requires a considerable amount of coordination to ensure that all areas are ready, with hardware in place, training completed, and enough support staff available.

- Phased by location—Going live with all functionality to be implemented in one location at a time. This strategy extends the duration of the activation activity, but provides some benefits. The staff from the areas that are already live can assist with providing support to the ones that follow. Holding a meeting after each phase to discuss lessons learned could provide continuous improvement for later phases.

- Phased by functionality—Going live in all locations with one feature at a time. An example would be to bring the admissions process live first for admission, discharge, and transfer and patient demographic information, followed by computerized practitioner order entry (CPOE) and then clinical documentation. This strategy also extends the duration of the activation and allows users to gradually get accustomed to the system before utilizing it fully. As above, meeting after each phase to discuss lessons learned could provide continuous improvement for future phases.

- Pilot—Going live initially with one location as a pilot test, and then following with everyone else in a phased big-bang process. This allows the team to learn from a small group before going live with the entire user community.

- Like for like—Going live with the same functionality that was in place prior to the project. Extra functionality is often added later through configuration management (discussed later in this chapter) or a later project. This strategy is often used when replacing a legacy system or during an upgrade. It helps to decrease the complexity of the activation and decreases the impact on the end users. There will always be some users who perceive this approach to be useless since they do not see an improvement.

## Implementing Solutions

You have taken enough time to properly plan how the system will be implemented. You have selected a project team with the right skills, chosen the right implementation strategy, identified what features will be implemented, and developed an outstanding communication plan. Now all you have to do is follow your plans.

This is when the project team takes the basic vanilla application the vendor provides and customizes it to meet the organization's needs. The vendor should provide training to the project team on how to make these changes. This includes configuring the clinical documentation data entry into notes or flow sheets, as well as the output as reports. Each order that can be placed for a patient, such as medications, diagnostic tests, diets, and consults, has to be configured in the system. Other items range from drop-down lists for a patient's religion during admission to how surgery will be scheduled. If there is a legacy system, the data conversion or loading of data also happens during this time.

Even if data is immigrated early, some data migration will have to occur during activation to ensure that all data is in the new system when it goes live. Care should also be taken to avoid duplication of data during the migration. Data validation after each migration is an important step that should be combined with an action plan to resolve duplicate records if they occur.

Part of the methodology should include how changes are handled during the project. There will be some requests to change the scope of the project or some requirements during the execution phase. Having a defined process for evaluating each request to determine its impact on the project helps prevent scope creep. The change management plan should identify who can submit changes, how changes are evaluated, what documentation is required, and who makes the final decision. A request may be approved, denied, or deferred to a later time. The project sponsors usually make the decision with the project manager facilitating the impact analysis.

Testing activities occur throughout the execution. A test plan, which should have at least been started during the planning phase, describes all the different testing activities to be completed during the project. Often the first testing activity is verifying that the hardware and application were installed correctly. Each of the initial environments, such as development, testing, or training, is required to ensure that the installations were successful. Testing will occur throughout the project based on the test plan and the different types of testing to be performed. For additional information on systems testing, refer to Chapter 6.

## System Integration to Support Business Requirements

It is rare in healthcare today to have a stand-alone system that does not share data with another in some way. The electronic health record (EHR) should include data from the lab and radiology systems so those who need to make medical decisions can view the results. Patient demographic information should be shared between the outpatient clinic, or office system, and the inpatient EHR so the patient does not need to provide the same information over and over again. Integration allows data to be in multiple systems without manual data entry. Some types of integration to be considered include the following:

■ Real-time data integration—Sharing of data nearly simultaneously when it is entered or modified, or when another defined trigger occurs. The standard for this type of integration is Health Level Seven (HL7), which defines the specifics surrounding the interface messages so what is sent from the source system is acceptable by the destination system.
■ Scheduled data integration—Sharing of data in a batch according to a predetermined time frame, such as nightly at midnight or every so many

hours. The data feed can be accomplished through formatted files or HL7 messages.

■ Integration of data from devices—Feeding of data from a specific device into an application. These devices can range from hemodynamic monitors, vital sign monitors, and anesthesia machines to ventilators. This type of interface helps decrease manual data entry, but may require the data to be verified before it becomes official within the system.

Integration utilizes an interface engine that receives information from the source system and either passes it directly to the destination system or makes some modification to the data before passing it along. For example, a modification would occur if the source system sent a patient's name as first name and last name, but the destination system could only accept a full name. The interface engine would accept the first and last names, combine them, and send the full name on. Different systems have different requirements for how the data is structured and where in the interface message they expect the specific data to be located. The interface message has sections, and a mapping document describes where each piece of data is expected to be and if the interface engine needs to do any manipulation.

## User and Operational Manuals and Training

As a project nears activation, it is necessary to educate the end users through documentation and training. If hands-on training is required, a training environment should be set up early in the project to allow the training team to develop materials and enter hypothetical patient data for any practice exercises that might be included. Training activities are tricky to schedule because they need to take place on the system that will actually be in use. As a result, the training environment cannot be fully set up until the entire configuration is completed and a copy created.

There are many factors that lead to the decision on what type of training should be provided. These include the organizational culture, extent of the change, number of users, users' work hours, and even the staff's comfort level with computers. Training can be done through computer-based training modules, lectures, demonstrations, hands-on exercises, or a combination of those.

Training should occur right before the activation so the users will retain what was taught. The timing depends on how many users need to be trained and how long the training classes will be. Experience shows that the best planning will not eliminate the need for just-in-time training. Inevitably, someone will not make it to class or will not remember how to do something. End-user manuals and quick reference guides along with the presence of support staff during the initial week or two will help fill this gap.

# Activation Planning and Immediate Postactivation Activities

Planning for the system to go live begins with the decision on implementation strategy discussed earlier in this chapter and continues through the remainder of the project. The organization should work with the vendor to define which activities can be completed in advance and which have to occur on the go-live day. The actual activities will depend on the specific project. If the organization is moving from a manual process to an automated one or is implementing a new system, the activation could be as simple as having users start using the system. When migrating from a legacy system or upgrading an existing system, the activation activities are more complex and include a period of time when the system is down, or unavailable. A detailed checklist of tasks that occur before and during the activation, whether downtime is scheduled or not, helps to ensure nothing will be missed or forgotten. A rehearsal of the activation provides an opportunity to test the process and fix any mistakes that occur. Evaluating the rehearsal helps to refine the process and the checklist to make the actual activation go more smoothly. It also boosts the project team's level of confidence because they have already done the tasks at least once, depending on how many rehearsals are conducted.

The planning for activation goes beyond the actual tasks that will occur to bring the system up. Other considerations should include where everyone will sit; if a command center will be set up so the entire team will be in one location; if food and drink will be available, especially if the activity will go beyond a few hours; if there will be a place for the staff to rest; what forms of communication will be available for anyone not in the command center; and how status updates will be communicated to the end users. How will issues requiring escalation be handled, and will the vendor be on-site or on the phone to provide assistance?

The type and duration of postlive support will depend on the impact of the change and the amount of just-in-time training expected. When implementing a new system in a clinic, the support staff might be available just before and during clinic hours for the first week. When implementing a new EHR in an acute setting, the support staff might be available around the clock for the first few weeks.

The users will almost immediately have suggestions for changing the system. Having a clear process for submitting requests for change will help users know their input is valuable. With that said, it is important not to make changes too early. Often the suggestions are just because the system, workflows, or processes are new and different from the ways the users have always done things. Unless suggestions are critical to patient care, they should just be documented for now. Critical issues should be taken care of right away. The rest of the suggested changes should be evaluated one to two months after activation to see if they are still needed.

# Managing Healthcare Information Systems

Once the system is live, it moves into operations and maintenance mode. During this time, the IT department must ensure that it continues to support the mission and goals of the organization and remains reliable and stable. During the implementation project, various processes should be put into place in preparation for this phase. These processes include configuration management, release management, customer support through a service desk, and resolution of any issues entered as trouble tickets. Documentation about how the system was configured feeds into good operations and maintenance documentation for resolving issues when they arise. Examples of operations and maintenance documentation include the following:

- Communication plan—Defines how end users communicate with the IT department about the new system. How will they request help for an issue? How will they request modifications to the system? How will they request help for general questions about how to use the system?
- Service desk knowledge base—Explains how to identify and resolve issues when users contact the service desk. This includes questions to ask and decision trees to help identify the resolution or the escalation process if an issue cannot be resolved. The escalation process should include how to approach the vendor if an issue cannot be resolved internally, as well as who has the authority to contact the vendor.
- Data flow documents—Identify where and how data flows from one system to another or from one location in the system to another, along with the dependencies between systems. This includes the triggers that prompt the data to flow, such as a change in the patient's location would trigger the information to be sent to update the lab system.
- Workflow documents—Explain end users' workflows and how the system fits into users' daily activities.
- Configuration management process—Defines how changes are made and what levels of approval and documentation are required for each change.
- Downtime procedures—Identify both what procedures end users will follow when the system is unavailable and what procedures the technical staff will follow to identify and resolve an issue causing downtime.
- Manuals—A group of documents ranging from end-user manuals to training guides and the configuration manual that provides step-by-step directions on how to make changes in the system.

Configuration management and release management are processes to control changes to the system, including software and hardware. They are involved in how changes are requested, the process for review and approval of changes, how changes are made and tested, and the process for releasing changes to the different environments to ensure that they are kept in sync and that each migration is verified. It is important that changes are made in a development environment, tested in a test environment, and verified in production. Conducting regression testing after the changes are made ensures the new modifications do not break something else. Controlling how and when changes are made in each environment is critical in avoiding unexpected negative results.

Working with the vendor on scheduling updates for small fixes, sometimes called hot fixes, to major upgrade releases will keep the system current while minimizing unexpected downtimes. Each new update should be evaluated prior to moving it through the configuration management process. If the update is large enough, it should be managed as a separate project.

Customer support is often provided through a help desk or a single phone number that goes to someone who can listen and help to resolve the issues the end users have. The calls may pertain to a bug, or issue with the system; a problem with the usability of the system; or a training or how-to question. Having a good knowledge base that allows the help desk staff to ask the right questions and provide enough information to resolve the issue during the first call can keep customer satisfaction high. For times when the service desk cannot resolve an issue, it is important to have a process for providing second-tier support. Often this is done through a help desk or ticket management system, but a custom database with workflows and notifications could work also. Timely feedback to the customer is important until the problem is resolved.

## Analyzing Data for Problems and Trends

Throughout the life cycle of any application, it is good practice to look for trends in usage as well as problems. Within the first year after an application goes live, analysis should occur to see if it actually met the need that was identified prior to its purchase. This is an evaluation of how well the goals leading to the investment were met and if the expected return on investment was realized. The results should be brought back to the governance committee for possible action, especially if the need was not met.

There are many reasons to collect data and look for trends. A researcher may want to look for levels of new system adoption over the months or years, evaluate user satisfaction with a system, or understand trends in system performance. The ways to collect data can be through surveys, user groups, or visits to the users. On the technical side, looking for trends in error reports, help desk logs, monitor logs, or unexpected downtimes will help the technical staff plan for improvements in system performance.

## Ensuring Critical Functions Are Repaired, Maintained, or Enhanced

The technical staff receives many different kinds of requests for change. These include feedback from users through help desk calls, rounds, user groups, and direct change requests. Some of these requests raise issues that must be fixed by the vendor or seek enhanced functionality not currently available. Vendors often provide updates, as mentioned earlier. Each change, or group of changes, should be evaluated and, if approved, prioritized. The smaller changes move through the configuration management process and are assigned and migrated according to the release management schedule. Larger requests or groups of requests should be managed as separate projects and follow the project management process.

## Business Continuity and Disaster Recovery Plans

The criticality of the system within the organization will define the disaster recovery and business continuity plans. The business continuity plan defines how an organization prepares for and maintains the business functions related to the defined system. This includes the operations and maintenance of the system to ensure stability, the process of resolving issues that could or do cause the system to be unavailable, how the business will continue without the system, and how to recover from an actual disaster.

The disaster recovery plan focuses on the technical aspects, such as data backup and recovery after the system goes down. Backups of the data are often done nightly and stored off-site on redundant servers or through a cloud computing provider, typically for an indefinite amount of time. There are hardware configurations that provide some level of continuity, such as automatic failover between clustered servers. Vendors can provide some options for how their systems can be configured. For critical systems, some organizations have off-site facilities where they can recover the system from backup if needed. Part of the disaster recovery plan, or a separate technical downtime plan, should include the steps to follow when the system goes down from causes other than a disaster. How the issue is identified and resolved, who is involved, and the process for a root cause analysis should all be included in this plan. These processes should be tested on a regular basis and updates should be made as needed.

The downtime plan focuses on business aspects, such as how to continue to operate without the electronic system. It includes procedures for communication, hard-copy forms for documentation, and plans for how data will be entered into the system once it becomes available again. Once users become dependent on the system for their work processes, they are reluctant to use manual processes. Regular reviews of the downtime plan and communication before any scheduled downtime will help with adoption, but support staff should be available to provide assistance whenever the downtime plan is required.

## Bibliography

1. HIMSS (Healthcare Information and Management Systems Society). *HIMSS Dictionary of Healthcare Information Technology Terms, Acronyms and Organizations.* 2nd ed. Chicago: HIMSS, 2010.
2. Schwalbe K. *Information Technology Project Management.* 4th ed. Cambridge, MA: Course Technology, 2006.
3. Houston S, Bove L. *Project Management for Healthcare Informatics.* New York: Springer, 2007.
4. Houston S. *The Project Manager's Guide to Health Information Technology Implementation.* Chicago: Healthcare Information and Management Systems Society, 2011.
5. Green M, Bowie M. *Essentials of Health Information Management Principles and Practices.* 2nd ed. Clifton Park, NY: Delmar Cengage Learning, 2011.
6. Project Management Institute. *The Guide to the Project Management Body of Knowledge.* 4th ed. Newtown Square, PA: Project Management Institute, 2008.
7. Morris P, Pinto J. *The Wiley Guide to Project, Program, and Portfolio Management.* Hoboken, NJ: John Wiley & Sons, 2007.

# Chapter 6

## Systems Testing and Evaluation

### Learning Objectives

At the conclusion of this chapter, the reader will be able to

- Design a formal testing methodology to demonstrate solutions meeting functional requirements (e.g., unit test, integrated test, stress test, and acceptance test)
- Implement internal controls to protect resources and ensure availability, confidentiality, and integrity during testing (e.g., security audits, versioning control, and change control)
- Validate implementations against contractual terms and design specifications
- Corroborate expected benefits are achieved (e.g., return on investment [ROI], benchmarks, and user satisfaction)

### Introduction

Healthcare organizations rely on information systems to manage clinical, administrative, financial, and legal aspects of daily operations. As technology advances and new healthcare systems are developed and marketed, stakeholders must weigh the risks of implementing or modifying systems and mitigate those risks as much as possible. A critical component of that risk mitigation strategy is testing and evaluating any new or modified system.

### Purpose of Systems Testing

The fundamental purpose of system testing is to provide knowledge to assist in managing the risks involved in developing, producing, operating, and sustaining systems and their capabilities.[1] Specifically, system testing provides knowledge of capabilities and limitations to the stakeholders for use in improving the system performance, and to the user community for optimizing system use and sustaining operations. Furthermore, system testing enables the stakeholders to identify the technical and operational limitations of the system under development so they can be resolved prior to production and deployment.[1] Information systems have become an integral part of healthcare operations and, as such, often have a direct impact on patient safety. With this in mind, identifying and testing for areas that are likely to be major patient safety risks is very important.

System testing and evaluation are performed on both hardware and software. Hardware testing includes evaluation of the physical components of the system (circuits, drives, internal components, etc.). Software testing is an investigation of the quality of a software product or service with the goal of finding any "bugs" and then fixing them before the product is released. Software testing can also provide an objective, independent view of the software that enables the business to appreciate and understand the risks of software implementation. Test techniques include, but are not limited to, executing a program or application with the intent of finding software errors or other defects. Comprehensive testing is a process of validating and verifying that a system

- Meets the requirements that guided its design and development
- Works as expected
- Can be implemented with the same functional characteristics across the entire organization
- Satisfies the needs of stakeholders[2]

Appropriate testing is critical for the success of any new or upgraded system. A study conducted by the National Institute of Standards and Technology (NIST) reported that software bugs (coding issues as well as integration challenges) cost the U.S. economy $59.5 billion annually.[3] More than a third of this cost could be avoided if better testing was performed; the earlier a defect is found, the cheaper it is to fix.

The first step in executing a successful test is creating a test methodology.

## *Test Methodology*

Different types of methodologies are used in the field of systems testing and quality assurance for today's complex healthcare information technology (IT) systems. Whether testing an enterprise-level system or a specific piece of code, the methodology is equally important. Due to the complexity of healthcare systems, many healthcare organizations adopt a buy-not-build strategy, outsourcing development to companies that specialize in that area. As a result, their IT staff often has only a partial picture of their system's development history. In such cases, a well-defined testing methodology is critical to ensure that the delivered system meets the needs of the healthcare organization. In formulating a testing methodology, different sets of test cases and testing strategies are prepared in order to verify that the system is as close to error-free as possible and capable of providing accurate and optimum outputs.[4] Testing scenarios vary widely among healthcare systems and are tailored for each organization by the test teams and stakeholders. Nonetheless, there is consensus among testing and standards professionals that any sound testing methodology should include the following key steps:

- Define the test strategy
- Develop testing tools
- Test execution
- Employ test controls
- Test reporting
- Final evaluation[4]

Each of these steps will be discussed in further detail in the following sections.

## Test Strategy

The test strategy is a formal description of how a system will be tested and is developed in order to address all levels of the testing process. The test team analyzes the requirements, writes the test strategy, and reviews the plan with the project team and various end users and other stakeholders. The test plan may include test cases, conditions, scripts, test environment, pass/fail criteria, and risk assessment. It will also define the testing scope and objectives, current business issues to consider during the test, testing roles and responsibilities, status reporting methods, test execution methods, industry standards to follow, test automation and tools, measurements and metrics, risks and mitigation, defect reporting and tracking, and change/configuration management.[5]

## Test Tools

Testing tools are widely available in the commercial market; the specific tools required will depend on the testing method(s) employed. Generally, system testing is performed either manually or through automation. Manual testing is simply direct human interaction with a system, testing for apparent defects. A member of the test team plays the role of an end user and tests most features of the application to ensure correct behavior. To ensure completeness of testing, the test team often follows a written test plan or script that leads them through a set of important test cases. Tools required for manual testing include a written test plan, test script, or scenarios to follow, and a method of recording and reporting the results. Although manual testing may find many defects in a system, it is a laborious and time-consuming process. In addition, it may not be effective in finding certain classes of defects not immediately apparent to the end user.

Automated testing may be performed through the use of special software (separate from the software being tested) that controls the execution of tests, compares actual outcomes to predicted outcomes, sets up test preconditions, and performs other test control and test reporting functions. The use of automated testing tools in healthcare is expanding, and there are many automated tools available that can be tailored specifically to an individual system's testing needs. One of the most significant benefits of test automation is the ability to duplicate the testing process. Once tests have been automated, they can quickly be run and repeated. This is often the most cost-effective method for systems that have a long maintenance life; even minor patches over the lifetime of a system can cause features to break that were working at an earlier point in time, so repeated testing is required for each patch or upgrade.[2]

## Test Execution

Performing and documenting the test activities is the primary focus of the testing methodology. Test professionals can use any number of methods to execute test events, and most fall into one of two categories: white-box testing or black-box testing.[2] These two approaches are based on the point of view a test engineer takes when executing test cases. White-box testing (also known as clear-box testing, glass-box testing, transparent-box testing, and structural testing) is a method of testing the *internal structures*, or workings, of a system, as opposed to its functionality; the tester is not concerned with what the system is supposed to do, but rather with how the system is supposed to operate on an internal level. Black-box testing is a method of software testing that tests the *functionality* of an application, as opposed to its internal structures or workings; the tester is only aware of what the system or application is supposed to do and has no knowledge of the internal operations of the system. A hybrid of the two approaches is known as gray-box testing, which is a combination of white-box and black-box testing approaches; the tester has some knowledge of internal structures and also understands the expected system functionalities. Gray-box testing is most useful when performing tests on existing systems that have been upgraded, patched, or modified.

Test methods are classified and executed based on the level of the test or the specific objective of the test. During system development, tests are performed at specific levels of development: unit-level testing, integration testing, and system testing. Test methods that are not associated with a specific level of development are classified by the testing objective, such as stress, acceptance, and regression testing.[2] Recently, healthcare organizations began adopting operational testing as well. Operational testing is focused on ensuring that the solution delivers the ROI and benefits that are expected. Users perform operational testing in a production environment while being observed by independent testers. Operational testing is often repeated every 90–180 days after deployment to ensure the system is being properly used and is delivering the intended results.

- *Unit testing* is performed by checking individual units of source code and sets of one or more computer program modules together with associated control data, usage procedures, and operating procedures to determine if they are fit for use. Intuitively, one can view a unit as the smallest testable part of an application. Unit tests are created by programmers and white-box testers during the development process.

- *Integration testing* involves combining individual software modules, applications, or units, and testing them as a group. Integration testing takes as its input modules that have been unit tested, groups them into larger aggregates, applies tests defined in an integration test plan to those aggregates, and delivers as its output the integrated system ready for system testing. Integration testing can be done using any of the box methods (white, black, or gray), but is best suited for gray-box testing, when the tester has some knowledge of the internal code of the individual units, as well as the expected system functionality.

- *System testing* is conducted on a complete, integrated system to evaluate the system's compliance with its specified requirements. System testing is one of the most common black-box testing methods and, as such, does not require knowledge of the inner design of the code or logic. System testing combines all of the integrated components that have successfully passed integration testing with software that has been integrated with hardware and tests them as a single system. The purpose of integration testing is to detect any inconsistencies between the software units that have been integrated (called assemblages) or between any of the assemblages and the hardware, as well as the exchange of data to external applications and systems.

- *Stress testing* is a form of testing that is used to determine the stability of a given system. It involves testing beyond normal operational capacity, often to a breaking point, in order to observe the results. The stress test puts a greater emphasis on robustness, availability, and error handling under a heavy load, rather than on what would be considered correct operation under normal circumstances. The goals of such tests may be to ensure the software does not crash in conditions of insufficient computational resources (such as memory or disk space), unusually high concurrency, or denial-of-service attacks.

- *Acceptance testing* is conducted to determine if the requirements of a specification or contract are met and to validate successful system implementation. Acceptance testing is usually created by business customers (the users or clients) and executed prior to accepting transfer of system ownership from the developer or vendor. Acceptance testing provides confidence that the delivered system meets the business requirements of sponsors, users, and other stakeholders. The acceptance test may also act as the final quality gateway, through which any quality defects not previously detected may be uncovered. Provided certain additional acceptance criteria are met (e.g., security testing, supportability and maintenance standards, usability standards, Section 508 compliance,[6] and standards compliance), system sponsors will normally sign off on a system as satisfying contractual requirements and deliver final payment to the vendor upon successful completion of acceptance testing. Acceptance testing is also done internally when major upgrades, patches, and the like are involved. The terms *acceptance testing, system testing,* and *integration testing* may be synonymous in some organizations and in some testing situations.

■ *Regression testing* is any type of system testing that seeks to uncover new bugs or errors in an existing, functional system that has been changed (by implementation of patches, enhancements, or configuration changes). It is common for new issues to be uncovered through the introduction of new systems. The intent of regression testing is to ensure that a planned change in software or hardware did not introduce new faults or defects into the production environment. A common method of regression testing includes repeating previously successful tests and checking to see if program behavior has changed or previously fixed faults have reemerged after a system change.

## Test Controls

System controls are implemented to protect the confidentiality, integrity, and availability of data and the overall management of a system during design, development, testing, and deployment. Some of the most common types of test controls include version controls (also called revision controls), security audits, and change controls.[2]

■ *Version control* (or revision control) tracks and provides control over changes to source code. Software developers and testers sometimes use version control software to maintain documentation and configuration files, as well as source code. As teams design, develop, and test software, it is common for multiple versions of the same software to be running in different sites and for the software's developers to be working simultaneously on updates. Often bugs or features of the software will be present in only certain versions due to the fixing of some problems and the introduction of new ones as the program develops. Therefore, for the purposes of locating and fixing bugs, it is vitally important to be able to retrieve and run different versions of the software to determine in which version(s) a problem occurs.

- *Security audits* are manual or automatic systematic, measurable technical assessments of a system or application. Manual assessments include interviewing staff, performing security vulnerability scans, reviewing application and operating system access controls, and analyzing physical access to the systems. Automated assessments include system-generated audit reports and software that monitors and reports changes to files and settings on a system. Systems that require security audits can include personal computers, servers, network routers, and switches.
- *Change control* is a formal process used to ensure that changes to a product or system are introduced in a controlled and coordinated manner. It reduces the possibility that unnecessary changes will be made to a system without forethought, introducing faults or undoing changes made by other users. Typical activities that would call for change control are patches to software products, system configuration changes, installation of new operating systems, upgrades to network routing systems, and changes to the electrical power systems supporting the infrastructure. Change control is also a means by which the number of changes in an environment at any one time is controlled.

## Test Reporting

Test reporting occurs throughout the testing process—not just at the conclusion of a test event. Stakeholders and sponsors may expect monthly, weekly, or even daily updates on current testing status, activities, schedules, and more. Test reporting can be challenging and should be planned out early in the testing process. Common challenges include tailoring test reports to your audience, clarifying confusion about the intent of testing, explaining how testing is actually done, and understanding which testing metrics are meaningful and why. At a minimum, test reports should address the mission of the test, system(s) or application(s) covered, organizational risk of deploying the system, testing techniques, test environment, updated testing status, and obstacles to testing.[7]

## Final Evaluation

For most testing projects, the most important deliverable is the final evaluation report, which contains the findings, conclusions, and recommendations of the system test. For successful system tests, the final evaluation should confirm to stakeholders that the system has achieved expected results and should specifically address how conducting the test will affect the anticipated outcomes or benefits. For example, if the results of a system test show that implementation of the system will significantly increase the organization's third-party insurance collections, the cost of conducting the test would be considered a sound investment and the benefits of the test would be clear. In addition, the final evaluation report should address the most common stakeholder questions at the conclusion of a test event, including (but not limited to)

- Does the system meet our quality and performance expectations?
- Is the system ready for users?
- What can we expect when *x* people simultaneously use the system?
- What are we risking if we go live with the system now?

Final evaluations may reveal the need for specific end-user training prior to the go-live event. Lessons learned from each test event should be leveraged by the team to improve the planning, execution, and evaluation of future tests. Beyond the go-live date, evaluation continues to play a critical role in a system's life cycle. Postimplementation evaluations are critical for measuring initial and long-term user satisfaction, system usability, business and patient care impacts and benefits, and the system's potential for expansion or integration with other organizational systems.

## References

1. DAU (Defense Acquisition University). *Defense Acquisition Guidebook*. Washington, DC: DAU, 2012.
2. Wikipedia. Software testing. July 2012. http://en.wikipedia.org/wiki/Software_testing (accessed November 18, 2015).
3. NIST (National Institute of Standards and Technology). Software errors cost U.S. economy $59.5 billion annually. Gaithersburg, MD: NIST, 2002. http://www.abeacha.com/NIST_press_release_bugs_cost.htm (accessed November 18, 2015).
4. Buzzle. Software testing methodologies. 2011. http://www.buzzle.com/articles/software-testing-methodologies.html (accessed November 18, 2015).
5. Testing Excellence. Test strategy and test plan. 2008. http://www.testingexcellence.com/test-strategy-and-test-plan/ (accessed November 18, 2015).
6. HHS (U.S. Department of Health and Human Services). HHS Section 508. Washington, DC: HHS, 2014. http://www.hhs.gov/web/section-508/index.html (accessed November 18, 2015).
7. Kelly M. Dimensions of a good test report. *InformIT*, March 24, 2006. http://www.informit.com/articles/article.aspx?p=457506 (accessed November 18, 2015).

# Chapter 7

## Systems Privacy and Security

### Learning Objectives

At the conclusion of this chapter, the reader will be able to

- Participate in defining organizational privacy and security requirements, policies, and procedures
- Assess privacy and security risks
- Mitigate privacy and security vulnerabilities
- Ensure user access control according to established policies and procedures
- Ensure confidentiality, integrity, and availability of data
- Define organizational roles (e.g., information security, physical security, and compliance)
- Develop data management controls (e.g., data ownership, criticality, security levels, protection controls, retention and destruction requirements, and access controls)
- Validate disaster recovery and business continuity plans
- Coordinate privacy and security audits
- Validate security features in the evaluation of existing and new system requirements

### Introduction

Concerns about privacy and security of health records are not new to the age of electronic health records (EHRs). In the days of paper records, patients had valid concerns about the privacy of their health information; they expected access to those records would be limited and their contents would remain confidential. What has changed in the era of EHRs is the ease with which health records could potentially be lost or breached, even from great distances, and the potential scale of the incidents.

One can imagine the loss or theft of a single patient's chart from a doctor's office or hospital even 10 years ago. What is much harder to imagine, in that era, is the theft of thousands of patients' financial information in a matter of mere seconds, or the felonious intrusion into a celebrity's health records by a malicious person located thousands of miles from the locked office of the celebrity's psychiatrist. In today's world, absent organizational understanding and adoption of appropriate privacy policies and security safeguards, the threat of those events is all too real.

## Defining Requirements, Policies, and Procedures

Today, numerous laws and regulations exist on international, national, and regional levels regulating the privacy and security of EHRs. As the use of technologies such as EHRs, personal health records (PHRs), health information exchanges (HIEs), and e-prescribing expands, the need for organizations to implement and maintain strong security will continue to be of high importance.

A primary area of focus for many laws and regulations is patient-sensitive health information that is transmitted or maintained in any form or medium. Those rules may impose restrictions on how organizations (including governments in some cases) may use or disclose health information.

In some cases, an individual organization may elect to put in place policies that further restrict access for a variety of reasons, especially when dealing with research that is on the front lines of medical science. For example, the presence in an individual's DNA of a certain genetic marker may not indicate anything today, but as science develops, that same marker could predict a condition that might have negative consequences for the patient.

Based on an understanding of requirements, top management will develop policies and procedures in support of organizational objectives. Policies describe an organization's rules and regulations. Procedures provide a stepwise accounting of how tasks are to be performed in order to ensure compliance with policies. Together, policies and procedures can be thought of as an organization's endeavor to put down in writing the rules and processes that its employees and business partners should follow. Before we explore the development of these plans at greater length, it is worth taking a moment to clearly define our terms. *Privacy* laws and rules deal with limits on the use and disclosure of health information. *Security* policies and procedures provide controls on electronic and physical access to health data. In the United States, for example, the protection of health information is now governed under the Health Insurance Portability and Accountability (HIPAA) Act of 1996, and more recently, updates were made through the Health Infomration Technology for Economic and Clinical Health (HITECH) Act in 2009. On a very basic level, the HIPAA Privacy Rule is the primary regulation pertaining to the privacy of health information. It defines what protected health information (PHI) is and specifies the entities that must keep it private. The HIPAA Security Rule is the primary regulation pertaining to the security of health information. It outlines what information security means in healthcare as well as the three safeguards for keeping PHI secure. These administrative, physical, and technical safeguards provide guidance for implementing information security practices as well as for assessing the risks posed by a covered entity's existing practices.[1,2]

## Risk Assessment

Once an organization has developed an awareness and understanding of applicable privacy and security laws and requirements, it should undertake an assessment of the organization's readiness with regard to each of those elements. That assessment should focus on identifying gaps between what is required and what actually exists within the organization's operations. A number of tools may be used in such an assessment.[3,4] Some examples include

- Review of current policies, procedures, contracts, and other documents relevant to privacy and security
- Organizational surveys or questionnaires that measure knowledge of, and compliance with, applicable privacy and security requirements
- Facility walk-throughs to identify areas where physical security limitations need to be addressed
- Technical penetration or intrusion attempts or other tests to assess security vulnerabilities
- Updated legislation, regulations, or international agreements that may drive new approaches
- Root cause analysis of any security breach that may have occurred since the last assessment

This information should serve to give the organization a realistic assessment of its risk. We can think of risk as the likelihood of a given incident occurring, as well as the adverse impact of such an incident. We often think of such risks in terms of threats—potential scenarios that would have a negative impact on security or privacy—and threat sources—persons or events with the ability to actualize a threat. Examples of threat sources include humans (e.g., malicious hackers and employee saboteurs), natural disasters (e.g., floods and earthquakes), and environmental events (e.g., power grid failure and nuclear or chemical accident). Threats and threat sources are dangerous to any organization that has not made itself entirely immune to them. We use the term *vulnerabilities* to describe flaws or weaknesses that allow exploits or events to result in a security breach or other violation of an organization's security policies.

## Vulnerability Remediation

The analysis resulting from a risk assessment should go a long way toward identifying the most significant vulnerabilities an organization faces. Additionally, audit reports, reports of atypical system behaviors, vendor advisories, and a system security analysis can be used to identify system vulnerabilities. Once those issues have been identified, the organization should embark on a remediation process to eliminate or mitigate the related risks. During the process of remediation, existing policies and procedures will be reviewed, new policies and procedures will be developed, education and training will take place, and controls will be put into place to safeguard critical systems and data. The controls include physical safeguards, administrative safeguards, and technical safeguards, which will be discussed below. With these tools at its disposal, an organization can decide to take one of two approaches to reduce risk to an acceptable level:

1. No action. The current risk level is deemed acceptable by the organization.
2. Mitigate. Implement safeguards to reduce risk to an acceptable level, along with policies and procedures in support of those safeguards.

## User Access Controls

To maintain data confidentiality, integrity, and availability, an organization must control access to systems and data. User access controls prevent access by unauthorized users. User access controls can be broken down into the following categories, sometimes termed the AAA, or triple-A, approach:[5]

■ Authentication
■ Access
■ Accounting

Authentication is the process of attempting to prove that users are who they say they are before allowing them to access a system. Three primary methods exist to authenticate users:

1. Something a user knows (e.g., personal identification number [PIN] or password)
2. Something a user has (e.g., smart card or token)
3. Something a user is (e.g., fingerprint, palm print, or retina scan)

Once a user has been authorized, or authenticated, an appropriate level of access must be set. Access privileges are ideally set to allow the minimum access necessary in order to perform a job. Role-based access is often defined by a user's role within the organization. For example, physicians generally have the ability to place orders and create and sign documents to which a nurse may not have access. A midlevel provider and medical student may each have subsets of the rights granted to a physician, while a pharmacist may have yet another set of privileges in the system.

Accounting is the final piece of the user access puzzle. Audit reports and other controls will provide assurance that users are not overstepping their bounds by accessing information that is not required for care delivery and may be forbidden by many privacy laws (e.g., looking up coworkers, neighbors, or celebrities in the system). Audit reports should be generated on both a scheduled and a random basis to ensure ongoing compliance.

## Confidentiality, Integrity, and Availability

A primary focus of healthcare information technology (IT) security is the area of confidentiality. Confidentiality is the process of limiting disclosure of a patient's personal information to comply with policies and regulations, and to maintain the trust that patients have placed in healthcare organizations.[6]

Two other areas that concern healthcare security professionals are integrity and availability of data. Integrity refers to the accuracy and completeness of data. To preserve the integrity of its health information, an organization must success-fully implement policies and procedures to protect the data from unauthorized modification, deletion, or destruction and to keep it consistent with its source. Additionally, the organization must provide auditing mechanisms to ensure data has not been altered, deleted, or destroyed in an unauthorized manner. Availability calls for information to be protected from any unplanned destruction, whether by accident, vandalism, natural disasters, and so on. Availability also makes certain health information is available to patients when they need it. Care must be taken to ensure that records will be available and survive the organiza-tion in the event of closure, merger, or similar events. This could also apply to other countries and their internal and external ties through treaties and the like.

## Organizational Roles

An expert who understands which privacy laws apply to an organization and how they should be properly interpreted plays a crucial role in most healthcare organizations. Laws in many jurisdictions require that each organization appoint an individual, sometimes with the title of chief information security officer, who is tasked with these responsibilities. Among this individual's tasks will be

- Assessing and maintaining knowledge of rules and regulations
- Developing policies and procedures

- Cultivating organizational and cultural awareness and developing educational plans in support of policies
- Managing appropriate access for external business partners and ensuring documentation exists in support of such access
- Monitoring compliance with policies
- Responding to complaints and other issues that arise
- Conducting or directing others to conduct scheduled and random access audits
- Investigating known security breaches and reporting information to appropriate regulatory or governmental agencies as required by law

As with privacy rules, it is critical for an organization to identify a person or persons who will be responsible for development of and compliance with security policies and procedures. Often, the first step in these activities is documentation of the organization's baseline state with regard to privacy and security. In many healthcare organizations, the compliance or risk management department serves this function. It is not unreasonable to expect that similar practices and procedures may also be present in other countries, but may be worded differently to reflect local laws, culture, regulations, and agreements.

## Data Management Controls

To ensure the security of protected data, a number of safeguards may be deployed. These safeguards seek to meet certain goals, including controlling electronic access to systems containing sensitive patient information or other private data; controlling physical access to locations or devices that may have ready access to secure data; managing data in transit, including e-mail and file transfer; and encryption of data on laptop computers, flash memory drives, or other devices that might be easily lost or stolen.

Safeguards can be categorized into three main groupings: administrative, technical, and physical. Administrative safeguards are administrative actions, policies, and procedures that an organization deploys in support of its security aims. Administrative safeguards include such actions as the ongoing education of employees on security requirements and scenarios in which data may or may not be used or disclosed, as well as developing policies and procedures that provide safeguards within the physical and technical realms.

Technical safeguards are electronic means of ensuring data is not accessible, or that it is encrypted in a way that makes it useless to a third party. Examples of technical safeguards would include the use of network firewalls, secure protocols on any public networks carrying patient data, and encryption of storage media on laptop computers and mobile devices.

The last type of measure, physical safeguards, consists of physical measures, policies, and procedures that protect electronic information systems from natural and environmental hazards, as well as unauthorized intrusion. Examples would include data centers that are located outside a floodplain and have redundant sources of power, and limited access to server rooms or areas where data may be accessed or damaged. One of the major threats security professionals face today is cybersecurity—or the unauthorized access and malicious attack of healthcare information systems and patient health information data, and more recently, ransomware - holding that patient health information "hostage" for payment.[7]

## Disaster Recovery and Business Continuity Plans

While everyone has responsibility for protecting patient privacy and ensuring healthcare data security, the healthcare IT security professionals must be involved in the development of an organization's disaster recovery and business continuity plans. Contingency plans in this area should include the following:

- Analysis of applications and data criticality. Applications and data should be prioritized in order of importance to the organization so a logical sequence of data recovery can be planned.
- Data backup plan. Detailed plans must be developed to ensure the existence of a retrievable backup copy of the organization's critical data.
- Disaster recovery plan. Procedures must be documented that define how to restore data after any loss, for any reason.
- Emergency-mode operation plan. Downtime plans should be spelled out that will enable the organization to continue to operate in emergency mode while access to electronic data is not possible.
- Testing and revision. All contingency plans must be routinely tested and revised to fill gaps that are discovered and to address changing organizational needs and infrastructure.

## Auditing

An essential component of an organization's security plans is the ability to audit all access to protected data. No matter how good an organization's policies and procedures are or how strenuously it works to limit access, individuals may still be able to access records they may not need to access to perform their daily duties. Audit reports enable an organization to identify any breaches or other policy violations, from employee snooping to a large criminal attack.

## Ongoing System Evaluation

Of course, ensuring security is an ongoing and critical process. Crucial to maintaining compliance is a continuous evaluation of the security features of existing and new hardware and software. Network diagrams that include the location and configuration of firewalls, servers, and routers must be maintained. Documentation of software and hardware, as well as vendor contact information, must be kept up-to-date. As new applications are introduced, technical and user interfaces and other data access points must be evaluated, and care must be taken to assess whether an application or interface might introduce new security vulnerabilities. Additionally, existing applications must be reevaluated on an ongoing and regular basis in the face of organizational changes and evolving local, national, and international attitudes, laws, and regulations.

## References

1. ONC (Office of the National Coordinator for Health Information Technology). Health information privacy, security and your EHR. Washington, DC: ONC. https://www.healthit.gov/providers-professionals/ehr-privacy-security (accessed November 10, 2015).
2. HHS (U.S. Department of Health and Human Services). Health information privacy. Washington, DC: HHS. http://www.hhs.gov/ocr/privacy/index.html (accessed November 10, 2015).
3. ONC (Office of the National Coordinator for Health Information Technology). Security risk assessment tool. Washington, DC: ONC. https://www.healthit.gov/providers-professionals/security-risk-assessment-tool (accessed November 10, 2015).
4. HIMSS (Healthcare Information and Management Systems Society). Risk assessment toolkit. Chicago: HIMSS. http://www.himss.org/library/healthcare-privacy-security/risk-assessment (accessed November 10, 2015).
5. Newman RC. *Computer Security: Protecting Digital Resources*. Sudbury, MA: Jones and Bartlett, 2010.
6. HIMSS (Healthcare Information and Management Systems Society). Privacy & security toolkit. Chicago: HIMSS, 2013. http://www.himss.org/library/healthcare-privacy-security/toolkit (accessed November 10, 2015).
7. HIMSS (Healthcare Information and Management Systems Society). 2015 HIMSS cybersecurity survey. Chicago: HIMSS, 2015. http://www.himss.org/2015-cybersecurity-survey (accessed November 10, 2015).

# ADMINISTRATION III

# Chapter 8

## Administration Leadership

### Learning Objectives

At the conclusion of this chapter, the reader will be able to

- Participate in organizational strategic planning (e.g., measure performance against organizational goals)
- Assess the organizational environment (e.g., corporate culture, values, and drivers)
- Forecast technical and information needs of an organization by linking resources to business needs
- Develop an information technology (IT) strategic plan and departmental objectives that align and support organizational strategies and goals
- Evaluate performance (e.g., goal/performance indicators and systems effectiveness)
- Evaluate effectiveness and user satisfaction of systems and services being provided
- Promote stakeholder understanding of IT opportunities and constraints (e.g., business and IT resources, budget, and project prioritization)
- Develop policies and procedures for information and systems management
- Comply with legal and regulatory standards
- Adhere to ethical business principles
- Employ comparative analysis strategies (e.g., indicators and benchmarks)
- Prepare and deliver business communications (e.g., presentations, reports, and project plans)
- Facilitate group discussions and meetings (e.g., consensus building and conflict resolution)
- Provide consultative services to the organization on IT matters
- Develop educational strategies regarding the information and management systems function
- Maintain organizational competencies on current IT technologies and trends

- Assure risk management is embedded in internal and external management processes and consistently applied (e.g., risk assessment and risk mitigation)
- Ensure quality standards and practices are followed by monitoring internal and external performance

# Introduction

Leadership is a skill that every member of any organization is responsible for understanding and, when appropriate, undertaking. In the healthcare sector, teams or responsible parties will come together and disband in both well-established and very informal processes. Teams may be made up of two and three individuals or, in project teams, can be quite larger in size. Leadership skills are necessary in all aspects of the work we do.

# Participation in Organizational Strategic Planning

Leaders are responsible for setting the strategic goals and priorities for the company, division, department, and new initiatives. A strategy is a formal or informal plan of action to achieve a goal. Regardless of where an organization is today, its strategies focus on where it would like to be at some point in the future. To outline and explain its strategies, an organization typically will use one or a series of statements that will be published for the benefit of the employees and customers. These statements express the mission, vision, values, and goals of the organization.

## Mission

The mission is a statement of why the organization exists—its purpose statement. Mission statements can vary from simple and concise to complex and hard to understand. The best mission statements are those that can be easily understood and remembered by any member of the organization or those that may be customers of your organization. Once read, it is not easily forgotten.

At the organizational level, it is typically the CEO and board of directors who set the mission of the company. The mission does not change with any regularity unless the business of the company or direction of the industry is changing as well. Nevertheless, each employee of the company has a responsibility to understand the mission to be sure that as they are evaluating their daily work, they can tie that work to the mission of the company.

## Vision

A second expression that a company uses is the vision statement. A vision is the company statement that defines where it wants to go or what it wants to be. The vision is what the company is striving to achieve as it completes the daily work, a futuristic perspective. The CEO and board also typically set the vision. Depending on how far the vision reaches into the future, it may be altered with more regularity than the mission.

## Values

The addition of values to corporate ideologies is much more recent than mission and vision. A list of values allows individuals to understand what the company supports and appreciates most. Values are often presented in a list that individuals can compare against in their own personal values, as well as the values that are built into the activities they undertake at work. Examples of a healthcare organization's values might include compassion, service, and respect. Employees should use the values as guides for their behavior at work and assess whether the values align or conflict with your work assignments. If an initiative lacks alignment or is in conflict with at least one value, it should be called into question.

## Goals

Goals are the measures to support vision accomplishment. The list of goals need to be SMART: specific, measurable, attainable, relevant, and time bound. Sample organizational goals include breaking even on Medicare reimbursement, leading America in clinical quality, and employing primary care providers of choice for the community. Clearly articulated goals that support the mission and vision serve as guides against which to measure the work.

# Organizational Environment

Every department of a large organization benefits from having a formalized plan that demonstrates how the work being performed aligns with the strategic goals and objectives of the organization. The complexity and detail of such a plan will vary by organization, as well as by the size and complexity of a department. For very small information management and systems departments, the question that arises is whether a full-fledged strategic plan is appropriate. A plan with objectives is a good idea regardless of the organization's size.

In many organizations, it will be satisfactory to create a table or spreadsheet that crosswalks the organizational vision and goals down through each of the individual projects or initiatives being worked on within a department or area. Companies often engage leaders in formal governance and leadership committees to promote understanding of the potential projects that may be coming in the next 12–18 months. A detailed plan is then created for that time period. Detailed planning much beyond 18 months out, other than for routine replacement, may be less valuable given the rapid changes in the information technology (IT) industry.

Maintaining a project crosswalk provides a visual summary of the initiatives being handled by an area of service. This crosswalk can then be used within the department and at administrative review sessions to demonstrate the linkage between vision, goals, and projects. Additionally, this same tool can serve as a link to the detailed work plans and project updates that are maintained by staff. In Figure 8.1, you can see how a series of projects are weighed by scoring each against the organization's goals and priorities. The resulting score and relative rank of each project is calculated and can be shared and help provide objectivity to project priorities.

## Forecasting Technical and Information Needs of an Organization

Leaders in healthcare IT provide assistance and direction in support of the goals and initiatives of the company. This requires a careful balance of leadership and support. It is important that all organizational leaders understand that operational goals direct IT and not the reverse. Unclear leadership responsibilities of those outside IT can put any organizational project at risk. All projects need operational leadership and, as necessary, IT operational and management support.

Information management and system leaders need to be keenly aware of organizational goals and be ready to actively recommend appropriate systems and technologies in support of those goals. Organizations that stay focused on goals will not catch the IT leader off guard. When goal deviation does occur, the IT leader needs to be ready to challenge the request to deviate from organizational goals and be prepared to quickly gather appropriate supporting materials to attend to the updated goals. Remaining focused on goals will help the IT leader and the organization to avoid creating the service gap that occurs when requested services surpass what the internal staff can provide.

New project requests are likely to come from a variety of sources. Some of the requests will be more fully developed than others. Requestors will need support in determining their project's scope, definition, and objectives, and, at times, in forming a relationship with a vendor that can undertake the request at hand. The IT leader needs to have a program evaluation staff that can sit with requestors and help them work through a new project request. Lacking resources and structure, customers may suggest a solution to a problem that has not been well defined. They need to understand new technology and infrastructure opportunities, such as leveraging the existing application portfolio and network services, integrating devices, exploring new vendor offerings, and providing internal and external consulting services.

All leaders need to know how to access the tactical steps that are in place to support the organizational goals. Focused goals will bring clarity to the tactics that need to be implemented. Be wary if an organization does not have the discipline to understand what is within its scope to accomplish in any defined time

| Index | Organizational goals and priorities (Request) | Exceptional care 29.00% | Effective and efficient use of resources 24.00% | Strategic growth 14.00% | Exceptional experience 9.00% | Nation leading research and education 9.00% | End user experience 5.00% | Innovation 5.00% | Sites impacted 5.00% | Score 0–9 | Relative rank |
|---|---|---|---|---|---|---|---|---|---|---|---|
|  | Example: Enhanced privacy | 1 | 3 | 3 | 9 | 1 | 1 | 1 | 1 | 2.48 | 28 |
| 1 | Home care/hospice | 9 | 3 | 1 | 3 | 1 | 3 | 3 | 9 | 4.48 | 15 |
| 2 | Transplant | 9 | 9 | 1 | 3 | 9 | 3 | 3 | 1 | 6.34 | 5 |
| 3 | Mobile devices | 1 | 3 | 1 | 1 | 1 | 9 | 9 | 9 | 2.68 | 26 |
| 4 | Nurse triage | 9 | 9 | 1 | 3 | 1 | 9 | 3 | 9 | 6.32 | 7 |
| 5 | Surgical clinic outreach | 9 | 3 | 1 | 3 | 1 | 9 | 1 | 1 | 4.38 | 16 |
| 6 | Anesthesia IntraOp U/S/R | 9 | 3 | 1 | 1 | 1 | 3 | 1 | 3 | 4 | 18 |
| 7 | EKG upgrade | 3 | 3 | 1 | 1 | 1 | 9 | 1 | 9 | 2.86 | 25 |
| 8 | Remote hospital growth | 9 | 9 | 1 | 9 | 1 | 3 | 1 | 1 | 6.06 | 8 |
| 9 | Remote clinic growth | 9 | 9 | 3 | 9 | 1 | 3 | 1 | 1 | 6.34 | 6 |
| 10 | Health clinics | 9 | 3 | 3 | 9 | 3 | 3 | 1 | 1 | 5.08 | 13 |
| 11 | HR system | 3 | 9 | 3 | 1 | 9 | 3 | 9 | 1 | 5.4 | 12 |
| 12 | MFM ClinDoc tools | 9 | 9 | 1 | 3 | 1 | 3 | 1 | 1 | 5.52 | 11 |
| 13 | Affiliate epic care link | 1 | 3 | 3 | 9 | 1 | 3 | 9 | 9 | 3.38 | 22 |
| 14 | CPM upgrade | 9 | 9 | 1 | 1 | 1 | 9 | 1 | 9 | 6.04 | 9 |
| 15 | Organizational analytics | 9 | 9 | 1 | 1 | 9 | 1 | 9 | 9 | 6.76 | 1 |

**Figure 8.1  Project rankings based on organizational goals and priorities.**

period. Leaders have a responsibility to serve as the organization's conscience regarding IT requests and service overextension. Activities must be clearly prioritized so that all leaders are operating from an identical institutional strategic plan.

Goals, strategies, and tactics will inevitably require both redirection and an occasional time-limited expansion of scope. Be aware of the personnel resources that are available in your scope of authority and their availability, and have a well-developed contingency plan for addressing resource needs when the unexpected occurs. This knowledge will help the organization remain flexible and make more efficient and well-thought-out decisions in matters requiring IT support.

Not only must IT leaders understand and support the organizational goals with their system-level knowledge and expertise, but they must also have a methodology that supports the organization's ability to measure activities against their stated goals and objectives. They must facilitate a process in which all leaders work together to define the organization's measures of progress and, ultimately, success. If agreement cannot be reached on a measure, it will be difficult to know when the related goal has been achieved.

The measures that are put in place can be used in internal benchmarking, in which the organization defines its current place, defines the objective, and then measures activity against both the starting point and the objective at regular reporting intervals. Local and national benchmarks may be available, but a contract may be required to use them. It can often be an expensive proposition to have access to such benchmark data.

Benchmarking data are available in many, but not all, aspects of IT management. Be sure that any benchmarks used are comparable to the data your organization is capable of supplying. Careful clarification on the front end may decrease the challenges of apples-to-oranges comparisons, but a few disparate data points may well remain.

## Developing the IT Strategic Plan

Among the many responsibilities of IT leaders is developing the IT strategic plan. In a very large organization, the IT strategic plan may serve as a reference tool for prioritizing the work that is to be done throughout the organization. In small or less complex organizations, the IT plan may be more appropriate as a section or addendum to the organizational strategic plan. When developing an IT strategic plan, it is important to include the input of organizational leaders and the staff responsible for the actionable components.

Begin the process of developing an IT strategic plan with copies of both the current IT plan and the organizational strategic plan. If the organizational plan has not been developed or refreshed in the last 12 months, then you must start the process by validating the strategies and tactics of the organizational plan first. The IT strategic plan must be perfectly aligned with all of the organizational priorities. If there is no previous IT plan to work from, myriad free templates and resources can be found on the web[1] and used as models of formatting and organization.

Consider taking the following steps to develop your IT plan:

■ Initiate the document by including the mission, vision, goals, and strategies of the organization. IT supports the business and therefore must be grounded in that business and its strategies.
■ Identify the current state of the systems and processes that support the business, and assess their effectiveness in meeting their stated functions.
■ Define the gap that exists between the functions that are or can be provided and those that need to be developed or procured.
■ Compare the timeline for staff to manage the development and costs associated with external development or purchase.
■ Identify who will take responsibility for the initiatives to be addressed.

The initial stages of the plan need to reinforce the idea that there is no such thing as an IT project. All projects are organizational and strategic in nature, and IT is only one component within the bigger initiative. Once top managers understand and agree to that, they will recognize why every major initiative will need to be sponsored by an operational leader or leaders. A well-developed plan will map the organizational strategies and the supporting applications and processes for each strategy. Once fully developed, the map will provide a visual representation of the current systems' status, an indicator of the expected useful lifeline of the systems or the gap that exists between the strategy and the needed technology.

The remainder of the plan can focus on the gaps—the gap analysis. The plan can outline the current state and desired future state. An approach to consider would be to evaluate the strengths, weaknesses, opportunities, and threats (SWOT) of the current organization. In cases where it is not likely that the gap can be bridged with a single process or system change, the plan needs to outline the stepping stones that can be laid out to achieve the desired outcome. As many of the steps may each take several years to complete, the plan's details need only focus on the first step or two, and then more high level for the remaining steps. This is practical, as the technologies and organizational priorities may change during the interval.

Finally, the plan needs to outline some of the more pure IT initiatives and personnel needs. Examples of this might include advanced technologies like voice over Internet protocol (VoIP), data center growth and capacity planning, network growth and development, and general systems refresh strategies. Elements considering the current and future resourcing needs, as well as the transition and succession plans for staff and leaders, help to ensure consistent leadership.

At some point staff will be leaving the company. Is there someone who has the appropriate education and skill set to step into an interim role? Does that person have the qualities to take on the role permanently? How about key managers and supervisors? Each leader should have a mentee within the organization who is being groomed and educated to move up when the time is appropriate. A well-prepared organization has the bench strength to maintain leadership continuity in the same way it has system redundancy to maintain continuity.

## *Implementing the IT Strategic Plan*

Once developed, the IT strategic plan needs to remain a living object and therefore must be regularly maintained. To achieve this, the document needs to be part of the organizational strategic plan and updated accordingly with any changes to its companion. The key IT objectives are visible to the entire department, so they have an opportunity to see and commit to each objective on a daily basis. Individuals' performance objectives can be tied back to this plan, and regular reports can be used as measures against the overall IT strategic plan. Finally, treat the plan itself as a project. Maintain a color-coded scorecard of goal progress and achievement for all to see.

# Evaluating Performance

Measures that monitor the ongoing effectiveness and progress of a department's activities are necessary for leaders to judge the performance of a department or work area. In an operational unit that has both projects and services, two types of measures will be necessary.

The development of a Gantt chart may be the most effective way of tracking a project. A Gantt chart includes a series of rows detailing each of the steps and substeps to be completed within the project. Each row has multiple columns identifying start dates, projected end dates, dependencies, responsible parties, completion percentage, and the like. The Gantt chart provides an excellent way of visualizing an entire project in both highly summarized and detailed ways. Commercial project-tracking software products are available, but many organizations effectively manage projects using a simple spreadsheet. An example of measuring a project against goals is included later in this chapter.

In departments where service is a component of the work done, it will be important to have a service-level agreement (SLA) with indicators that are tracked at regular intervals. The expected service level can be internally derived, negotiated with the customers, or driven by externally agreed-upon benchmarks. Service-level parameters can best be measured using a dashboard visualization tool. A dashboard is a series of graphs or tables that indicate the current performance, the historic performance for an appropriate time interval, the expected quality of services, and if appropriate, the acceptable level of variation below and above the stated goal. In addition to the quality-of-service goal, there may be a stretch goal, though it is not usually on a control chart. The stretch goal is

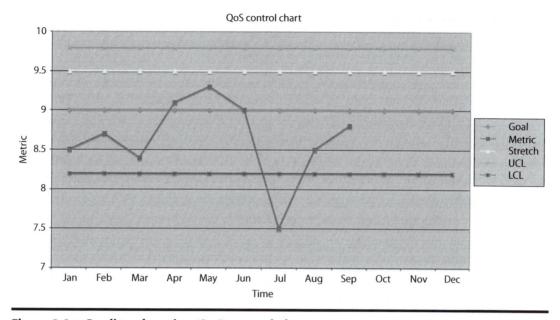

**Figure 8.2  Quality-of-service (QoS) control chart. UCL, upper control limit; LCL, lower control limit.**

typically an internally desired target that exceeds any quality-of-service parameters that have been agreed to.

A typical dashboard includes a series of control charts. Control charts are statistical representations of the graphs discussed above. They add lines representing the upper and lower control limits. This takes into account that there will be natural variation in the results represented around a mean. To the extent that a series of points begins to move in one direction or the other, it will become necessary to review the process looking for special-cause variation. In any business, variation will often increase costs. In healthcare, variation may also signal changes in the quality of patient care, and therefore warrants immediate attention and understanding. A sample quality-of-service control chart is presented in Figure 8.2.

## Evaluating Effectiveness and User Satisfaction

At times, organizational leaders may find that they have become too detached from the organization and the stakeholders they are serving. IT leaders may be especially prone to this because they often work in a separate location from where care services are provided or because the complexity of their work slowly removes them from the day-to-day environment of care.

Regular departmental and system assessments will prevent isolation and enhance communication with stakeholder communities throughout the organization. The assessments need to include the effectiveness of both the systems supported and the services provided.

Measuring system effectiveness needs to start with a baseline analysis. This ties in very nicely with the earlier discussion of understanding service-level benchmarks. It is important to have both an objective and a subjective assessment of the quality metrics. A simple example of this can be seen in an assessment of system availability. Ninety-nine percent uptime for a computer system sounds highly efficient and tracks very nicely along a control chart. Customers, however, report that they struggle with the average of 1.75 hours of system downtime each week, even though that falls within the 1% deemed acceptable. A customer assessment helps the leader understand the customer's point of view. The 24/7 healthcare environment has expectations of 99.999% system availability.

A baseline assessment can be accomplished in several ways. Face-to-face interviews have value for systems that affect only a small number of stakeholders, especially when they work in disparate parts of the company. Unit rounding will be effective when actual observation of the system in use is needed. What better way to demonstrate an interest in stakeholders' work than to be present in their environment? Typically, it is most efficient to meet with a group of users together. This can be done by going to departmental or unit meetings that are already scheduled. Alternatively, you may choose to call a town hall meeting to look at a general situation or a focus group to examine specific situations. Both can be organized as either physical or virtual meetings.

The baseline assessment is designed to gather data regarding the systems that the stakeholders are using and the way they are being used. Take the time to understand the stakeholders' expectations of system availability and performance. Listen to their past internal and external experiences, and pay special attention if they note adverse changes in systems performance. Use the assessment time to accept feedback regarding opportunities for system operating improvements. Be clear that not all requests can be accommodated, but remain open-minded to what will result if some meaningful feedback is directly addressed.

Once the baseline is determined, commit to a regular process of follow-up analyses. Identify the interval that is most appropriate. If the organization concurs with an initial assessment that the performance of IT systems and services is satisfactory, then an annual follow-up assessment will be sufficient. A lower than desirable assessment warrants a prompter turnaround and more frequent follow-up. Regular communication or monthly status reports should address commitments to improvement. Effectiveness should be reassessed at regular intervals agreed on with customers.

The process for the follow-up assessment can be accomplished by telephone or web-based surveys. Providing easily accessible feedback tools within the applications themselves will prompt regular responses. Customers will appreciate the availability of immediately accessible feedback because it will enable them to avoid making calls to the help desk.

Departmental effectiveness needs to be differentiated from system effectiveness as you do your assessment. The distinction is necessary because customers and stakeholders have a multitude of different needs. The methodology for retrieving feedback about the two can be essentially the same, but the objectives will be different. In the departmental assessment, the value is in understanding how the personnel respond and relate to others within the organization.

Departmental effectiveness is measured using interpersonal metrics reported by customers. Leaders have an advantage because they have also had the opportunity to receive customer service. A typical first impression of customer service is formed by the response time to inquiries. Keep in mind that customers are providing clinical services and therefore are not typically in one physical location for more than a few moments at a time. Any response time greater than just a couple of minutes is likely to cause dissatisfaction. A popular service management framework to consider is the Information Technology Infrastructure Library (ITIL).[2]

Additional factors to consider evaluating include

- Do staff empathize with the concerns and frustrations of customers?
- Do staff communicate regularly with customers when they are working on a problem that takes more than a short time to resolve?

## Promoting Stakeholder Understanding of IT Opportunities and Constraints

Health information and management systems leaders have a responsibility to discuss the opportunities and systematic limitations of using information systems to address organizational goals and objectives. Leaders must assist stakeholders in understanding where there are opportunities to be gained through the use of technology. Equally important is the leaders' ability to temper enthusiasm by explaining any limitations that must be understood as well.

The initiation of a project charter is a critical juncture in IT's support of the organization. Success can be achieved using a well-articulated and accepted process that facilitates understanding and communication between the leader and the stakeholders. A method for initiating a project is via the utilization of an SBARC. SBARC is an acronym for situation, background, assessment, recommendation, and communication. This is an extension of the SBAR (minus the communication step) developed at Kaiser Permanente by Michael Leonard.[3] The one- to two-page SBARC proposal helps to frame a situation or request and a method of addressing it. It is an easy way to document a situation and proposed approach to a very wide audience. The simplicity of the tool makes it easy for a knowledgeable team member to complete and provides a concise summary for leaders to assess prior to committing to a full project proposal or a *pro forma* financial plan.

The SBARC process begins a discussion of the key goals and objectives of an initiative and frames some of the potential strategies for resolution. As appropriate, the SBARC may be followed up with a more formal business planning process and *pro forma* financial plan. A disciplined approach to framing and initiating projects ensures that the stakeholder and the project team members are operating from an identical framework. Ways of assessing the process improvement needs might include the utilization of either a Lean (production practice looking at resource consumption) or Kaizen (continuous improvement processes) methodology as a tool for optimizing the performance of a system. Once developed, the framework includes the deliverables of the project, along with the cost and timing, together defined as the scope of the project.

A well-written plan that has been signed off on by all stakeholders will help to eliminate the opportunity for scope creep to infiltrate the project. Scope creep is a common event in the life of a project. New opportunities or events will warrant that new analyses occur. A disciplined analysis following the project planning approach outlined above will weigh the merits of new opportunities in the context of the project as a whole. This is referred to as scope or project change control management. If a value-added suggestion is made and approved, then the plan is amended and communication undertaken. Scope creep is the undisciplined addition of new goals, objectives, and milestones that may have a negative effect on the cost or timeline of a project. This occurs when inadequate analysis of suggestions are allowed to work their way into the process. An effective way of eliminating scope creep is to anticipate it and have a method of reviewing recommended changes in scope with the project's leadership team on a regular basis.

At times, a more appropriate method of project planning is the agile methodology. Using this approach, initial objectives are expressed and a series of sprints are defined. At the end of each sprint, the team members review the product and suggest enhancements to be included in the next sprint interval. This method allows for more flexible development cycles.

## Developing Policies and Procedures for Information and Systems Management

The implementation of policies and procedures within an organization facilitates the standardization of actions and operations for employees, patients, and guests. Often, policies and procedures can be implemented in any portion of the organizational structure, from the entire company to the very smallest operation. Leaders face two questions: Is the policy really needed? If so, at what level of the organization must that policy be implemented? To maintain their accreditation in the United States, a healthcare organization is required to have a defined set of policies on information management and security and privacy policies. IT leaders in other countries will need to understand the accreditation standards that apply to their operations.

Prior to policy implementation, consider for what purpose you are developing a policy, and whether it is necessary to have a policy and procedure to govern that activity or process. If so, do not begin from scratch. Peers, both locally and nationally, have addressed many of the issues you face, and those same peers will have advice and examples to share. Start with a local survey of your peers. This has the advantage of helping you establish local networking connections and begin to create a community standard for the policy in discussion.

If local support is not available, then move to national peer groups, but ask yourself why you may be in front of the curve for your particular community. You can always look to organizations like Healthcare Information and Management Systems Society (HIMSS),[4] International Federation of Health Information Management Associations (IFHIMA),[5] and International Medical Informatics Association (IMIA)[6] or other national professional associations or societies allied to the field. These organizations will all have examples of a variety of policies.

A reason for *not* adopting a particular policy or procedure is your inability to audit and report on the effectiveness of the policy in question. If you do not have the ability to audit, then you run the risk of a challenge by health system accreditors. Do what is measurable, measure what you do, review what you have measured, and act on the results of what you have reviewed.

Be prepared to act on the results of your audit measurements, and make sure that the implications of failing to adhere to a policy are built into the policy itself. The consequences of noncompliance, when embedded within the policies and procedures, will help close the loop for employees. If there needs to be room for exceptions, those exceptions must be outlined as part of the policy as well. Once again, if there are no consequences for deviation from policy, then you must ask yourself whether there is a need for the policy in the first place.

On some occasions, policies and procedures are used as much for education and training as for any other purpose. A good example of this is a password policy. It is inevitable that a challenge will be brought forward regarding the implementation of a password policy. As most, if not all, systems allow the definition of the policy to be incorporated directly into the software, it really is unnecessary to have a separate policy because the system will not allow staff to create a password that does not meet the standard. In this case, a policy explaining the risks of weak password construction, in addition to meaningful education on how to create a strong password that is easy to remember, might be a better overall strategy.

## Complying with Legal and Regulatory Standards

The discipline of information and management systems includes a complex web of legal, regulatory, accreditation, and other compliance issues. Each country is going to have its own sources of oversight. IT leaders have a responsibility for knowing the sources of those standards in their own country. In the United States, navigation of meaningful use, e-prescribing, conditions of participation, and Health Information Portability and Accountability Act (HIPAA) is just the beginning of this complex responsibility. Effective leaders need to either understand the many nuances of these standards or have easy access to individuals who can assist in their understanding. Those individuals include the corporate compliance officer or equivalent, legal counsel, and the lead Joint Commission liaison, among others.

Depending on the size of the organization, all of the responsibilities may fall on the shoulders of one individual. Most likely, though, the responsibilities will be distributed around the organization, with those individuals coming together under the auspices of a corporate compliance committee, a Joint Commission International (JCI)[7] steering committee, or perhaps an audit and education committee. The information that these individuals are responsible for is ever changing. Their knowledge comes from several key documents, most of which are available directly or by purchase over the Internet. In the United States, the information can be obtained from the Centers for Medicare & Medicaid Services (CMS),[8] and internationally, from JCI.[7]

The two most influential sources of standards for healthcare organizations in the United States are CMS and the Joint Commission, formerly known as the Joint Commission on Accreditation of Healthcare Organizations.

CMS can be found at https://www.cms.gov/. CMS is within the Department of Health and Human Services (HHS). The key operating document for a hospital that receives any funding from CMS is "Conditions for Coverage and Conditions of Participations." The details of this framework are found at https://www.cms. gov/Regulations-and-Guidance/Legislation/CFCsAndCoPs/. A healthcare organization is held to these conditions in order to receive funds for services. On a day-to-day basis, the *Federal Register* serves as the "the official daily publication for rules, proposed rules, and notices of Federal agencies and organizations, as well as executive orders and other presidential documents," and the first and last indications of proposed rule changes.[9]

JCI is located online at http://www.jointcommissioninternational.org/. It serves as the voluntary accreditation body for more than 100 countries throughout the world. Accreditation is accomplished by complying with a comprehensive list of standards published by JCI. Organizations meet the standards through preparation, followed by a scheduled site review by a team of JCI surveyors.

## Adhering to Ethical Business Principles

Corporate financial implosions and evidence of legal and ethical impropriety bring the need for organizational and leadership ethics to the forefront. As an organizational leader, it is important to the practice of your profession and your position as a role model to your staff that you adhere to an identifiable code of business or corporate ethics.

In the context of your role, you must understand and adhere to the corporate code of ethics and values as established by the administration or board of directors of the organization where you work. On one end of the spectrum, business ethics are meant to ensure that all members of the organization are complying with local, state, and federal laws in the work that they do, and that they as individuals feel both compelled and safe to report any activities that are not within the scope of the law. Both large and small organizations will have a person or department charged with corporate compliance.

Corporate compliance programs are made up of a set of basic elements. Senior management must be aware of and involved in the process of compliance. Policies and procedures must reflect the organization's procedures for achieving compliance. Education about compliance must be given to both management and employees. And there must be both monitoring programs and disciplinary procedures to act on those who do not adhere to the compliance approaches. Actions need to be in the best interest of the company and absent of any financial gain for individuals or for any member of their immediate family.

At the other end of the spectrum, business ethics extend the concepts of fairness and equity both inside and outside the organization. The organization is a member of the business and local communities, and there is an implied duty to be a contributor to those communities.

## Employing Comparative Analysis Strategies

Organizational leaders need to understand more than their own departmental goals, measures, and metrics. IT leaders are often part of the operational leadership of the entire organization. They need to understand the organization's overall financial and budgetary reports, its comparative benchmarks, and its overall performance.

### Budgets

To understand how the organization is doing financially, it is necessary to be able to read and understand a budget spreadsheet. Typically, such reports will be summarized and reviewed by the financial leaders of the company. These reports include the annual budgets by line item and the projected budget and expenditures to date. Variances between budgeted and actual expenditures to date will be reported, and there may also be a column that enables comparison with actual expenses for the most recent historic comparable period of time. This often consists of last year's expenses for the same time period. Many expenses are spread evenly over the year and are easy to predict, measure, and compare. Other expenditures have unique timing considerations that, if not understood, can lead to a false understanding of the reports. Revenue and expenses that are recognized on a semiannual or quarterly basis can make year-to-date results appear far from expected, especially if the budget is constructed with an even distribution of those same expenses and revenues. A well-constructed budget report will include notations explaining the timing of events.

An organization will classify many of its expenses as either capital or operating expenses. Capital expenses are treated as assets and have enduring value to the organization. Each asset is then depreciated over a period of time that depends on the expected useful life of the asset. An asset with a useful life of five years will then have a depreciation expense of one-fifth of its original value, which then shows up as an operating expense in the annual budget. This depreciation expense may show up in either IT or the operating department to which the asset was attributed. Expenses that would typically be classified as operating include salaries, benefits, maintenance, travel, utilities, and supplies.

## Other Financial and Nonfinancial Indicators

Financial and nonfinancial indicators are measured to compare one organization to the next or against national benchmarks. Days in accounts receivable, or A/R days, is an expression of the average amount of time it takes for the organization to receive payment from payers after the bills have been submitted to the guarantor. The discharged not final billed (DNFB) is an indicator of the expected amount of money to be billed to the guarantor, but not yet submitted due to outstanding documentation or procedural issues. Both of these indicators are important, as they represent money due to the organization but not yet received. Cash available to the organization is referred to as the day's cash on hand and represents the number of days the organization could continue to operate if no further new funds were received by the organization. The larger the number, to a point, the better it is for the organization.

## Benchmarks

In addition to the previously discussed benchmarks specifically for information and management systems, there are benchmarks for organizational operations. These too are made up of both internal and external comparisons. The internal benchmarks are usually set by operations or the board of directors and are often reflections of the financial indicators listed above. Typically, the organization will set its goals for the number of days in A/R and days cash on hand. External benchmarks may include additional financial indicators, but are likely to reflect quality, safety, regulatory, or accreditation measures.

## Quality Indicators

Quality indicators may be set by state or federal government agencies or payers to the organization. They may serve as goals to be met and aggregate data to establish benchmarks. Each country may have its own voluntary or required quality benchmarking processes. In the United States, the HHS CMS has several quality reporting programs depending on the type of setting. Other indicators are available from external services, such as the University HealthSystem Consortium or Premier®. These entities will take extracts of your organization's data and aggregate them with comparable data from other organizations. This information is then distributed back to the data contributors so that each organization can compare its own results with different slices of the healthcare continuum. The advantage of these external comparison groups is that they enable an organization to compare itself to other organizations of like size, educational service, payer mix, geographic location, and so forth. The downside is that some of these programs are subscription services that provide comparisons only to paid subscribers.

## Preparing and Delivering Business Communications

Leadership skills are going to be assessed on a regular basis from both written and verbal communication, as well as the ability to organize and manage a typical business meeting. Organized meeting preparation assists the attendees in understanding the goals and objectives of the time invested. Well-prepared documents outline the topics and time to be spent on each issue. An example of a comprehensive meeting agenda is presented in Figure 8.3.

A departmental template for all meeting agendas and minutes will help to facilitate this communication. This creates a uniform method of communication that allows the staff to learn how to identify issues, actions, and decisions in a consistent way. Each variation in formatting adds a level of complexity for the customer.

The agenda template in Figure 8.3 starts with the organization's name and the committee's name. Each header defines the section to follow. "Meeting Information" states the date, time, and location of the meeting, while the subsequent section, "Attendees," lays out the expected participants and the roles they will play. The agenda itself lists each of the discussion points, the expected outcomes, the parties responsible to lead the discussion, and the time limit for the presentation, discussion, and decision, if necessary.

The "Committee Action Items" and "Committee Action Register" sections list the pending actions from the most recent meeting and other prior meetings, respectively. These sections enable all parties to have a comprehensive understanding of the status of all action items that remain open. Lacking those sections, it would be easy for a busy committee to lose track of items that have lower levels of priority than others. It is acceptable to push back the date of some deliverables, but those changes should be made in a transparent way with the support of the committee as a whole.

The remaining sections of the agenda keep a record of actions and issues that are yet to be resolved. "Open Issues" lists items that were not completed by the desired action during the previous scheduled meeting. Any item that has been tabled will be left in the "Open Issues" section. "New Issues" serves as a tracking section for the meeting record keeper and the chair. This location is used to add issues that will need attention or completion in the time between meetings.

| Organization name | Name of your committee |
|---|---|

**Meeting information**

| Meeting name: | November ITSC | Meeting date: | 11/28/2007 |
|---|---|---|---|
| Time: | 7:00 am to 9:00 am | Location: | Room 106 |

**Attendees**

| Names: | ☐ Chairperson<br>☐ Attendee 1 | ☐ Attendee 2<br>☐ | ☐ Attendee 3<br>☐ |
|---|---|---|---|

November guests:
☐ Guest 1 and reason for attendance
☐ Guest 2 and reason for attendance

**Agenda**

| Discussion point | Expected outcome | Responsible party | Time (min) |
|---|---|---|---|
| Agenda review | Agree to meeting goals | | 5 |
| Prior meeting review | Approve prior meeting minutes<br>Review/update action items<br>Review/update issues status | | 5 |
| Item 1 | Discussion v. decision | | 10 |
| Item 2 | Discussion v. decision | | 10 |
| Item n | Discussion v. decision | | 30 |

**Committee action items**

| Action item | Comments/Progress made | Responsible party | Completion date | | Status |
|---|---|---|---|---|---|
| | | | Original | Revised | |
| 2008 IS budget | • Send 2008 IS budget communication to ITSC committee members | | 10/31/07 | | |
| Data center approval request — November board | • Send data center summary information to ITSC committee members | | 11/2/07 | | |
| Tactical plan for all IS initiatives | • Listing of all current and requested service requests for IS<br>• Tool will become a part of decision-making process<br>• Draft to be presented at October ITSC for approval | | 12/20/07<br>Awaiting System Capital Project Approval Process | | |

**Committee action register — pending items**

| Action item | Comments/progress made | Responsible party | Completion date | | Status |
|---|---|---|---|---|---|
| | | | Original | Revised | |

**Figure 8.3  Meeting agenda template.**

| Organization name | Name of your committee | | | | |
|---|---|---|---|---|---|
| Complete IS 5-year assessment/estimate of infrastructural requirements and associated cost | • Expand 5-year incremental costing grid to include expense/capital impacts related to replacement equipment/upgrades, etc. (known costs of doing business) | | TBD | | |
| Develop ITSC dashboard | • Define metrics — situational/operational | Team | TBD | | |

| Open issues (from previous meetings) | | | |
|---|---|---|---|
| Issue | Action taken or required | Assigned to | Status |
| | | | |

| New issues raised | | |
|---|---|---|
| Issue | Action taken or required | Assigned to |
| | | |
| | | |

| Tentative future meeting agendas | | | |
|---|---|---|---|
| Dicussion point | Planned outcome | Responsible party | Time (min) |
| Simple sign-on/CCOW/biometric access technology | Establish strategy for technology access<br>• Educate committee on capabilities pros/cons, complexity, and implementation impacts<br>• Decide how to perform exploration — funding<br>• Potential to neutral/external party with industry expertise define scope | Team | |

| Key decisions made |
|---|
| |

| Meeting minutes | | |
|---|---|---|
| Discussion point | Discussion Notes | Time (min) |
| Agenda review | Meeting began at 7:00 am. | |
| Prior meeting review | | |
| Item 1 | | |
| Item 2 | | |
| Item n | | |
| Adjourn | Meeting adjourned at 9:00 am. | |

**Figure 8.3 (Continued)   Meeting agenda template.**

● ◖ ◎ ↑ ↓ ◖ ●  Status History

| Area | Topic | Apr-05 | May-05 | Jun-05 | Jul-05 | Aug-05 | Sep-05 | Oct-05 |
|---|---|---|---|---|---|---|---|---|
| Project assessment | Overall status | ◎ | ◖↑ | ◖ | ◖ | ◖ | ◖ | ◖ |

| Area | Topic | Apr-05 | May-05 | Jun-05 | Jul-05 | Aug-05 | Sep-05 | Oct-05 |
|---|---|---|---|---|---|---|---|---|
| Project management | Staffing | ◎ | ◎ | ◎ | ◖↑ | ◖ | ◖ | ◖ |
|  | Detailed project plan | ◎ | ◎ | ◎ | ◎ | ◎ | ◎ | ◎ |
|  | Implementation progress | ◎ | ◖↑ | ◖ | ◖ | ◖ | ◖ | ◖ |
|  | Communication | ◎ | ◖↑ | ◖ | ◖ | ◖ | ◖ | ◖ |
|  | Change management | ◎ | ◖↑ | ◖ | ◖ | ◖ | ◖ | ◖ |
| Go live | On schedule | ◎ | ◎ | ◎ | ◎ | ◎ | ◎ | ◎ |

| Area | Topic | Apr-05 | May-05 | Jun-05 | Jul-05 | Aug-05 | Sep-05 | Oct-05 |
|---|---|---|---|---|---|---|---|---|
| Cadence | Staffing and | | | ◎ | ◖↑ | ●↑ | ● | ● |
|  | Workflows | | | ◎ | ◖↑ | ◖ | ◖ | ◖ |
|  | Reporting needs | | | ◎ | ◎ | ◎ | ◎ | ◎ |
|  | System build | | | | ◎ | ◎ | ◎ | ◎ |
|  | Testing | | | | | | | |
|  | End-user training | | | | | | | |
|  | Postlive activities | | | | | | | |
| HIM | Staffing and | | | ◖ | ◖ | ◖ | ◖ | ◖ |
|  | Workflows | | | ◎ | ◖↑ | ◖ | ◖ | ◖ |
|  | Reporting needs | | | ◎ | ◎ | ◎ | ◎ | ◎ |
|  | System build | | | | ◎ | ◎ | ◎ | ◖↑ |
|  | Testing | | | | | | | |
|  | End-user training | | | | | | | |
|  | Postlive activities | | | | | | | |

**Figure 8.4  Status report for EHR implementation.**

Presentation and communication skills help define a leader. Leaders speak clearly and with authority. Let the audience know the purpose and the desired outcome of your presentation. Is the purpose to inform or to have an action result from the materials presented? During the presentation, include all the information that attendees need to understand, but highlight the key points rather than every detail. At the close, restate both the purpose and the desired outcome and address any questions or concerns, as this prevents disruption and loss of continuity during the presentation.

Project communication plans and status reports are important materials for everyone from project and organizational leaders through line staff. Figure 8.4 shows an example of a project status report for an organization's EHR implementation. Specific issues and subissues are identified with both a color-coded and a numeric indication of their status. Each issue also includes the specific current completion date. This report does not reflect the project budget. The budget status needs to be reported on a regular basis and clearly demonstrates the status overall and year-to-date. All variances, greater than a predetermined amount, need to be explained.

Like other communications, status documents need to provide an initial brief summary and follow with necessary supporting documentation. For project communications, the timeline and the completion status are the best first materials for review. In a project status report, a color-coded summary of tasks and status provides valuable visual clues. Use of arrows also provides quick indicators of the general direction of the elements compared to their immediately preceding status. Keep the reports simple by using red, yellow, and green to identify tasks that are out of compliance, at risk, or on track, respectively. Status reports need only be a single page with a table of color-coded tasks, a summary of the issues related to the tasks' color codes, the responsible parties for each task, and the estimated date of resolution or completion.

## Facilitating Group Discussions and Meetings

As important as it may be for a leader to direct a conversation, it is equally important to know how to facilitate a group through a difficult discussion. This differs somewhat from a typical business meeting. Knowing the issues, controversies, and positions of meeting participants helps to manage the discussion. Construct meeting agendas with consideration for the time it will take to resolve issues, and keep controversial decisions at the top of the agenda or as the sole item so there will be adequate time for discussion and resolution. If able, meet with key committee members in advance and begin a process of negotiation and education.

Complex decisions and controversial topics can make meeting management a challenge. Become familiar with *Robert's Rules of Order*[10] and define the expected rules of participation with committee members at the formation of the committee or at the beginning of any particularly challenging meeting in which you might anticipate conflict or debate. Keep a record of all motions and seconds. Record the essence of key discussions, including the names of participants when there is dissension. Ideally, decisions will be arrived at by consensus, but when necessary, keep a detailed record of the vote. As the discussion leader, do not let any committee members dominate the conversation, especially if they do not wait their turn in the queue. Ask speakers to clarify whether they are speaking in favor of or against the particular motion. Do not hesitate to clarify whether a member is contributing new insights to the discussion or just echoing another's thoughts. In the interest of time, the focus needs to be on contributions.

The committee chairperson must not dominate the conversation. The chair carefully guides the conversation through the selection of speakers, asks probing and clarifying questions, and contributes or highlights commentary as necessary. Use the straw poll as a tool. Identify those in favor of a motion and those who can live with the motion. If some attendees cannot live with the motion as stated, they should be asked to offer an alternative motion that serves the goals of all parties at the table. This keeps attendees accountable for problem solving.

## Providing In-House Consulting Services

Consulting services are frequently purchased when personnel resources are in short supply or when a specific skill is lacking within the organization. Most frequently, an organization goes to the outside to facilitate a large initiative when internal resources cannot be spared. It is possible to retain professional services on an issue-by-issue basis or to keep a firm on retainer. Additionally, an organization could supply in-house consultation as a means of managing, staffing, or advising on any manner of need.

In-house consultation can be provided by individuals on an as-needed basis, but larger organizations are beginning to implement a project management office (PMO).[11] The IT and facility/plant management departments and staff often have the greatest depth of experience in managing large and complex projects at any organization, and the PMO may grow out of one or both of those areas. The PMO has personnel who are trained or certified in project management methodology as sponsored by the globally recognized Project Management Institute, Inc.[12]

Staff of the PMO are skilled at meeting with operational personnel to understand the detailed requirements of the project at hand and translate those requirements into a plan for execution. They understand the processes of resource gathering, project planning, and project scope management, as well as the tools for visualizing the life of the project. They have the skills to manage development of the project's *pro forma* financial statements and the ongoing project budget. As the organization moves from IT projects to strategic operational projects with IT components, the IT project leaders can begin to alter their focus from operational leadership to true project management.

IT leaders may also serve as the voice of internal expertise. As departments throughout the healthcare organization begin to automate, they may need guidance or advice as to how to incorporate technologies into their workflow. The IT leaders or the PMO can provide innovation support to explore existing technologies to implement or watch for these departments. Partnership between the operational and technology experts creates an opportunity for innovation.

## Developing Educational Strategies for IT Staff

Leaders are hired due to a combination of their experiences and skills. They will likely select individuals to work for them based on similar criteria. The staff will continue to gain experience as they do their jobs, but there is very little opportunity for them to continue their education and expand their knowledge unless someone creates opportunities for them. Education can be provided in many ways and at relatively little overall cost.

At the very least, education needs to be valued. Commit to the time it will take for staff to complete further education, and commit to supporting the cost of the education as well. Encourage staff to broaden their skills by taking opportunities to stretch their current skills or cross-train in areas that are beyond their current experiences. When it becomes tempting to reduce costs by eliminating educational support, also consider how much it will cost to recruit new staff and whether the skills sought are those the current staff may be lacking.

Initiate your educational support by creating low-cost educational opportunities for the staff. Ensure that staff members are signed up as members of all the vendor user groups, both locally and nationally. Take advantage of professional societies, interest groups, and other local educational opportunities as well. Many of these sponsor local presentations and educational dinner meetings as conveniences to their members. Societies like HIMSS offer both local and national membership. In many cases, education is free and is often available in multiple media formats so that individuals can attend in person or via webcasting, webinars, and other telecasting options. Many vendors will also make free educational opportunities available to the staff.

When funds are available, consider having staff take turns attending vendors' user conferences or professional society conferences. That way, staff members are able to go to conferences every couple of years. Ask those staff who go to take time to explore specific educational sessions of interest to the whole organization. Upon the conference attendee's return, arrange for a team luncheon at which that person can report on information learned and share any gathered materials. Most societies and large user groups make their conference presentations available online, so it is very easy to share content with staff.

As noted earlier, succession planning is an important part of the overall IT planning process. An investment in education and the thoughtful application of the new skills expands the capabilities of the IT staff and helps to ensure a well-balanced, mature, and knowledgeable department.

## Staying Current on IT Technologies and Trends

The overall education of the IT team members extends beyond the applications they service and the immediate issues and objectives that are at hand. Team members need to stay connected to a variety of disciplines related to their specific sphere of expertise. The greatest opportunity for this added education comes from within the organization itself. Listen to the feedback of colleagues and peers. Be engaged and ask questions to become more knowledgeable. So much of the work we do overlaps with the work of others. Knowledge will expand your effectiveness in the work you do.

Outside of your own colleagues, a valuable educational resource is the media and printed press. *The Guardian, Healthcare IT News, People's Daily,* and the *Wall Street Journal* are often the first to pick up on and report trends or activities that have national or international significance in many disciplines. Take the time to review the headlines and articles in order to stay up on current events. Organizational leaders will be regularly asked to comment on materials in those publications.

Many publications now offer really simple syndication (RSS) or other services that will e-mail the headlines or article titles that align with subjects you are interested in. With so many potential sources of new information, having the option to push material of selected interest is a time-saver. Given the option of being proactive or reactive, a successful leader will choose the former path.

## Managing Risk

A key piece of the IT planning process integrates with the organizational efforts to manage risk. Issues of risk can be addressed along two dimensions. The first is magnitude of risk: If the event does occur, how big of an impact will it have on the organization, process, or project? The second dimension is the likelihood of the risk: What is the best estimate of the likelihood that the risk event will in fact occur? Within each dimension, the risk is low, medium, or high and assigned a point value of 1 to 3, respectively.

The tool shown in Figure 8.5 depicts these two dimensions in a matrix. The values of each pair of dimensions are multiplied to generate a numeric score. A score of 1 is the lowest risk, while a score of 9 indicates the greatest risk. Color-coding the scores highlights the degree of risk being borne.

Organizations' risk management strategies will vary depending on their tolerance for risk. Typically, scores of 6 or higher will warrant the creation of a contingency plan. A contingency plan is an alternative path, project, or process that would be considered in the event that the primary path is disrupted. A simple example would be a backup plan to print and distribute paper reports in the event that the electronic distribution process is disrupted for longer than a preset amount of time. Within any one very large project, there are likely to be multiple smaller contingency plans to account for any individual event that may occur.

Risk management and business continuity planning are taking on great prominence in healthcare. Leaders have the responsibility to bring to light the full effects of system loss and the costs associated with mitigating those risks. The solutions are often expensive and will create considerable conversation, especially around the likelihood of any particular event happening.

|  |  | Magnitude of risk | | |
|  |  | Low 1 | Medium 2 | High 3 |
|---|---|---|---|---|
| Likelihood of risk occurring | Low 1 | 1 | 2 | 3 |
|  | Medium 2 | 2 | 4 | 6 |
|  | High 3 | 3 | 6 | 9 |

**Figure 8.5 Risk matrix.**

## Quality Standards and Practices

Oversight for an IT department, especially one that has responsibilities for software development, requires careful attention to quality control standards. The Institute of Medicine (IOM) has produced many publications citing issues with patient quality and safety, including *Health IT and Patient Safety: Building Safer Systems for Better Care*.[13] While a U.S. publication, the principles and recommendations set forth have international relevance.

Software as delivered and its subsequent configuration by IT staff require comprehensive and regular review to ensure safe and high-quality performance. Quality assurance begins with the staff that implement and configure the software technically. Performance can be measured against testing results provided by the software vendors themselves and internally developed quality assurance scripts. As an example, external quality and patient safety organizations such as the Leapfrog Group[14] can provide testing to ensure appropriate decision support and alerts for computerized practitioner order entry (CPOE) programs.

Leaders must set clear expectations, or a plan, for the quality standards to be delivered and then measure, report, and modify the plan to continually improve on the products delivered. Publishing current performance, as well as goals and objectives, will remind the entire department of the expectations and aspirations for which the group is striving.

## References

1. McNickle M. 5 tips for creating a strategic plan for IT. *Healthcare IT News*, March 29, 2012. http://www.healthcareitnews.com/news/5-tips-creating-strategic-plan-it (accessed November 30, 2015).
2. ITIL. http://www.itil-officialsite.com/home/home.aspx (accessed November 30, 2015).
3. Institute for Healthcare Improvement. SBAR toolkit. Cambridge, MA: Institute for Healthcare Improvement. http://www.ihi.org/resources/Pages/Tools/SBARToolkit.aspx (accessed November 30, 2015).
4. HIMSS (Healthcare Information and Management Systems Society). Privacy & security. Chicago: HIMSS. http://www.himss.org/library/healthcare-privacy-security/toolkit (accessed November 30, 2015).
5. IFHIMA (International Federation of Health Information Management Associations). http://www.ifhima.org/ (accessed November 30, 2015).
6. IMIA (International Medical Informatics Association). http://www.imia-medinfo.org/new2/ (accessed November 30, 2015).
7. Joint Commission International. http://www.jointcommissioninternational.org/ (accessed November 30, 2015).
8. CMS (Centers for Medicare & Medicaid Services). Conditions for coverage (CfCs) & conditions of participations (CoPs). Baltimore: CMS. http://www.cms.gov/Regulations-and-Guidance/Legislation/CFCsAndCoPs/index.html?redirect=/CFCsAndCoPs (accessed November 30, 2015).

9. Federal Register. https://www.federalregister.gov/policy/about-us (accessed November 30, 2015).
10. *Robert's Rules of Order.* http://www.robertsrules.org/ (accessed November 30, 2015).
11. Price MP. *Business Driven PMO Setup.* Plantation, FL: J. Ross Publishing, 2009.
12. Project Management Institute. https://www.pmi.org/ (accessed November 30, 2015).
13. Institute of Medicine. *Health IT and Patient Safety: Building Safer Systems for Better Care.* Washington, DC: National Academies Press, 2011.
14. The Leapfrog Group. http://www.leapfroggroup.org/ (accessed November 30, 2015).

# *Chapter 9*

# Administration Management

## Learning Objectives

At the conclusion of this chapter, the reader will be able to

- Define roles, responsibilities, and job descriptions for information technology (IT)–related functions
- Assure staff competency in information and management systems skills
- Manage projects and portfolios of projects (e.g., initiate, plan, execute, control, and close)
- Manage relationships with vendors (e.g., contract cost, schedule, support, maintenance, and performance)
- Facilitate steering committee meetings and topics
- Assure adherence to industry best practices (e.g., change control and project management)
- Maintain system, operational, and department documentation
- Provide customer service (e.g., service-level management, request tracking, and problem resolution)
- Manage budget and financial risks
- Manage customer relationships with business unit leaders

## Introduction

As you move from Chapter 8 on administration leadership to this chapter on administration management, it is important to understand that today's health-care information technology (IT) professionals must possess both leadership and management skills to be effective. Understanding management concepts is vital to being an effective member of the leadership team. Management principles address matters such as resource allocation, staffing, and initiating and directing ongoing department management. This chapter covers principles related to department management, contract management, financial management, IT service management and documentation, and customer service and customer relationships.

# Roles and Responsibilities for IT-Related Functions

The increased adoption of technology in healthcare has expanded the role of IT. In addition to traditional or general IT functions, the field of healthcare IT has created new roles and responsibilities. Healthcare IT is the area of IT involving the design, development, creation, use, and maintenance of information systems for the healthcare industry. Healthcare IT includes electronic coding, accounting, and billing systems; electronic medical records (EMRs) or electronic health records (EHRs); and clinical or departmental applications, such as lab, radiology, pharmacy, and nutrition. Health informatics, a discipline that is closely aligned with healthcare IT, is the study of resources and methods for the management of healthcare information. Health informatics includes medical informatics, nursing informatics, clinical informatics, and biomedical informatics.

IT-related careers in healthcare can be found in many different types of organizations. These include hospitals and healthcare provider systems, healthcare payer organizations, health information exchanges, community health centers, long-term care facilities, ambulatory centers and small physician practices, educational institutions and academic medical centers, government agencies and the military, vendor organizations, and consulting companies. Both general IT and healthcare IT roles exist in these organizations. Individuals with a clinical background who are interested in a career in healthcare IT will find excellent opportunities in most of the aforementioned organization types. Those from general IT making a transition to healthcare IT without prior medical or clinical experience may find job opportunities difficult to attain, largely due to intense competition and high number of applicants.[1]

## *Senior Management Roles and Responsibilities*

Board of director, executive management, and medical executive committee support are essential for the success of IT in a healthcare organization. The chief information officer (CIO) is generally the most senior-level IT executive. In many health systems, this role also carries the vice president or senior vice president designation. Additional IT-related leadership roles can include the chief medical information officer (CMIO), the chief nursing information officer (CNIO), the chief technology officer (CTO), the chief information security officer (CISO), IT department directors and chairs, and physician and nurse champions. Recently, health systems have developed new roles, such as the chief innovation officer, chief applications officer, and chief privacy officer positions, to meet the dynamic and complex technology environment.

## General IT Roles and Responsibilities

Healthcare organization IT departments are staffed with internal full-time employees (FTEs) or outsourced staff that support traditional IT-related roles. Job descriptions for these roles are categorized as senior level, midlevel, and junior level, and typically include titles such as director, manager, architect, analyst, engineer, technician, administrator, programmer, and developer. Common areas that these roles are responsible for include applications, clinical and business intelligence, data warehouse and database administration, data center, directory services, help desk, IT security, mobile applications, server, network, telecommunications, storage, systems integration, backup, messaging, collaboration, technical documentation, policies and procedures, virtualization, and website.

## Healthcare IT Roles and Responsibilities

To meet the evolving technology demands of healthcare organizations, particularly in light of the increased usage of EHRs, many clinical, business, and project-related roles now require healthcare IT knowledge and a blend of clinical, management, and technical experience. Some of the more in-demand clinical and business positions are analyst roles. These include specialty roles covering systems, administrative support, applications, clinical systems, reports, finance, supply chain, human resources and payroll, revenue cycle, decision support, interfaces, and clinical and business intelligence. Other important healthcare IT roles have positions in informatics, clinical engineering, go-live events, implementation consulting, integration, project management, quality assurance, and usability.

## Careers in Healthcare IT

The U.S. Office of the National Coordinator for Health Information Technology (ONC) identified six healthcare IT workforce roles that healthcare organizations will need to fill as they deploy EHRs:[2,3]

1. Practice workflow/information management redesign specialist. Workers in this role assist in reorganizing the work of a provider to take full advantage of the features of healthcare IT to improve care delivery.
2. Implementation manager. Workers in this role provide on-site management of mobile adoption support teams for the period of time before and during implementation of a new healthcare IT system in clinical and public health settings.
3. Implementation support specialist. Workers in this role provide on-site user support for the period of time before and during implementation of healthcare IT systems in clinical and public health settings. These individuals will provide support services above and beyond what is provided by the vendor to be sure the technology functions properly and is configured to meet the needs of the redesigned practice workflow.

4. Clinician/practitioner consultant. This role is similar to the practice workflow and information management redesign specialist, but brings to bear the background and experience of a licensed clinician or public health professional.
5. Software support technician. Workers in this role maintain systems in clinical and public health settings, including patching and upgrading of software. They also provide one-on-one support in a traditional help desk model to individual users with questions or problems.
6. Trainer. Workers in this role use adult learning principles to design and deliver training programs to employees in clinical and public health settings.

## Achieving Staff Competency in Information and Management System Skills

### *Employee Development*

Employee development is a key component in ensuring that healthcare IT staff attain the necessary competency in information and management system tools and skills. Mastering those skills, along with developing the soft skills needed to collaborate and work together as a team, is essential in ensuring the success of the organization. Staff improvement programs provide employees with the proficiencies and qualifications needed for advancement within the organization, and help staff form positive attitudes and interpersonal skills to work effectively. Employee development can be provided through training and in-service programs, certification classes, community college or university educational courses, conferences and workshops, professional association involvement, and self-study through books, industry magazines, videos, and online resources.

### *Organizational Training and In-Service Programs*

Training and in-service programs may originate from several sources. Human resources typically have responsibility for organization-wide training requirements (e.g., security and safety regulations, discriminatory practices, and quality improvements). Supervisory, management, and leadership development may be designed and offered by a leadership department within the organization or through human resources. The department or group in which an employee works provides programs such as in-service or online training. In addition, IT projects for information and management system deployments usually include a training budget for system developers, administrators, and end users who will be supporting and using the product.

### *Job-Related IT Certifications*

IT-based certifications have long been a mainstay of IT education and professional credentials. Certifications have two main advantages. First, they provide a framework by which technical staff can learn and gain a level of proficiency in a specific IT-related topic. Second, a certification provides the recipients with a credential showing they have a defined body of knowledge in a specific area. Although a certification by itself will not qualify a person for a new job or promotion, it does demonstrate that the individual has mastered the basic level of a specific knowledge area, and is often viewed as a positive contributing factor in the decision of whom to hire. It is recommended that clinicians keep their clinical licensure and certifications active and up-to-date, even if they are no longer in a clinical role. Similarly, IT professionals should also consider keeping their IT certifications active, particularly those certifications that are in high demand in healthcare IT.

The Certified Professional in Healthcare Information and Management Systems (CPHIMS) certification is an essential credential for all healthcare IT management, management engineering and process improvement professionals, U.S. military personnel, and consultants. Developed and sponsored through HIMSS, eligible candidates become certified by passing the challenging CPHIMS Examination. The CPHIMS certification verifies that individuals have the knowledge necessary to be successful in healthcare IT. CPHIMS-certified individuals are members of an elite group of healthcare professionals with demonstrated expertise in the important categories of healthcare and technology environments, IT systems, leadership, and management.

Many of today's highly sought-after healthcare IT certifications can be obtained only by employees of organizations that are engaged in a specific vendor product deployment, such as an EHR or healthcare information systems project. However, healthcare systems also value generally available certifications, particularly if they are in the process of deploying related methodologies throughout their organization. These include certifications such as the Project Management Professional (PMP®), Information Technology Infrastructure Library (ITIL), and Lean Six Sigma.

## *Miscellaneous Professional Development*

Healthcare IT professionals should consider other professional development and education opportunities. These are particularly useful in helping individuals become well rounded and remain current in the rapidly evolving healthcare environment. Employees are typically responsible for the costs of their professional development, but many companies pay for such education as a benefit of employment. Several of the more common sources of professional development are healthcare IT conferences and workshops; programs sponsored by national and local professional associations, such as HIMSS; university certificate programs and bachelor's, master's, and doctorate degrees in healthcare IT, informatics, information management, and information systems; and self- or group study using books, industry magazines or journals, videos, and such online resources as white papers, webinars, conferences, and training.

## Performance Evaluation

Performance evaluation is an important tool healthcare administrators can utilize to monitor and improve employee competencies. Performance evaluation is the ongoing process in which employees' work, outcomes, attitudes and interpersonal skills, professional growth, and adherence to organizational values are assessed and feedback is provided. In the evaluation process, the employee's actual performance is compared against the expected performance. In order to be effective and objective, the performance evaluation process must start with specific and measurable performance goals. The performance goals should be defined and communicated to the employee at the start of the year.

A variety of methods can be used in the performance evaluation process, the most common being the rating scale. The scales will specify personal traits and behaviors expected, such as teamwork, communication skills, adherence to values, dependability, and initiative. Also specified will be specific job attributes, such as quality and quantity of work.[4] Each trait or behavior is accompanied by a range of numbers or words that the evaluator marks to indicate an employee's level of performance.

Some organizations use the 360-degree method of performance appraisal. In this method, other individuals are asked to rate the employee on specific criteria. Raters may include individuals who work with the employee on teams, subordinates, peers in the same department, employees in other departments, and sometimes outside customers and vendors. The employee is also given the opportunity to perform a self-assessment. The results of all these assessments are taken into consideration in the final evaluation that is completed for the employee. In this process, it is important to provide confidentiality to the raters for the evaluations they provided.

During the performance appraisal process, it is important for the manager to provide feedback to employees at regular intervals during the year. Employees should never be surprised during a formal appraisal that they were found to be performing at a less than adequate level. In addition, it gives them an opportunity to improve performance. Alternatively, if an employee is performing at an excellent or exceptional level, the interim positive feedback will help to preserve that positive behavior. Although interim reviews can be done formally or informally, it is advisable to complete a formal, written interim review if an employee's performance requires improvement.

When disciplinary action is needed, it must be taken based on clear facts and with documented justification. If disciplinary action is needed, it should be done progressively over time—starting with verbal discussions, then utilizing written and verbal communication, and possibly ending with termination. This approach provides consistent communication to the employee about what needs to be done to resolve the problem. Communication may be oral at first. If the problem persists, documentation should be completed in the form of notes to the employee's personnel record and written warnings with substantive examples of the inadequate performance. At all steps during the process, it is advisable to communicate with and seek the advice from the human resources department.

## Managing Projects and Project Portfolios

Another major role of the IT professional is project management. Project management methodology is used in healthcare organizations to successfully implement new and complex IT systems. Project management is the discipline of planning, organizing, securing, managing, leading, and controlling resources to achieve specific goals. A project is a temporary endeavor with a defined beginning and end. The temporary nature of projects stands in contrast with organizational operational initiatives, which consist of repetitive, permanent, or semipermanent functional activities. Hospitals that support both project and functional initiatives are called matrixed organizations. In cases where multiple interdependent projects exist, program management is used to manage all the projects as a group.

Health systems with multiple independent projects and resources that require a formalized framework for tracking, allocating, and managing them effectively often adopt project portfolio management (PPM). PPM is the centralized management of processes, methods, and technologies used by project managers (PMs) and project management offices (PMOs) to analyze and collectively manage a group of current or proposed projects based on numerous key characteristics. As the PPM landscape has been evolving rapidly, healthcare organizations are looking to manage their project initiatives through a single, enterprise-wide system called enterprise project portfolio management (EPPM).

In contrast to the traditional approach of combining manual processes, desktop project tools, and best-of-breed PPM applications for each project portfolio environment, EPPM takes a more integrated and top-down approach to managing all project-intensive work and resources across the enterprise.

Project management has the following phases:

- Initiating phase. In this phase, project stakeholders are identified, the project charter and the preliminary scope statement are developed, and the project charter is approved.
- Planning phase. This phase involves planning the project scope, quality and risk management, and schedule. The project scope is defined through creating the project management plan, developing the scope management plan, and creating the work breakdown structure (WBS). Quality and risk management planning involves identifying and analyzing risks and planning the risk responses. The project schedule is developed by defining and sequencing activities, estimating activity resources and duration, determining the project schedule, and planning human resources.

- Executing phase. This phase involves directing and managing project execution; acquiring, developing, and managing the project team; performing quality assurance; and procuring project resources.
- Monitoring and controlling phase. This phase involves managing the integrated change control process; controlling quality; controlling changes in cost, schedule, and scope; measuring performance; and monitoring and controlling risks. An effective change control methodology will address both reactive and requested changes, and will include processes for categorizing changes and determining how changes will be requested, reviewed, and implemented.
- Closing phase. This phase involves releasing the final deliverables to the customer, handing over project documentation to the organization, terminating supplier contracts, releasing project resources, and communicating project closure to all stakeholders. The final step is to undertake a postimplementation review to identify the level of project success and note any lessons learned for future projects.

According to the Project Management Body of Knowledge (PMBOK®) Guide, project management consists of nine knowledge management areas:[5]

1. Project scope management involves ensuring all the required work is performed to complete the project successfully. Scope creep is a key reason why many projects fail. Project scope management is accomplished by defining and controlling what is included in the project and what is not. Project scope management activities include the scope plan, scope definition, WBS, scope control, and scope verification.
2. Project time management involves developing and controlling the project schedule. Project time management components include activity definition, activity sequencing, activity resource scheduling, activity duration, schedule development, and schedule control.
3. Project cost management involves estimating the project cost and ensuring the project is completed within the approved budget. Accordingly, cost management includes the cost estimate, cost budgeting, and cost control.
4. Project human resource management consists of obtaining, developing, and managing the team who will perform the project work.
5. Project procurement management encompasses managing the acquisition of products and services from external sources in order to complete the project. Project procurement management includes planning acquisitions, negotiating contracts with sellers, selecting sellers, administering contracts with sellers, and closing contracts.
6. Project risk management focuses on the identification of project risks and appropriate responses. Project risk management includes identifying risks, performing a risk analysis, developing a risk response plan, and monitoring and controlling risks.

7. Project quality management involves ensuring the project satisfies its objectives and requirements. Project quality management includes performing quality planning, quality assurance, and quality control.
8. Project integration management consists of the integration of the various project activities. Project integration management includes developing the project management plan, directing and managing project execution, monitoring and controlling the project work, and closing the project.
9. Project communications management ensures project information is generated and distributed promptly. Project communication management activities include planning communication, distributing needed information to project stakeholders in a timely fashion, reporting the project performance and project status, and resolving issues among the stakeholders.

The PM is an important stakeholder in bringing projects to successful completion. The PM is responsible for working with project sponsors, the project team, and others involved in the project to meet project goals and deliver the project within budget and on schedule. The PM should also control the assigned project resources to best meet project objectives; manage project scope, schedule, and cost; report on project progress; and facilitate and resolve issues, conflicts, risks, and other obstacles to project success.

## Managing Vendor Relationships

Healthcare CIOs are increasingly turning to vendors for the expertise and support they need to meet the technology requirements of their organizations. This reliance on vendor partnerships enables vendors to play a key role in the success of many healthcare organizations. A well-managed vendor relationship will result in increased customer satisfaction, reduced costs, better quality, and better service from the vendor. If problems arise, a well-managed vendor will be quick to remedy the situation. Vendor management is not simply negotiating the lowest price possible. It involves working with vendors on contract performance, schedules and costs, product functionality, and support and maintenance agreements in order to mutually benefit both organizations.

The vendor management process begins with selecting the right vendor for the right reasons. This involves analyzing business requirements, performing a vendor search, selecting the winning candidate, and successfully negotiating the contract. The contract should be carefully considered to ascertain that restrictions or exclusions, penalties, and terms are beneficial to both parties. Once the relationship with the vendor has begun, vendor performance must be monitored at all times, with particular attention to the requirements that are most critical to the healthcare organization. Regular communication between the vendor and the healthcare organization will help to avoid misunderstandings and address issues before they become problems.

Three common pitfalls should be avoided in order to achieve successful vendor management.[6] First, it is important not to confuse vendor selection with vendor management. Equal importance needs to be given to managing the vendor relationship during and after the selection and contracting phases. Second, do not select a vendor based on price alone. Instead, give priority to a vendor that understands the value of developing a relationship that is mutually beneficial. Third, do not forget to evaluate how your vendor relationships affect your business. In addition to examining service-level agreements (SLAs) and contract fulfillment, IT leadership determines whether an engagement has brought value to the organization and whether both parties have received a return on their relationship.

The following 10 vendor management principles will enable healthcare organizations to build effective relationships with their suppliers and service providers:[7]

1. Use project management methodology. Due to the high visibility and accountability of today's complex healthcare projects, attention should be given to the basics of project management, such as creating a well-defined and properly planned project, recruiting effective project sponsorship, clarifying roles and responsibilities, establishing formal change control management, and ensuring effective issue management.
2. Understand vendor management is multifaceted. Effective vendor management involves evaluation and selection, contract development, relationship management, and delivery management.
3. Be aware of the contract details. This includes understanding what the vendor is responsible for, managing the project and vendor according to the contract, and understanding what incentives motivate the vendor.
4. Formal documentation is key. All changes to the project and communications must be in writing and formally controlled.
5. Contract complexity should be consistent with project risk. The procurement process and the contract's level of detail should correspond to the level of project risk.
6. Include all important deliverables in the contract. Important deliverable specifications; the methodology used to create the deliverable; specific resources, roles, and responsibilities; planned communications; deliverable acceptance criteria; and project success criteria should be included in the contract.
7. Management commitment is key. Senior management's commitment and flexibility are important to making the vendor–customer partnership work.
8. Focus on benefiting both the customer and the vendor. Both parties to the contract should give high priority to developing mutually beneficial resolutions should issues and tensions arise.
9. Clarify contractual terms and expectations. All terms and processes in the contract should be reviewed, explained, and clarified to avoid conflicts and misunderstandings.

10. Ensure vendor and customer roles and responsibilities are clear. All parties' roles and responsibilities should be precisely defined in the contract. Particular attention should be paid to interactions between the procurement department and the project team, the contract administrator and the PM, and the vendor's PM, sales team, and accounting and legal departments.

## Facilitating Steering Committee Meetings

In today's complex healthcare environment, steering committees are essential in providing guidance and practical direction for IT project and operational initiatives. According to the Computer Economics IT Management Best Practices 2011–2012 study, nearly 80% of all IT organizations have steering committees, and 69% of those organizations make full use of their committees.[8] The use of IT steering committees ranks first as the most mature IT management practice out of 15 practices covered in the study.

A steering committee is defined as an advisory committee, usually made up of high-level stakeholders or experts, which provides guidance on key issues such as company policy and objectives, budgetary control, marketing strategy, resource allocation, and decisions involving large expenditures.[9] IT steering committees are a best-practice approach in healthcare organizations for aligning strategic business and IT priorities. Steering committees, which usually include executives and department heads, focus on three main tasks: IT strategic planning, project prioritization, and project approval. Clear mandates and a real ability to influence decision making through executive participation increase the value of IT steering committees.

To ensure success in this important area of IT governance, healthcare CIOs should consider adopting four strategies:

1. Create a committee charter that includes the desired outcomes. This should help everyone understand the role and purpose of the group, which includes promoting improved communication and recognizing the partnership required for a successful IT deployment.
2. Establish a scope that reflects a corporate-wide perspective. The broader focus will be helpful when mediating conflicts in priorities or departmental perspectives that may not be in the best interest of the entire organization.
3. Consider indicating the specific level of authority of this group and its role in decision making. For example, the committee may be identified as a coordinating body that will resolve priorities, endorse proposals prior to approvals, and monitor progress of major IT initiatives, but will have no role in budget approval or other departmental expenditure decisions.
4. Designate someone other than the CIO to chair the IT steering committee. Assigning a non-IT person, such as the chief operating officer (COO), CMIO,

or chief finance officer (CFO), to chair the group communicates the message that IT is accepted as a critical resource and recognized as such by the entire organization.

To form an effective IT steering committee and keep it on track, three important steps should be considered:[10]

1. It is important to develop a case by aligning IT priorities with strategic business priorities. Focus on core IT strategic objectives and not IT resource allocation. In addition, stress shared decision making and foster a culture of communication between business units.
2. Develop a steering committee charter. It should outline the key tasks and responsibilities of the committee.
3. Keep the IT steering committee small and schedule regular meetings. Ensuring the membership is consistently informed, engaged as often as needed based on the project scope and timelines, and includes executive decision-making authority, is critical to the success of the IT steering committee.

The use of IT steering committees is a proven method of driving better IT and business alignment, particularly in the area of IT governance, strategic planning, and project prioritization and approval. By developing IT steering committees with clear objectives, strong executive participation, and a commitment to meeting regularly, IT leaders can significantly improve the value of IT to the business units.

## Adhering to Industry Best Practices

IT management has matured as an organizational function over the years. As a result, certain policies and standards have been adopted by many of the top-performing IT organizations. Some of these are well-established disciplines and are commonly accepted as industry best practices or benchmarks. Industry best practices are methods or techniques that have consistently shown results superior to those achieved by other means. In addition, industry best practices can evolve as improvements are discovered.

A recent survey of more than 200 IT organizations identified the following 15 IT management best practices:[11]

1. Regular meeting of the executive IT steering committee
2. Regular meeting of the IT change control board
3. Periodic testing of the disaster recovery plan
4. Auditing of IT security policy compliance
5. Multiyear IT strategic planning

6. User satisfaction surveying
7. Use of PMO
8. Benchmarking IT spending levels
9. Publishing IT performance metrics
10. IT project portfolio management
11. Use of IT asset management system
12. Conducting postimplementation audits
13. ITIL adoption, which encompasses service strategy, service design, service transition, service operation, and continual service improvement
14. Use of IT balanced scorecard
15. Active contribution to open-source projects

# Developing System, Operational, and Department Documentation

## System Documentation

System documentation includes the documents that support analysis, decision making, acquisition, and implementation processes. It also addresses system features and functional and technical requirements. Systems analysis documentation includes the information gathered in the process of "collecting, organizing, and evaluating data about IT system requirements and the environment in which the system will operate."[12] It also includes documents such as functional requirements, design specifications, requests for information and proposals, and related vendor responses. Also considered part of system documentation are procedure manuals, computer programs, and machine operating manuals; details of standards compliance; and records of the initial system testing process and results (e.g., data collection and input procedures).

## Operational Documentation

Operational documents relate to ongoing systems operations and maintenance. They include information about ongoing testing of systems and results, audit processes, and database management, as well as training manuals. Operational documents also encompass implementation time frames, flowcharts, and progress reports; data backup and recovery procedures; and system retirement, tuning, and logistic support requirements.

## Department Documentation

Department policies and procedures (P&Ps) help to guide the processes and actions employees should use to perform their work, and are essential for healthcare organizations to achieve various accreditations. A department or organizational policy formalizes what is expected or required of employees, among other things. A procedure document describes how an outcome is to be accomplished. Therefore, policies and procedures serve two purposes: (1) they set performance requirements that can be used to motivate or discipline employees, and (2) they serve as ongoing references for employees and orientation documents for new hires.[12] In developing P&Ps, the following steps are useful: (1) identify a need; (2) draft a policy or procedure that addresses the need; (3) get management approval; (4) distribute the approved document to employees and educate them on its contents; (5) revise, replace, or withdraw the policy or procedure as needed; and (6) coordinate with human resources, corporate compliance, or other areas when applicable.

Department P&Ps will address elements such as security (e.g., access control, entity authentication, audit trails, data encryption, firewall protection, and virus checking), privacy protection (definitions of access rights and instructions for handling specific information and patients), and information retention and availability of medical information. In addition, communication of medical information, management of licensed software, handling of service requests, the IT strategic plan, and the IT budget should be addressed. It is also important to consider change management, project management, and process improvement; development methods and standards; and copyrights and ownership in department P&Ps.

## Providing Customer Service

Healthcare is primarily a people business—it calls for the organization to be particularly customer focused, or customer centric. HIMSS defines customer centric as "placing the customer as the center or focus of design or service."[13] It is excellence in service that distinguishes the IT department as responsive and knowledgeable, or as customer centric. There are several specific factors and approaches to consider in organizing the customer service functions in the IT department.

### Service-Level Management

IT departments undertake many tasks; therefore, SLAs are needed to define the service levels to be met. It is desirable to cover each incoming service request with an SLA that documents the specific levels of service expected and the metrics that will be used to evaluate them. The SLA should also address which resources will be provided, including the level of assistance that can be supplied and who will supply it. Also, the SLA should detail the reporting mechanisms. Specifically, how will performance be monitored and communicated, can issues be tracked, and how much time is allowed to elapse between the reporting of an issue and its resolution?

## *Request Tracking*

In managing an SLA, the IT department will need to implement request-tracking processes, which include help desk triage, issue tracking, and user satisfaction surveys. As part of the help desk triage, each reported problem should be assigned a priority level and worked on accordingly. Issue tracking, which is the ongoing monitoring of open, new, and closed service requests, can help identify possible larger problems. It also warns of the need to focus additional resources on requests that are approaching the time limit specified in the SLA statement. Upon completion of a service, users will respond to a user satisfaction survey assessing how well the IT department technician met the service objectives. The survey can be a short question, such as "Are you satisfied with the service you received?" The surveys reflect users' perceptions, which drive the overall IT perception and, if necessary, give IT management a chance for service recovery—an attempt to correct any dissatisfaction users may have. User feedback usually generates excellent opportunities for employees involved in providing service.

The most measured IT area is usually the help desk. A key measure of effectiveness is the first-call resolution rate—the number of service requests that are resolved during the initial call to the service technician. A first-call resolution rate of 70% means most problems are being diagnosed and resolved on the phone with the customer, and therefore not being transferred to someone else for resolution. That rate is not only good for customers who get their problems fixed immediately, but also good for the other members of the IT department, who will not have to take time away from other assignments to help resolve a customer's problem. First-call resolution is high if service technicians are well trained and materials for reference and troubleshooting are readily available.

Another help desk measure is the call abandonment rate, the percentage of times callers hang up without speaking to a technician. If average wait times are high, the call abandonment rate will probably be high as well. The longer callers have to wait, the more likely they are to give up. This is a serious problem for the help desk, even if superb services are provided to callers who finally get through to speak to someone.

Other metrics include system performance rates related to uptime and response time. High availability and fast response times are important, particularly with widely used systems or those used in direct patient care.

## *Problem Resolution*

In theory, the customer should be pleased anytime the service-level goals are met. If a customer is disappointed, other customers probably feel the same way, even if they are not saying so and SLA goals are being met. In resolving inconsistencies such as these, consider whether a customer's expectations were met, and if not, an explanation is in order. For example, if a customer's survey response indicates the technician should have simply gone to the local office supply store and purchased a replacement drive, explain why policy prohibits that practice. In resolving these issues, it is also important to understand the customer's perspective and ask, "Does the policy make sense or is the customer possibly right?"

## Managing Budget and Financial Risks

### *Financial Risk Management*

It is important for healthcare organizations to make sound decisions in order to manage financial and budget risks. Without a solid understanding of financial risks and their impact, they cannot be expected to make the right decisions about their capital and operating investments. The fundamental idea behind managing financial risk in healthcare is to reduce and protect against the inherent unpredictability of future costs.

Enterprise risk management (ERM) is a proven methodology that organizations use to manage overall risk. While ERM has been used to address clinical, human resource, and legal risks in the hospital setting, it has not been frequently applied to financial risk management. This could be due to the complex and highly specialized nature of the tax-exempt capital markets, which can be intimidating to many risk management professionals. In spite of its complexity, financial risk can be handled in the same four steps as other forms of risk:

1. Identification—Listing financial risks that can occur as a result of either negative factors or favorable events (e.g., when unexpected success leads to exponentially increased demand for services)
2. Quantification—Assessing the likelihood or probability a risk-related event will occur and the magnitude of its impact
3. Risk response—Determination and implementation of a response to the risk, such as acceptance, transference, mitigation, or avoidance
4. Monitoring—Continuous review of existing and future risks

Core financial skills are needed to reduce the risks associated with IT investments. Today's IT professionals should be knowledgeable about budgeting and planning; financial purchasing options, such as capitalized and depreciated assets; operating expenses; basic accounting principles and standards; financial models and methods; and compliance regulations. In addition, the IT professional should use a broad range of methods and tools, such as return on investment (ROI) calculations, budget-tracking tools, revenue creation reports, monthly financial reports and variances, technology pilots where available, SLAs to improve vendor performance, and soliciting buy-in for IT initiatives from business and clinical unit executives to minimize and reduce IT procurement risks.

## Budget Risk Management

Managing budgets is one of the basic disciplines that all managers must master. An organized approach to developing and maintaining the budget will go a long way in helping reduce risks. In addition, to prepare for the possibility that some risks will not be managed successfully, a risk contingency budget should be created. Funds from the risk contingency budget can then be used to prevent a project from going over budget.

For today's IT managers, having solid budgeting and forecasting skills is critical in reducing budget risk. Understanding the annual budget cycle is important, particularly in avoiding the fiscal year-end crises that often occur as organizations attempt to balance their budgets. The business requirements for expenses should be accurately assessed. The budget should be developed in detail. At the line-item level, capital and operating expenditures should be differentiated and long-range capital planning should be identified. Capital expenditures are payments by the organization for fixed assets, such as buildings and equipment. Capital expenses are incurred when a company buys assets that have a useful life of more than one year and are typically depreciated. The long-range capital plan, which covers five years or more, should be the result of an executive review process that determines the proper mix of existing assets and new investments needed to fulfill the healthcare organization's mission, goals, and objectives, and should reflect the priorities for the year. Operating expenditures are incurred in the course of ongoing, day-to-day business activities and include payments for rent, utilities, salaries and benefits, training, software maintenance fees, and telecommunications. Operating expenses relate to items that have a useful life of one year or less and are not depreciated.

It is important for a consistent model or software system to be used to manage the budget. Budget risk can be addressed by paying attention to contracts and maintenance fee increases, and by adjusting and reforecasting the expenditures. Healthcare organizations may be required to make budget reductions; therefore, maintaining multiple budget scenarios is important. These can be reserved for times when revenue is low, when critical enhancements are made, or when revenue-generating projects are planned.

The following important steps should be considered when managing budgets:[14]

- Negotiate an effective budget to start with. Spending the necessary time at the beginning of a project will eliminate budget challenges later in the project schedule.
- Plan for unexpected expenses. This will allow for flexibility should unforeseen expenses arise.
- Prepare early for year-end budget activities. Finalizing budgets at the end of the fiscal year is an important and time-consuming activity. It is best to start planning for this early or on an ongoing basis.

- Stay close to budget. Attempt to finish as close to budget expectations as possible and avoid being significantly over or under budget, as this will affect the following year's budget allocations.
- Account for cost allocations. Identify charges or transfers that may occur to or from other departments to your department.
- Understand the key budget numbers. Know all the critical numbers for your department, and be aware if any of the numbers are wrong.

## Managing Customer Relationships with Business Leaders

Customer relationship management (CRM), a widely accepted practice in healthcare, is an organization's approach to interactions with customers, patients, vendors, and other business associates.[15] CRM involves using proven methods to attract new customers, retain current customers, and reestablish relationships with past customers. It also involves leveraging technology, such as the Internet and social media, and traditional marketing techniques to organize, automate, and synchronize business processes. Using CRM, healthcare organizations can achieve increased quality and efficiency, reduced overall costs, and greater profitability.

Unlike many industries that are product driven, healthcare organizations are uniquely service driven, ultimately aimed at developing relationships to improve patient loyalty by getting the right information at the right time to everyone involved in the continuum of care. By customizing service offerings to better meet customer expectations, and by continuously training and rewarding employees for delivering exceptional customer service, healthcare organizations can achieve profitable customer relations not only with patients, but also with payers, regulators, vendors, and other stakeholders.

To improve customer satisfaction levels, a comprehensive systems approach is recommended.[16] It is critical to set a clear customer experience strategy. Customer service involves more than creating an organizational slogan. To establish a good strategy, it is important to understand the organization's vision and mission; determine the organization's customer service direction, slogan, and values; share the customer service strategy by using a comprehensive communications program; emphasize customer service is a key responsibility for each department; and ensure the customer service strategy aligns with the other organizational strategies.

Selecting the right team and developing, motivating, and managing staff members are two important areas of consideration. Interpersonal skills and the right attitude are two qualities critical for employees to possess when providing customer service. Emphasizing functional expertise, technical competence, and knowledge is less important, and many of these can be taught. Employees working directly with the customer need to understand the organization's culture and learn key communication skills. Four steps needed to build a culture of excellent customer relations are as follows: (1) provide training in key skills needed to deliver excellent personal service, (2) use ongoing coaching and feedback to reinforce improved customer relations, (3) regularly measure and monitor performance levels, and (4) reward performance with both monetary and nonmonetary awards.

Effective service delivery creates efficient customer interaction, eliminating the need for third-party intervention to keep customers satisfied. To help ensure a positive customer experience, it is important to identify preferred service delivery processes, review critical success points in those processes, and determine service standards and objectives. In addition, it is vital to establish service delivery procedures to maximize material service and create SLAs to improve customer satisfaction.

Regardless of how well trained the staff is or how effective the organization's current service delivery processes are, opportunities for improvement can always be identified. It is important that problems and issues be resolved quickly by building continuous improvement into the service delivery procedures. To properly manage the customer experience, it is necessary to identify where opportunities for improvement are by actively soliciting customer feedback; teach staff how to handle customer complaints effectively by using the correct blend of empathy, apology, and resolution; focus on the root of the problem and not just the symptoms; and be proactive in seeking to prevent issues instead of reacting to events that have already occurred.

Although senior management support is vital for creating and maintaining a successful CRM program, involving midlevel management in the change process and empowering them to be key change agents is essential. To do this, it is vital to engage the management team early and often, to involve management members in formulating the customer service strategy, and to develop managers' coaching skills so they are able to understand and reinforce key personal service skills. In addition, management should include managers as facilitators during training sessions; reward managers for establishing, monitoring, and updating service delivery processes; and motivate managers to be examples to their teams.

Delivering outstanding service requires the building of a culture that focuses on customer relations. This can involve changing all aspects of an organization's service delivery. The investment of time and effort can be significant, but the rewards can be enormous, building long-term patient and customer loyalty and helping to ensure business profitability.

## Summary

With the increased adoption of healthcare IT, new roles and responsibilities in healthcare IT management are being developed. Managers are looking to ensure their staff members are properly trained and educated. Today's leaders require a blend of clinical awareness; experience in operational, financial, and project management; and technical knowledge to be successful. Healthcare organizations are increasingly turning to vendors and consultants for the expertise and support they need to meet their IT requirements. Stakeholder management using effective steering committees, implementation of industry best practices, and experience with well-defined customer service processes are necessary skills for healthcare administrators. By maintaining the appropriate documentation, giving careful attention to financial and budget risks, and managing customer relationships, healthcare organizations will continue to experience success.

# References

1. Santiago A. How to break into a career in healthcare IT. 2014. http://healthcareers. about.com/od/administrativeandsupport/p/HealthITjobs.htm (accessed April 22, 2016).
2. Health IT workforce roles and competencies. 2010. https://www.healthit.gov/sites/ default/files/health_it_workforce_6_month_roles_as_of_06_03_10.pdf (accessed April 22, 2016).
3. ONC (Office of the National Coordinator for Health Information Technology). Get the facts about Health IT Workforce Development Program. Washington, DC: ONC. https://www.healthit.gov/sites/default/files/get_the_facts_workforce_develop-ment.pdf (accessed April 22, 2016).
4. Longest B, Rakich S, Darr K. *Managing Health Services Organizations.* 4th ed. Baltimore: Health Professions Press, 2000, pp. 536–550.
5. PMBOK. *A Guide to the Project Management Body of Knowledge.* 4th ed. Newton Square, PA: Project Management Institute, 2008, pp. 13, 43.
6. Perelman D. Six steps to successful vendor management. *eWeek,* May 17, 2007. http://www.eweek.com/c/a/IT-Infrastructure/Six-Steps-to-Successful-Vendor-Management (accessed April 22, 2016).
7. Horine G. *Absolute Beginner's Guide to Project Management.* 2nd ed. Indianapolis: Que Publishing, 2009.
8. Trembly A. IT steering committees: Do they have any power? *Insurance Networking News,* August 19, 2001. http://www.insurancenetworking.com/blogs/return_of_ the_guru/it_steering_committee_ce_it_management_best_practices-28649-1.html (accessed April 22, 2016).
9. Business Dictionary. Steering committee. http://www.businessdictionary.com/defini-tion/steering-committee.html (accessed April 22, 2016).
10. Info-Tech Research Group. Establish an effective IT steering commit-tee. London: Info-Tech Research Group. http://www.slideshare.net/ Info-Tech/establish-an-effective-it-steering-committee?qid=641c8d4e-c43e-4f38-894d-a880ba8ea8b8&v=qf1&b=&from_search=1 (accessed April 22, 2016).
11. Computer Economics. IT management best practices: Adoption and growth of 15 IT disciplines. Irvine, CA: Computer Economics. http://www.computereconomics.com/ page.cfm?name=IT_Management_Best_Practices (accessed April 22, 2016).
12. Austin CJ, Boxerman SB. *Information Systems for Healthcare Management.* Chicago: AUPHA/Health Administration Press, 2005, p. 283.
13. HIMSS (Healthcare Information and Management Systems Society). *HIMSS Dictionary of Healthcare Information Technology Terms, Acronyms and Organizations.* 3rd ed. Chicago: HIMSS, 2013, p. 35.

14. Owen J. *The Leadership Skills Handbook.* 2nd ed. San Francisco: Jossey-Bass, 2012.
15. Shaw R. *Computer Aided Marketing & Selling.* London: Butterworth Heinemann, 1991.
16. Nash D, Nash S. Customer relationship management: 6 steps from customer service. North Yorkshire, UK: Team Technology. http://www.teamtechnology.co.uk/customerservice2.html (accessed April 22, 2016).

# *Chapter 10*

# Questions

## Chapter 1: The Healthcare Environment

### Question 1
Among the multiple types of hospital ownership, which is not a common model?
  A. Public (government) owned and managed
  B. Private, not for profit (nonprofit)
  C. Physician owned
  D. Private, for profit

### Question 2
Hospitals may be classified many different ways. Which of the following statements is true regarding hospital classification?
  A. Private hospitals are always for-profit organizations
  B. Urban, rural, and children's hospitals are classified by their geographic locations
  C. Rural hospitals are most frequently classified as teaching hospitals
  D. Hospitals may be classified in more than one way; for example, an urban hospital might also be classified as a government-owned hospital or as a general hospital

### Question 3
An ambulatory surgery center would be best classified as
  A. A teaching hospital
  B. An outpatient care setting
  C. A general hospital
  D. A rehabilitation hospital

### Question 4
From the perspective of the healthcare delivery organization, payments generally come from three types of entities:
  A. Employers, employees, and government entities
  B. Government-financed and managed programs, insurance programs managed by private entities, and patients' personal funds

C. National health systems, national insurance systems, and multipayer systems

D. Uninsured, underinsured, and insured

## Question 5

In considering the purpose for interrelationships among healthcare organizations, identify the purpose below that is correct:

A. Enable access to comprehensive care services from only one healthcare organization

B. Ensure effective transfers of care facilitated by the provision of essential health information

C. Facilitate obtaining appropriate rewards for care referrals

D. Facilitate marketing of healthcare services regardless of patients' consent

## Question 6

Ensuring the general portability of healthcare is facilitated by

A. Health information exchanges (HIEs) such as Canada's Health Infoway and the U.S. HIE programs, including the Nationwide Health Information Network (NHIN)

B. The Organisation for Economic Cooperation and Development (OECD)

C. Insurance programs administered by private entities

D. The secondary use of healthcare information

## Question 7

An example of the secondary use of a patient's health information would be when the information is shared

A. To support transfer of the patient's care between two providers

B. Through an authorized health information exchange to support the portability of care

C. In support of a diagnostic test required to further the treatment of a patient

D. With public health officials for statistical reporting or in support of clinical research

## Question 8

In the financial reimbursement area, the interrelationships between healthcare organizations

A. Are unrelated to the efficiency of healthcare claims processing

B. May assure government payers that quality healthcare services have been delivered

C. Do not support private insurance organizations in their assessment of the quality of delivered healthcare services

D. Are designed to maximize reimbursement for covered healthcare services

## Question 9

Key information technology and information management professionals in healthcare organizations include the

A. Chief information officer (CIO), chief executive officer (CEO), and chief medical information officer (CMIO)

B. Chief information officer (CIO), chief security officer (CSO), and chief medical information officer (CMIO)

C. Chief information officer (CIO), chief financial officer (CFO), and chief technology officer (CTO)

D. Chief information officer (CIO), chief executive officer (CEO), and chief nursing informatics officer (CNIO)

## Question 10
Nongovernment professional associations may perform regulatory roles for their profession. Which of the following is *not* a typical role for a professional association?

A. Determining qualifications for a profession by defining professional examination criteria

B. Making laws and regulations regarding reimbursements for their profession

C. Issuing a code of conduct to guide professional behavior

D. Implementing disciplinary procedures for those in their profession

# Chapter 2: The Technology Environment

## Question 1
Patients have an expectation that healthcare providers will keep health information entrusted to them

A. Private and secure

B. Available Monday through Friday

C. On paper

D. Available for research

## Question 2
Data warehouses include

A. Data from one hospital only

B. Information from the patient

C. Data from many different applications

D. Financial data only

## Question 3
Interface engines support

A. Interoperability and data integration

B. Manual connections to financial systems

C. Cloud storage of patient information

D. Encryption of patient-identifiable data

## Question 4
Telehealth can be used to

A. Constrain patients to specific providers

B. Provide specialist care to patients in rural areas

C. Prohibit transfers of patients

D. Mandate admissions to academic medical centers

### Question 5

mHealth applications can address

A. Medical records

B. Global health initiatives

C. Issues concerning supply chain inventory

D. Only cell phones

## Chapter 3: Systems Analysis

### Question 1

What system will give informative guidelines to practitioners regarding medication and procedures, including warning systems relating to high-risk medications and processes?

A. Clinical decision support system (CDSS)

B. Computerized practitioner order entry (CPOE)

C. Picture archiving and communication system (PACS)

D. Electronic health record (EHR)

### Question 2

When defining problems and opportunities, major areas of change can occur in the following areas:

A. Analytical, supervisory, financial, and administrative

B. Clinical, administrative, financial, and application

C. Supervisory, administrative, financial, and clinical

D. Application, analytical, administrative, and financial

### Question 3

When defining requirements, what is the key to implementing safe, sustainable, and cost-effective IT practices?

A. Quality tools

B. Sustainment plan

C. Control plan

D. Project plan

### Question 4

Sustainable controls for IT implementation can result in

A. Uncontrolled security

B. Serving minimum purpose possible

C. Determining what is practical for local area implementation and testing

D. Satisfying integration with policy regulations

### Question 5

When performing cost–benefit analysis, important variables to be considered include

A. Sustainability versus total costs per month

B. Time and cost of implementation

C. Impact on internal parties

D. Process mapping

## Question 6

The benefits of developing proposals in support of integrating healthcare practices can include

A. Secure information sharing

B. Minimal communication between various localized care providers

C. Stand-alone architectures for various equipment and software applications

D. Enhanced efficiency in the communication flow

## Question 7

When presenting your analysis to your executive leadership, key elements may include

A. Possible changes in the project implementation that can be driven by changes in technology standards

B. Requirements that may change, affecting the strategic capability of the proposal

C. Sensitivity to challenges or changes in the internal environment that may rely on the establishment of a support team within the organization

D. Expectations that the implementation of analysis and subsequent proposals will rely on the presence of standard operational processes in the internal environment

## Question 8

When managing projects and resources, it is important to have a work plan that

A. Is aimed at establishing a generic implementation setup for a project

B. Includes equipment costs

C. Plans the intended workflow processes by managing personnel

D. Analyzes processes and evaluates outcomes

## Question 9

Promotion and application of system analysis can include

A. Evaluating past operational situations in an average healthcare facility

B. Identifying the minor problems in processes with respect to optimization of IT use

C. Identifying primary solutions to problems through the implementation of IT policies

D. Evaluating alternative solutions' alignment with the specific objectives set out in the plan

## Question 10

What are possible characteristics that you may encounter when analyzing future healthcare IT trends?

A. Integration of possible entities within an organization in preparation for standardization

B. Alignment with emerging trends on the local IT platform
C. Loss of a low volume of business due to nonalignment of health sector players
D. Importance of implementing an operational work plan to align the health-care sector with current IT trends

## Chapter 4: Systems Design

### Question 1
All of the following are parts of a request for information (RFI) except
  A. Background
  B. Submittal information
  C. Cost requirements
  D. Introduction

### Question 2
The following roles are typically represented in a system design team except
  A. Technical lead/architect
  B. Board member
  C. Information security officer
  D. Procurement

### Question 3
Which of the following must be considered during system design?
  A. System monitoring
  B. Disaster recovery
  C. Availability
  D. All of the above

### Question 4
Detailed technical specifications address all of the following except
  A. System monitoring
  B. Programming language
  C. Security and data encryption
  D. Government regulations

### Question 5
If the design team decides that the system should be built rather than bought, the following more technical roles should be brought onto the design team except
  A. Data modeler
  B. Application developer
  C. Legal
  D. Technical architect

**Question 6**

Unclear or poorly written technical requirements can lead to any of the following except

A. Positive vendor relationships
B. Vendors submitting high bids
C. Inability of the vendor to deliver
D. Litigation

# Chapter 5: Systems Selection, Implementation, Support, and Maintenance

**Question 1**

Functional requirements could include the following:

A. Printers
B. Workflow redesign
C. Backup and recovery plans
D. System documentation

**Question 2**

Which is a characteristic of a request for proposal?

A. A collection of documents with high-level requirements
B. A collection of documents with detailed requirements
C. May or may not include costing information
D. An informal request for information

**Question 3**

Implementation execution includes the following:

A. Definition of the team's roles and responsibilities
B. Decision on implementation strategy
C. Planning for how to manage organizational changes
D. System configuration or build

**Question 4**

The implementation strategy in which all functionality is implemented in one location followed by everywhere else is called

A. Phased by location
B. Big bang
C. Pilot
D. Phased by functionality

**Question 5**

End-user training should be completed at what point in the implementation?

A. During the activation
B. Right before the activation
C. As early as possible
D. Right after planning

### Question 6

Planning for activation should include which of the following?

A. Completing a root cause analysis
B. Scheduling postlive support staff
C. Defining the testing plan
D. Configuration management

### Question 7

After the system is live, which of these should be measured and evaluated?

A. System usability
B. Duration of the implementation
C. Quantity of printers
D. Number of vendors responding to the request for proposal (RFP)

### Question 8

The business continuity plan includes

A. The release management plan
B. The disaster recovery plan
C. The risk management plan
D. The configuration management plan

# Chapter 6: Systems Testing and Evaluation

### Question 1

The fundamental purpose of information systems testing is

A. To give leadership the information necessary to perform a build versus buy analysis
B. To give end users an opportunity to provide inputs regarding system development and functionality
C. To manage risks of developing, producing, operating, and sustaining systems
D. To justify the expense of the proposed system to the board of directors

### Question 2

Test tools include manual and automated tools. Which of the following is a manual test tool?

A. Automation software
B. Black-box test
C. Antivirus program
D. Test script

### Question 3

Testing performed to validate successful system implementation is called

A. Acceptance testing

B. Integration testing

C. System testing

D. Stress testing

## Question 4

System controls are implemented to protect the confidentiality, integrity, and _____ of data during testing.

A. Usability

B. Availability

C. Format

D. Security

## Question 5

Test reporting occurs throughout the testing process and, at a minimum, should address

A. The test team members and their experience levels

B. The estimated cost of the test

C. The expected outcomes of the test

D. The mission of the test

# Chapter 7: Systems Privacy and Security

## Question 1

Access privileges for each role should be set

A. To provide the maximum access necessary

B. To provide the minimum access necessary

C. Based on the user's request

D. Based on the user's physical location

## Question 2

Which of the following is typically among the responsibilities of a chief information security officer?

A. Assessing rules and regulations

B. Validating integrity of backups

C. Developing encryption algorithms

D. Approving all individual access requests

## Question 3

The AAA, or triple-A, approach deals with which area?

A. Financial auditing

B. Physical safeguard

C. User access controls

D. Security auditing

### Question 4

What should an IT analyst do if she suspects there may have been a loss of data that may contain multiple patients' sensitive health information?

- A. Contact the organization's risk management or compliance department
- B. Inform all affected patients
- C. Notify the government regulatory department in charge of the relevant regulations
- D. Purge other database records that may be accessed using this health information

### Question 5

Locked doors, property control tags on devices, and employee identification badges are all examples of what?

- A. Technical safeguards
- B. Physical safeguards
- C. Audit controls
- D. Access management

## Chapter 8: Administration Leadership

### Question 1

The company's statement that defines where it wants to go or what it wants to be is known as the

- A. Mission statement
- B. Vision statement
- C. Statement of values
- D. Statement of goals

### Question 2

A control chart typically contains each of the following *except* the

- A. Stretch goal
- B. Upper control limit
- C. Mean
- D. Lower control limit

### Question 3

An SBARC includes each of the following *except* the

- A. Situation
- B. Background
- C. Assessment
- D. Constitution

### Question 4

Each of the following is a recommended initial assessment tool *except*

- A. Face-to-face interviews
- B. Web surveys

C. Unit or departmental meetings

D. Focus group meetings

## Question 5

The international organization that serves as a voluntary accrediting, quality, and safety organization is

A. Project Management Institute (PMI)

B. Centers for Medicare & Medicaid Services (CMS)

C. Joint Commission International (JCI)

D. International Federation of Health Information Management Associations (IFHIMA)

## Question 6

The actions of doing good, being honest, and acting fairly are all components of a sound

A. Business impact analysis

B. Systems design

C. Corporate mission

D. Business ethics position

## Question 7

Successful conflict resolution is achieved through a mutual focus on

A. Eliminating the differences of opinion or positions

B. The common ground of the parties in conflict

C. Understanding the personality types of the parties in conflict

D. A proposed solution provided by the mediator

## Question 8

Which of the following items is *not* typically a part of the IT strategic plan?

A. Current systems state

B. Desired future systems state

C. A summary of IT initiatives supporting organizational goals

D. The IT project sponsors for each initiative

# Chapter 9: Administration Management

## Question 1

IT workforce roles that healthcare providers will need as they transition to EHRs include

A. Revenue cycle manager, software support technician, and trainer

B. Clinician/practitioner consultant, implementation support specialist, and payroll manager

C. Materials management consultant, clinician/practitioner consultant, and trainer

D. Implementation support specialist, clinician/practitioner consultant, and trainer

### Question 2
A project manager has been assigned to manage the implementation of a new clinical system. The project manager is responsible for
 A. Appointing the project steering committee from hospital management
 B. Delivering project objectives within budget and on schedule
 C. Delegating project scope decisions to the appropriate team members
 D. Reporting change requests to the CIO for approval or rejection

### Question 3
When undertaking a new project assignment, the *best* order of approach is
 A. Initiate, plan, control, execute, and close
 B. Plan, initiate, execute, control, and close
 C. Control, plan, initiate, execute, and close
 D. Initiate, plan, execute, control, and close

### Question 4
An advisory committee made up of high-level stakeholders or experts who provide guidance on key issues such as company policy and objectives, budgetary control, marketing strategy, resource allocation, and decisions involving large expenditures is called
 A. An IT steering committee
 B. A system development life cycle committee
 C. A vendor selection committee
 D. A policies and standards committee

### Question 5
An important step to *avoid* when managing budgets is to
 A. Negotiate a good budget at the close of the budget cycle
 B. Stay close to budget
 C. Beware of cost allocations
 D. Use proven budget tools and techniques

### Question 6
The widely accepted practice in healthcare for managing an organization's interactions with customers, patients, vendors, and other business associates is
 A. Enterprise risk management
 B. Project portfolio management
 C. Customer relationship management
 D. Project quality management

# Chapter 11

# Answer Key

## Chapter 1: The Healthcare Environment

### Question 1
Among the multiple types of hospital ownership, which is not a common model?
Correct answer: C. Physician owned.

### Question 2
Hospitals may be classified many different ways. Which of the following statements is true regarding hospital classification?
Correct answer: D. Hospitals may be classified in more than one way; for example, an urban hospital might also be classified as a government-owned hospital or as a general hospital.

### Question 3
An ambulatory surgery center would be best classified as
Correct answer: B. An outpatient care setting.

### Question 4
From the perspective of the healthcare delivery organization, payments generally come from three types of entities:
Correct answer: B. Government-financed and managed programs, insurance programs managed by private entities, and patients' personal funds.

### Question 5
In considering the purpose for interrelationships among healthcare organizations, identify the purpose below that is correct:
Correct answer: B. Ensure effective transfers of care facilitated by the provision of essential health information.

### Question 6
Ensuring the general portability of healthcare is facilitated by
Correct answer: A. Health information exchanges (HIEs) such as Canada's Health Infoway and the U.S. HIE programs, including the Nationwide Health Information Network (NHIN).

### Question 7
An example of the secondary use of a patient's health information would be when the information is shared
Correct answer: D. With public health officials for statistical reporting or in support of clinical research.

### Question 8
In the financial reimbursement area, the interrelationships between healthcare organizations
Correct answer: B. May assure government payers that quality healthcare services have been delivered.

### Question 9
Key information technology and information management professionals in healthcare organizations include the
Correct answer: B. Chief information officer (CIO), chief security officer (CSO), and chief medical information officer (CMIO).

### Question 10
Nongovernment professional associations may perform regulatory roles for their profession. Which of the following is *not* a typical role for a professional association?
Correct answer: B. Making laws and regulations regarding reimbursements for their profession.

## Chapter 2: The Technology Environment

### Question 1
Patients have an expectation that healthcare providers will keep health information entrusted to them
Correct answer: A. Private and secure.

### Question 2
Data warehouses include
Correct answer: C. Data from many different EHRs.

### Question 3
Interface engines support
Correct answer: A. Interoperability and data integration.

### Question 4
Telehealth can be used to
Correct answer: B. Provide specialist care to patients in rural areas.

### Question 5
mHealth applications can address
Correct answer: B. Global health initiatives.

# Chapter 3: Systems Analysis

### Question 1
What system will give informative guidelines to practitioners regarding medication and procedures, including warning systems relating to high-risk medications and processes?
Correct answer: A. Clinical decision support system (CDSS).

### Question 2
When defining problems and opportunities, major areas of change can occur in the following areas:
Correct answer: B. Clinical, administrative, financial, and application.

### Question 3
When defining requirements, what is the key to implementing safe, sustainable, and cost-effective IT practices?
Correct answer: D. Project plan.

### Question 4
Sustainable controls for IT implementation can result in
Correct answer: C. Determining what is practical for local area implementation and testing.

### Question 5
When performing cost–benefit analysis, important variables to be considered include
Correct answer: B. Time and cost of implementation.

### Question 6
The benefits of developing proposals in support of integrating healthcare practices can include
Correct answer: A. Secure information sharing.

### Question 7
When presenting your analysis to your executive leadership, key elements may include
Correct answer: A. Possible changes in the project implementation that can be driven by changes in technology standards.

### Question 8
When managing projects and resources, it is important to have a work plan that
Correct answer: D. Analyzes processes and evaluates outcomes.

### Question 9
Promotion and application of system analysis can include
Correct answer: D. Evaluation of alternative solutions' alignment with the specific objectives set out in the plan.

### Question 10
What are possible characteristics that you may encounter when analyzing future healthcare IT trends?
Correct answer: A. Integration of possible entities within an organization in preparation for standardization.

## Chapter 4: Systems Design

### Question 1
All of the following are parts of a request for information (RFI) except
Correct answer: C. Cost requirements.

### Question 2
The following roles are typically represented in a system design team except
Correct answer: B. Board member.

### Question 3
Which of the following must be considered during system design?
Correct answer: D. All of the above.

### Question 4
Detailed technical specifications address all of the following except
Correct answer: B. Programming language.

### Question 5
If the design team decides that the system should be built rather than bought, the following more technical roles should be brought onto the design team except
Correct answer: C. Legal.

### Question 6
Unclear or poorly written technical requirements can lead to any of the following except
Correct answer: A. Positive vendor relationships.

## Chapter 5: Systems Selection, Implementation, Support, and Maintenance

### Question 1
Functional requirements could include the following:
Correct answer: B. Workflow redesign. (All others are nonfunctional requirements.)

### Question 2
Which is a characteristic of a request for proposal?
Correct answer: B. A collection of documents with detailed requirements. (All others are characteristics of an RFI.)

**Question 3**

Implementation execution includes the following:
Correct answer: D. System configuration or build. (All others are part of implementation planning.)

**Question 4**

The implementation strategy in which all functionality is implemented in one location followed by everywhere else is called
Correct answer: C. Pilot.

**Question 5**

End-user training should be completed at what point in the implementation?
Correct answer: B. Right before the activation.

**Question 6**

Planning for activation should include which of the following?
Correct answer: B. Scheduling the postlive support staff.

**Question 7**

After the system is live, which of these should be measured and evaluated?
Correct answer: A. System usability.

**Question 8**

The business continuity plan includes
Correct answer: B. The disaster recovery plan.

# Chapter 6: Systems Testing and Evaluation

**Question 1**

The fundamental purpose of information systems testing is
Correct answer: C. To manage risks of developing, producing, operating, and sustaining systems.

**Question 2**

Test tools include manual and automated tools. Which of the following is a manual test tool?
Correct answer: D. Test script.

**Question 3**

Testing performed to validate successful system implementation is called
Correct answer: A. Acceptance testing.

**Question 4**

System controls are implemented to protect the confidentiality, integrity, and _____ of data during testing.
Correct answer: B. Availability.

### Question 5
Test reporting occurs throughout the testing process and, at a minimum, should address
Correct answer: D. The mission of the test.

## Chapter 7: Systems Privacy and Security

### Question 1
Access privileges for each role should be set
Correct answer: B. To provide the minimum access necessary.

### Question 2
Which of the following is typically among the responsibilities of a chief information security officer?
Correct answer: A. Assessing rules and regulations.

### Question 3
The AAA, or triple-A, approach deals with which area?
Correct answer: C. User access controls.

### Question 4
What should an IT analyst do if she suspects there may have been a loss of data that may contain multiple patients' sensitive health information?
Correct answer: A. Contact the organization's risk management or compliance department.

### Question 5
Locked doors, property control tags on devices, and employee identification badges are all examples of what?
Correct answer: B. Physical safeguards.

## Chapter 8: Administration Leadership

### Question 1
The company's statement that defines where it wants to go or what it wants to be is known as the
Correct answer: B. Vision statement.

### Question 2
A control chart typically contains each of the following *except* the
Correct answer: A. Stretch goal.

### Question 3
An SBARC includes each of the following *except* the
Correct answer: D. Constitution.

## Question 4
Each of the following is a recommended initial assessment tool *except*
Correct answer: B. Web surveys.

## Question 5
The international organization that serves as a voluntary accrediting, quality, and safety organization is
Correct answer: C. Joint Commission International (JCI).

## Question 6
The actions of doing good, being honest, and acting fairly are all components of a sound
Correct answer: D. Business ethics position.

## Question 7
Successful conflict resolution is achieved through a mutual focus on
Correct answer: B. The common ground of the parties in conflict.

## Question 8
Which of the following items is *not* typically a part of the IT strategic plan?
Correct answer: D. The IT project sponsors for each initiative.

# Chapter 9: Administration Management

## Question 1
The U.S. Office of the National Coordinator for Health Information Technology (ONC) identified six healthcare IT workforce roles that healthcare providers will need as they transition to EHRs. These include
Correct answer: D. Implementation support specialist, clinician/practitioner consultant, and trainer.

## Question 2
A project manager has been assigned to manage the implementation of a new clinical system. The project manager is responsible for
Correct answer: B. Delivering project objectives within budget and on schedule.

## Question 3
When undertaking a new project assignment, the *best* order of approach is
Correct answer: D. Initiate, plan, execute, control, and close.

## Question 4
An advisory committee made up of high-level stakeholders or experts who provide guidance on key issues such as company policy and objectives, budgetary control, marketing strategy, resource allocation, and decisions involving large expenditures is called
Correct answer: A. An IT steering committee.

## Question 5

An important step to *avoid* when managing budgets is to
Correct answer: A. Negotiate a good budget at the close of the budget cycle.

## Question 6

The widely accepted practice in healthcare for managing an organization's interactions with customers, patients, vendors and other business associates is
Correct answer: C. Customer relationship management.

# Chapter 12

# Acronyms

**AAA:** authentication, access, and accounting (triple-A approach)

**AAAASF:** American Association for Accreditation of Ambulatory Surgery Facilities

**AAAHC:** Accreditation Association for Ambulatory Health Care

**ACA:** Affordable Care Act

**ACHC:** Accreditation Commission for Health Care, Inc.

**ACO:** accountable care organization

**ACR:** American College of Radiology

**ADE:** adverse drug event

**ADM:** automated dispensing machine

**AHIMA:** American Health Information Management Association

**AMIA:** American Medical Informatics Association

**AMP:** Applied Measurement Professionals, Inc.

**ASP:** application service provider

**ASTM:** American Society for Testing and Materials

**AO:** accreditation organization

**AOA:** American Osteopathic Association/Healthcare Facilities Accreditation Program

**AR:** accounts receivable

**ASC:** ambulatory surgery center

**ATA:** American Telemedicine Association

**ATM:** asynchronous transfer mode

**BI:** business intelligence

**BPM:** business process management

**BPMN:** Business Process Model Notation

**BPR:** business process reengineering

**BYOD:** bring your own device

**CAH:** critical access hospital

**CAHIMS:** Certified Associate in Healthcare Information and Management Systems

**CAP:** College of American Pathologists

**CBI:** clinical and business intelligence

**CDA:** clinical document architecture

**CDC:** Centers for Disease Control and Prevention

**CDS:** clinical decision support

**CDSS:** clinical decision support system

**CEO:** chief executive officer

**CFO:** chief financial officer

**CHAP:** Community Health Accreditation Program

**CHC:** community health center (in Canada)

**CHCF:** California HealthCare Foundation

**CHIM:** Certification in Health Information Management (in Canada)

**CHIO:** chief health information officer

**CHIP:** Children's Health Insurance Program (in the United States)

**CHPS:** Certified in Healthcare Privacy and Security

**CIO:** chief information officer

**CISO:** chief information security officer

**CISSP:** Certified Information Systems Security Professional

**CLIA:** Clinical Laboratory Improvement Amendments

**CMIO:** chief medical information officer

**CMS:** Centers for Medicare & Medicaid Services

**CNIO:** chief nursing information officer

**COO:** chief operating officer

**CoP:** conditions of participation

**COTS:** commercial off-the-shelf [solution]

**CPHIMS:** Certified Professional in Healthcare Information and Management Systems

**CPOE:** computerized practitioner order entry (or computerized provider order entry)

**CPT:** current procedural terminology

**CPU:** central processing unit

**CRM:** customer relationship management

**CSO:** chief security officer

**CT:** computed tomography

**CTO:** chief technology officer

**DAMA®:** Data Management International

**DICOM:** Digital Imaging and Communications in Medicine

**DMAIC:** define, measure, analyze, improve, and control

**DMS:** document management system

**DNFB:** discharged not final billed

**DNVHC:** DNV Healthcare

**eHealth:** healthcare practice supported by electronic processes and communication

**EHR:** electronic health record

**eMAR:** electronic medication administration record
**EMM:** electronic materials management
**EMR:** electronic medical record
**EPPM:** enterprise project portfolio management
**ERM:** enterprise risk management
**FDA:** Food and Drug Administration (in the United States)
**FTE:** full-time employee
**GB:** gigabyte
**GDP:** gross domestic product
**GP:** general practitioner
**GUI:** graphical user interface
**HCPC:** Health and Care Professions Council
**HHA:** home health agency
**HHS:** Department of Health & Human Services
**HIE:** health information exchange
**HIM:** health information management
**HIMSS:** Healthcare Information and Management Systems Society
**HIPAA:** Health Information Portability and Accountability Act
**HIT:** health information technology
**HITECH Act:** Health Information Technology for Economic and Clinical Health Act
**HITSP:** Healthcare Information Technology Standards Panel
**HL7:** Health Level Seven
**HRSA:** Health Resources and Services Administration
**HSCIC:** Health and Social Care Information Centre
**ICD:** International Statistical Classification of Diseases and Related Health Problems
**ICU:** intensive care unit
**IDS:** integrated delivery system
**IEEE:** Institute of Electrical and Electronics Engineers
**IFHIMA:** International Federation of Health Information Management Associations
**IHE:** Integrating the Healthcare Enterprise
**IM:** information management
**IMIA:** International Medical Informatics Association
**IOM:** Institute of Medicine
**IP:** Internet Protocol
**IPv4:** Internet Protocol version 4
**IPv6:** Internet Protocol version 6
**ISC²:** Information Systems Security Certification Consortium, Inc.
**ISPOR:** International Society for Pharmacoeconomics and Outcomes Research
**IT:** information technology
**ITIL:** Information Technology Infrastructure Library
**JCI:** Joint Commission International

**KPI:** key performance indicator

**LAN:** local area network

**mHealth:** mobile health

**ME-PI:** management engineering and process improvement

**MPLS:** multiprotocol label switching

**MRI:** magnetic resonance imaging

**NHIN:** Nationwide Health Information Network (in the United States)

**NHS:** National Health Service (in the United Kingdom)

**NIST:** National Institute of Standards and Technology

**NPI:** National Provider Identifier

**OECD:** Organisation for Economic Cooperation and Development

**ONC:** Office of the National Coordinator

**OPT:** outpatient physical therapy provider

**P&Ps:** policies and procedures

**PA:** physician assistant

**PA-C:** physician assistant–certified

**PACS:** picture archiving and communication system

**PCP:** primary care provider

**PHI:** personal health information

**PHR:** personal health record

**PM:** project manager

**PMBOK:** Project Management Body of Knowledge; PMBOK Guide

**PMO:** project management office

**PMP:** Project Management Professional

**PPM:** project portfolio management

**PQRI:** Physician Quality Reporting Initiative

**PQRS:** Physician Quality Reporting System

**RAM:** random access memory

**RDBMS:** relational database management system

**RFI:** request for information

**RFID:** radio frequency identification

**RFP:** request for proposal

**RHC:** rural health clinic

**RHIA:** Registered Health Information Administrator (in the United States)

**RHIO:** regional health information organization

**RHIT:** Registered Health Information Technologist (in the United States)

**ROI:** return on investment

**RPO:** recovery point objective

**RSS:** really simple syndication

**RTO:** recovery time objective

**SAE:** self assessment exam

**SBARC:** situation, background, assessment, recommendation, and communication

**SLA:** service-level agreement

**SMART:** specific, measurable, attainable, relevant, and time bound
**SNOMED:** Systematic Nomenclature of Medicine
**SUS:** Secondary Use Services (in United Kingdom)
**SWOT:** strengths, weaknesses, opportunities, and threats
**TCP:** transmission control protocol
**UMM:** usability maturity model
**URL:** uniform resource locator
**UX:** user experience
**VoIP:** voice over Internet protocol
**VPN:** virtual public network
**WAN:** wide area network
**WBS:** work breakdown structure
**WHO:** World Health Organization
**XPDL XML:** Process Definition Language

# Appendix

## Contents

CPHIMS Candidate Handbook ...............................................................192
About HIMSS .......................................................................................192
   HIMSS Vision ...............................................................................193
   HIMSS Mission .............................................................................193
   Statement of Nondiscrimination.................................................193
HIMSS Certification Program Examinations...................................193
   Testing Agency.............................................................................193
CPHIMS Certification Program........................................................194
   CPHIMS Eligibility Requirements..............................................194
CPHIMS Examination ........................................................................194
CPHIMS Examination Preparation....................................................201
   Review the Content Outline........................................................201
   Complete the CPHIMS Self-Assessment Examination (SAE) ...........201
   The CPHIMS Review Guide, Third Edition ...............................201
   HIMSS Dictionary of Healthcare IT Terms, Acronyms, and Organizations .... 202
   HIMSS Learning Center CPHIMS Review Course......................202
   Use Other Study Resources.........................................................202
CPHIMS Examination Administration................................................202
   Computer Administration at AMP Assessment Centers ............203
   Special Administration: Laptop or Paper/Pencil ......................203
   Testing Outside of the United States .........................................203
   Special Arrangements for Candidates with Disabilities ...........204
Adhering to Professional Standards of Conduct .............................204
CPHIMS Examination Application and Scheduling Process............205
   Online Application and Scheduling...........................................206
   Paper Application and Scheduling .............................................207
   Rescheduling or Canceling a CPHIMS Examination .................208
On the Day of the CPHIMS Examination .........................................208
   Reporting for the CPHIMS Examination.....................................208
   On-Site Security ...........................................................................209
   Identity Verification .....................................................................209

Use of Calculators.................................................................................210

Inclement Weather or Emergency ........................................................210

Failing to Report for the CPHIMS Examination .................................210

Taking the CPHIMS Examination ............................................................210

Rules for CPHIMS Examination ...........................................................212

Copyrighted Examination Questions....................................................213

Following the CPHIMS Examination .......................................................213

Score Reports........................................................................................213

How the CPHIMS Passing Score Is Set................................................214

Passing the CPHIMS Examination........................................................215

Failing the CPHIMS Examination.........................................................215

Scores Canceled by HIMSS .................................................................215

Score Confidentiality ...........................................................................216

Administrative Matters .........................................................................216

Duplicate Score Report....................................................................216

Name and Address Change ............................................................216

Renewal of CPHIMS Certification ...........................................................216

Failing to Renew..................................................................................217

Appeals ....................................................................................................217

Checklist for Becoming Certified............................................................218

Certified Professional in Healthcare Information and Management Systems

(CPHIMS) ................................................................................................219

Examination Application ......................................................................219

Request for Special Examination Accommodations ............................... 222

Documentation of Disability-Related Needs........................................... 223

## CPHIMS Candidate Handbook

This Candidate Handbook provides information about the Certified Professional in Healthcare Information and Management Systems (CPHIMS) program, including CPHIMS eligibility, examination administration policy, and process, as well as the CPHIMS Examination application.

A copy of the most up-to-date version of this Candidate Handbook can be downloaded here: http://www.himss.org/health-it-certification/cphims/handbook. The most current version of the Candidate Handbook supersedes any other version.

## About HIMSS

HIMSS is a cause-based, global enterprise producing health IT thought leadership, education, events, market research, and media services around the world. Founded in 1961, HIMSS encompasses more than 61,000 individuals, of which more than two-thirds work in healthcare provider, governmental, and not-for-profit organizations across the globe, plus more than 640 corporations and 450 not-for-profit partner organizations, that share this cause. HIMSS, headquartered in Chicago, serves the global health IT community with additional offices in the United States, Europe, and Asia.

### HIMSS Vision

Better health through information technology.

### HIMSS Mission

Globally, lead endeavors optimizing health engagements and care outcomes through information technology.

### Statement of Nondiscrimination

HIMSS does not discriminate among candidates on the basis of age, gender, race, color, religion, national origin, disability, or marital status.

## HIMSS Certification Program Examinations

HIMSS conducts certification examinations for programs in healthcare information and management systems:

- CPHIMS (Certified Professional in Healthcare Information and Management Systems)
- CAHIMS (Certified Associate in Healthcare Information and Management Systems)

Each certification examination is designed to test a well-defined body of knowledge representative of professional practice in healthcare information and management systems. Successful completion of a certification examination is an indicator of broad-based knowledge in healthcare information and management systems. Certification examinations conducted by HIMSS are independent of each other. Each leads to a certification credential in healthcare information and management systems.

Content of each examination was defined by an international or national role delineation study. The study involved surveying practitioners in the field to identify tasks that are performed routinely and considered important to competent practice. Each edition of a certification examination is developed through a combined effort of qualified subject matter experts and testing professionals, who construct the examination in accordance with the Examination Content Outline.

### Testing Agency

HIMSS contracts with Applied Measurement Professionals, Inc. (AMP) to assist in the development, administration, scoring, score reporting, and analysis of the CPHIMS Examination.

## CPHIMS Certification Program

The CPHIMS certification program promotes the healthcare information and management systems field through certification of qualified individuals and the following program elements:

■ Recognizing formally those individuals who meet the eligibility requirements of CPHIMS and pass the examination
■ Requiring certification renewal through continued personal and professional growth in the practice of healthcare information and management systems
■ Providing an international standard of requisite knowledge for certification, thereby assisting employers, the public, and members of health professions in assessing healthcare information and management systems professionals

### *CPHIMS Eligibility Requirements*

Candidates who meet eligibility requirements and pass the CPHIMS Examination attain the CPHIMS designation. HIMSS reserves the right, but is not obligated, to accuracy of information supplied by or on behalf of a candidate.

Eligibility for the CPHIMS Examination requires fulfilling one (1) of the following requirements:

■ Baccalaureate degree from an accredited college or university plus five (5) years of information and management systems experience,* three (3) of those years in a healthcare setting.**
■ Graduate degree or higher from an accredited college or university plus three (3) years of information and management systems experience,* two (2) of those years in a healthcare setting.**

*Information and management systems experience refers to work experience in systems analysis; design; selection, implementation, support, and maintenance; testing and evaluation; privacy and security; information systems; clinical informatics; and management engineering.*

**Includes experience with a provider of health services or products to a healthcare facility (e.g., hospital; healthcare consulting firm; vendor; federal, state, or local government office; academic institution; payer; or public health).*

## CPHIMS Examination

The CPHIMS Examination is structured as follows:

■ Composed of 115 multiple-choice questions. A candidate's score is based on 100 of these questions. Fifteen (15) are "trial" or "pretest" questions that are interspersed throughout the examination.

- A candidate is allowed two (2) hours in which to complete the CPHIMS Examination.
- The CPHIMS Examination is based on the three (3) major content areas listed in the Content Outline.
  - Each content area is further defined in the Content Outline by a list of tasks representative of that job responsibility.
  - The number of CPHIMS Examination questions devoted to each major content area is included in the Content Outline.
- CPHIMS Examination questions are categorized by the following cognitive levels:
  - *Recall (RE):* The ability to recall or recognize specific information
  - *Application (AP):* The ability to comprehend, relate, or apply knowledge to new or changing situations
  - *Analysis (AN):* The ability to analyze and synthesize information, determine solutions, and/or evaluate the usefulness of a solution

| CPHIMS Examination Detailed Content Outline (effective March 1, 2013) | Cognitive Level | | | TOTAL |
|---|---|---|---|---|
| | *Recall* | *Application* | *Analysis* | |
| **1. General** | **22** | **6** | **0** | **28** |
| A. Healthcare environment<br>　1. Articulate characteristics and services of different types of healthcare organizations (e.g., hospitals, clinics, ambulatory centers, community health organizations, healthcare payers, regulators, research, and academic).<br>　2. Recognize the various types of interrelationship models of care within and across healthcare organizations.<br>　3. Differentiate the roles and responsibilities of healthcare information and management systems professionals within the organizational structures in which they work.<br>　4. Describe the roles governmental, regulatory, professional, and accreditation agencies play related to healthcare and their impact on clinical outcomes and financial performance. | 10 | 4 | 0 | 14 |

| *CPHIMS Examination Detailed Content Outline (effective March 1, 2013)* | Cognitive Level | | | |
| --- | --- | --- | --- | --- |
| | Recall | Application | Analysis | TOTAL |
| B. Technology environment<br>1. Describe various technologies that support the healthcare environment.<br>2. Articulate the characteristics of applications commonly used in healthcare organizations (e.g., clinical, administrative, financial, and consumer).<br>3. Identify future trends and key issues in healthcare technologies (e.g., HIE, interoperability and standards, telehealth, and privacy and security). | 12 | 2 | 0 | 14 |
| **2. Systems** | **3** | **22** | **15** | **40** |
| A. Analysis<br>1. Describe the major components of the systems analysis process with regard to IT implementation in healthcare.<br>2. Articulate the problem that can be resolved through proper policies based on IT.<br>3. Explain the current and developing trends in IT systems analysis.<br>4. Perform a cost–benefit analysis of a proposed initiative.<br>5. Identify the project management stages that are most important to the systems analysis phase. | 2 | 10 | 4 | 16 |
| B. Design<br>1. Identify system designs to accommodate business processes.<br>2. Develop requests for information and/or requests for proposals.<br>3. Ensure compatibility of software, hardware, network components, and medical devices.<br>4. Ensure compliance with applicable industry, regulatory, and organizational standards.<br>5. Ensure a process exists to incorporate industry, technology, infrastructure, legal, and regulatory environment trends. | 0 | 3 | 3 | 6 |

| CPHIMS Examination Detailed Content Outline (effective March 1, 2013) | Cognitive Level | | | TOTAL |
|---|---|---|---|---|
| | Recall | Application | Analysis | |
| 6. Design an information infrastructure that supports current and anticipated business needs (e.g., business continuity and disaster recovery). 7. Evaluate existing and emerging technologies to support organization's future growth and strategy. 8. Employ effective data management practices. | | | | |
| C. Selection, implementation, support, and maintenance 1. Facilitate solution selection criteria. 2. Select and review team members. 3. Conduct solution selection activities (e.g., demonstrations, site visits, and reference checks). 4. Employ organizational change management techniques in support of solution implementation. 5. Provide knowledge transfer through user and operational manuals and training. 6. Execute the implementation of solutions. 7. Integrate systems to support business requirements. 8. Manage healthcare information systems (e.g., operate and upgrade). 9. Analyze data for problems and trends (e.g., error reports, help desk logs, surveys, performance metrics, and network monitoring). 10. Prioritize issues to ensure critical functions are repaired, maintained, or enhanced. 11. Incorporate solution into organizational disaster recovery and business continuity plans. 12. Develop system and personnel downtime procedures. | 0 | 4 | 3 | 7 |

| CPHIMS Examination Detailed Content Outline (effective March 1, 2013) | Cognitive Level | | | TOTAL |
|---|---|---|---|---|
| | *Recall* | *Application* | *Analysis* | |
| D. Testing and evaluation<br>1. Design a formal testing methodology to demonstrate solutions meet functional requirements (e.g., unit test, integrated test, stress test, and acceptance test).<br>2. Implement internal controls to protect resources and ensure availability, confidentiality, and integrity during testing (e.g., security audits, versioning control, and change control).<br>3. Validate implementations against contractual terms and design specifications.<br>4. Corroborate expected benefits are achieved (e.g., return on investment, benchmarks, and user satisfaction). | 0 | 2 | 3 | 5 |
| E. Privacy and security<br>1. Participate in defining organizational privacy and security requirements, policies, and procedures.<br>2. Assess privacy and security risks.<br>3. Mitigate privacy and security vulnerabilities.<br>4. Ensure user access control according to established policies and procedures.<br>5. Ensure confidentiality, integrity, and availability of data.<br>6. Define organizational roles (e.g., information security, physical security, and compliance).<br>7. Develop data management controls (e.g., data ownership, criticality, security levels, protection controls, retention and destruction requirements, and access controls).<br>8. Validate disaster recovery and business continuity plans.<br>9. Coordinate privacy and security audits.<br>10. Validate security features in the evaluation of existing and new system requirements. | 1 | 3 | 2 | 6 |

| CPHIMS Examination Detailed Content Outline (effective March 1, 2013) | Cognitive Level | | | TOTAL |
|---|---|---|---|---|
| | Recall | Application | Analysis | |
| **3. Administration** | **5** | **18** | **9** | **32** |
| A. Leadership | 3 | 10 | 9 | 22 |
|   1. Participate in organizational strategic planning (e.g., measure performance against organizational goals). | | | | |
|   2. Assess the organizational environment (e.g., corporate culture, values, and drivers). | | | | |
|   3. Forecast technical and information needs of an organization by linking resources to business needs. | | | | |
|   4. Develop an IT strategic plan and departmental objectives that align and support organizational strategies and goals. | | | | |
|   5. Evaluate performance (e.g., goal/performance indicators and systems effectiveness). | | | | |
|   6. Evaluate effectiveness and user satisfaction of systems and services being provided. | | | | |
|   7. Promote stakeholder understanding of information technology opportunities and constraints (e.g., business and IT resources, budget, and project prioritization). | | | | |
|   8. Develop policies and procedures for information and systems management. | | | | |
|   9. Comply with legal and regulatory standards. | | | | |
|   10. Adhere to ethical business principles. | | | | |
|   11. Employ comparative analysis strategies (e.g., indicators and benchmarks). | | | | |
|   12. Prepare and deliver business communications (e.g., presentations, reports, and project plans). | | | | |
|   13. Facilitate group discussions and meetings (e.g., consensus building and conflict resolution). | | | | |
|   14. Provide consultative services to the organization on IT matters. | | | | |
|   15. Develop educational strategies regarding the information and management systems function. | | | | |

| CPHIMS Examination Detailed Content Outline (effective March 1, 2013) | Recall | Application | Analysis | TOTAL |
|---|---|---|---|---|
| 16. Maintain organizational competencies on current IT technologies and trends. | | | | |
| 17. Assure risk management is embedded in internal and external management processes and consistently applied (e.g., risk assessment and risk mitigation). | | | | |
| 18. Ensure quality standards and practices are followed by monitoring internal and external performance. | | | | |
| B. Management | 2 | 8 | 0 | 10 |
| 1. Define roles, responsibilities, and job descriptions for IT-related functions. | | | | |
| 2. Assure staff competency in information and management systems skills. | | | | |
| 3. Manage projects and portfolios of projects (e.g., initiate, plan, execute, control, and close). | | | | |
| 4. Manage relationships with vendors (e.g., contract cost, schedule, support, maintenance, and performance). | | | | |
| 5. Facilitate steering committee meetings and/or topics. | | | | |
| 6. Assure adherence to industry best practices (e.g., change control and project management). | | | | |
| 7. Maintain system, operational, and department documentation. | | | | |
| 8. Provide customer service (e.g., service-level management, request tracking, and problem resolution). | | | | |
| 9. Manage budget and financial risks. | | | | |
| 10. Manage customer relationships with business unit leaders. | | | | |
| **Total** | **30** | **46** | **24** | **100** |

Cognitive Level spans Recall, Application, Analysis.

# CPHIMS Examination Preparation

The method of preparation and amount of time spent preparing for the CPHIMS Examination can be driven by the candidate's preferred study style, level of professional experience, or academic background. Some methods of preparation may include but are not limited to the following methods.

## *Review the Content Outline*

Candidates who have passed the CPHIMS Examination report that study should begin by reviewing the CPHIMS Examination Content Outline. Review the content categories and related tasks. Identify and focus review on tasks that you do not perform regularly or with which you are not familiar. Remember that all questions in the CPHIMS Examination are job related/experience based and test the application and analysis of information, not just the recollection of isolated facts.

## *Complete the CPHIMS Self-Assessment Examination (SAE)*

A Self-Assessment Examination (SAE) for the CPHIMS Examination is an online tool created by HIMSS to simulate the CPHIMS Examination. This tool is available for purchase at http://store.lxr.com/dept.aspx?id=49.

The 100-question online practice examination was developed using the same procedures as the CPHIMS Examination, and conforms to examination specifications in content, cognitive levels, format, and difficulty. Feedback reports from the SAE provide an opportunity to evaluate and remedy less than desirable performance before taking the CPHIMS Examination. The questions presented in the SAE are not from the past CPHIMS Examinations and are different from the questions contained on the current CPHIMS Examination.

## *The CPHIMS Review Guide, Third Edition*

The *CPHIMS Review Guide, Third Edition*, is available in softcover and eBook versions. Whether you're taking the CPHIMS Examination or simply want the most current and comprehensive overview in healthcare information and management systems today, this updated publication has it all. For those preparing for the CPHIMS Examination, this book is an ideal, supplementary study guide. The content reflects the Examination Content Outline covering healthcare and technology environments; systems analysis, design, selection, implementation, support, maintenance, testing, evaluation, privacy, and security; and administration leadership and management. Candidates can challenge themselves with the sample multiple-choice questions at the end of the book. The review guide may be purchased here:

https://www.crcpress.com/HIMSS-Dictionary-of-Healthcare-Information-Technology-Term-Acronyms-and/Himss/9781938904288?utm_source=himss.org&utm_medium=weblink&utm_campaign=HWP37_bookstore&promo=hwp37.

## HIMSS Dictionary of Healthcare IT Terms, Acronyms, and Organizations

This dictionary was developed and extensively reviewed by industry experts. The resource includes

- Definitions of terms for the IT and clinical, medical, and nursing informatics fields
- Acronyms, with cross-references to current definitions
- Academic and certification credentials commonly used in healthcare and IT

For more information and to order a copy, visit https://www.crcpress.com/go/himssbookstore?utm_source=marketplace.himss.org&utm_medium=weblink&utm_campaign=mainStorePage.

## HIMSS Learning Center CPHIMS Review Course

The HIMSS Learning Center offers three options to assist candidates in preparing for the CPHIMS Examination.

- Option 1: Online course only
- Option 2: Virtual instructor-led training only (four live webinars offered at various times throughout the year)
- Option 3: Online course and virtual instructor-led training combo (available at various times throughout the year) For more information and the upcoming schedule, visit http://himsslearn.org/.

## Use Other Study Resources

HIMSS recommends that study for the CPHIMS Examination focus on references and programs that cover the information summarized in the CPHIMS Examination Content Outline. It should not be inferred that questions in the CPHIMS Examination are selected from any single reference or set of references, or that study from specific references guarantees a passing score on the examination. For information about references, study guides, and review sessions offered by HIMSS, visit http://www.himss.org/health-it-certification.

# CPHIMS Examination Administration

The CPHIMS Examination is administered in the following ways:

- On computers at AMP Assessment Centers worldwide
- During special administrations at conferences, meetings, or other specially arranged sessions

In accordance with the Americans with Disabilities Act (ADA), special arrangements can be made for candidates with a disability.

## Computer Administration at AMP Assessment Centers

The primary mode of delivery of the CPHIMS Examination is by computer at AMP Assessment Centers geographically distributed throughout the world. Assessment Center locations, detailed maps, and directions are available at www.goAMP.com.

For computer administrations at AMP Assessment Centers, a candidate who meets eligibility requirements for the CPHIMS Examination may submit an application and fee at any time. A candidate must make an appointment for testing and take the CPHIMS Examination within ninety (90) days from confirmation of eligibility from AMP. The CPHIMS Examination is administered by appointment only Monday through Saturday at 9:00 a.m. and 1:30 p.m., with the exception of holidays. Candidates are scheduled on a first-come, first-served basis.

| If AMP is contacted by 3:00 p.m. CST on | Depending on availability, the examination may be scheduled as early as |
|---|---|
| Monday | Wednesday |
| Tuesday | Thursday |
| Wednesday | Friday/Saturday |
| Thursday | Monday |
| Friday | Tuesday |

## Special Administration: Laptop or Paper/Pencil

The CPHIMS Examination may be offered on laptop or in paper-and-pencil format during conferences or meetings. A candidate who meets eligibility requirements and submits an application and fee for receipt by the posted deadline is allowed to test. Different application procedures apply for special administrations. Contact HIMSS for information on how to apply for a special administration.

## Testing Outside of the United States

Candidates who are eligible for the CPHIMS Examination and wish to take the CPHIMS Examination outside of the United States may be accommodated. International AMP Assessment Center locations may be found by visiting www.goAMP.com.

## *Special Arrangements for Candidates with Disabilities*

HIMSS complies with applicable provisions of the Americans with Disabilities Act (ADA) and strives to ensure that no individual with a disability is deprived of the opportunity to take the CPHIMS Examination solely by reason of that disability. Through its agents, HIMSS will provide reasonable accommodation for a candidate with a disability who requests timely accommodation by completing and timely submitting the Request for Special Examination Accommodations form included in this Candidate Handbook to AMP.

AMP Assessment Centers are equipped with Telecommunication Devices for the Deaf (TDD) to assist deaf and hearing- impaired candidates. TDD calling is available 8:30 a.m. to 5:00 p.m. (CST) Monday through Friday at 913-895-4637.

This TDD phone option is for individuals equipped with compatible TDD machinery. Additionally, wheelchair access is available at all AMP Assessment Centers.

A candidate with a visual, sensory, or physical disability that prevents taking the examination under standard conditions may request special accommodations and arrangements. For either a computer or a special administration of the CPHIMS Examination, complete the Request for Special Examination Accommodations form included in this Candidate Handbook and submit it with a CPHIMS Examination application and fee at least 45 days prior to the CPHIMS Examination date desired.

# Adhering to Professional Standards of Conduct

HIMSS is responsible to its candidates, employers, the healthcare information and management systems profession, and the public for ensuring the integrity of all processes and products of its certification programs. As such, HIMSS requires adherence to these Professional Standards of Conduct by all who have achieved certification through successful completion of its programs. A candidate's signature on the application for the CPHIMS Examination attests to ongoing agreement to adhere to the following Professional Standards of Conduct.

Professional Standards of Conduct: An individual who is awarded certification by HIMSS agrees to conduct himself/herself in an ethical and professional manner. This includes demonstrating practice-related behavior that is indicative of professional integrity. By accepting certification, the individual agrees to the following:

■ Maintain professional competence.
■ Demonstrate work behavior that exemplifies ability to perform safely, competently, and with good judgment.

- Conduct professional activities with honesty and integrity.
- Avoid discriminating against any individual based on age, gender, race, color, religion, national origin, disability, or marital status.
- Avoid conflicts of interest.
- Abide by the laws, rules, and regulations of duly authorized agencies regulating the profession.
- Abide by rules and regulations governing programs conducted by HIMSS.

Infraction of these Professional Standards of Conduct is misconduct for which granting of a certification or renewal of a certification may be delayed or denied, or for which a certification may be revoked by HIMSS.

*Reporting Violations.* To protect the international credential and to ensure responsible practice by its credential holders, HIMSS depends on its candidates, professionals, employers, regulatory agencies, and the public to report incidents that may be in violation of these Professional Standards of Conduct. A certified individual who has violated these standards should voluntarily surrender his/her certification.

Written reports of infraction of these standards may be sent to HIMSS, Professional Certification, 33 West Monroe Street, Suite 1700, Chicago, Illinois 60603-5616 USA. Only signed, written communication will be considered.

HIMSS will become involved only in matters that can be factually determined, and commits to handling any situation as fairly and expeditiously as possible. During its investigation and decision, HIMSS will protect the confidentiality of those who provide information to every possible extent. The named individual will be afforded a reasonable opportunity to respond in a professional and legally defensible manner, in accordance with policies established by HIMSS.

## CPHIMS Examination Application and Scheduling Process

After fulfilling the CPHIMS eligibility requirements, a candidate may apply to AMP for the CPHIMS Examination in one (1) of the following ways:

- Online application (available at www.goAMP.com; requires credit card payment for fees)
- Paper application (included in this Candidate Handbook)

Documentation of eligibility does not need to be submitted with a CPHIMS Examination application. HIMSS reserves the right, but is not obligated, to verify accuracy of information supplied by or on behalf of a candidate. If selected for an audit, the candidate will be asked to submit documentation as proof of meeting the eligibility requirements.

To apply for the CPHIMS Examination, an eligible candidate must submit the appropriate fee (see below) with a complete CPHIMS Examination application to AMP.

| | |
|---|---|
| HIMSS individual organizational affiliate member | $270 U.S. |
| HIMSS regular, corporate, or student member | $300 U.S. |
| Nonmember | $375 U.S. |

*(Chapter-only and online-only members are not eligible for the member rate.)*

■ Payment may be made by credit card (VISA, MasterCard, American Express, or Discover) or by company check, cashier's check, or money order made payable to AMP. Cash and personal checks are not accepted.

■ Examination-related fees are nonrefundable.

■ For computer administrations at AMP Assessment Centers, candidates may request to reschedule a scheduled appointment up to two (2) business days prior to the scheduled administration. The CPHIMS Examination may be rescheduled once without incurring an additional fee. The new date must be within 90 days of AMP confirming receipt of the original application. A candidate may *reschedule the CPHIMS Examination a second or additional time* by submitting to AMP a written request including their name, address, identification number, and the *$75 U.S. rescheduling fee*. A new CPHIMS Examination application is not required. The CPHIMS Examination must be rescheduled within 90 days of AMP confirming receipt of the original application. For payment by credit card, the credit card number and an expiration date must be included.

■ Credit card transactions that are declined are subject to a $25 U.S. handling fee. A certified check or money order for the amount due, including the handling fee, must be submitted to AMP to cover a declined credit card transaction.

■ Candidates who fail a CPHIMS Examination and apply to retake the CPHIMS Examination must pay the full examination fee as listed above.

## Online Application and Scheduling

*(For computer administrations at AMP Assessment Centers only)*

Complete the application and scheduling process in one online session. Visit www.goAMP.com and select "Schedule/Apply for an Exam." Follow the online instructions for accessing the application.

If you are a current member of HIMSS, you are eligible for a reduced HIMSS member rate for the CPHIMS Examination fee. When prompted, enter your membership number, name, and address exactly as they appear in HIMSS's membership database. Your preferred mailing and e-mail addresses designated in HIMSS's membership database are used for all records and communications. For information on your membership record, please contact HIMSS at *HIMSS Individual Member Services* at membersupport@himss.org.

After completing the CPHIMS Examination application and submitting credit card payment information (VISA, MasterCard, American Express, or Discover), AMP confirms the candidate's certification of eligibility and prompts the candidate to schedule a CPHIMS Examination appointment or supply additional eligibility information, respectively. The candidate must schedule a CPHIMS Examination date that is within 90 days of AMP confirming receipt of the CPHIMS Examination application.

## *Paper Application and Scheduling*

*(For computer administrations at AMP Assessment Centers only)*

Complete and submit to AMP a CPHIMS Examination application with the appropriate fee. Candidates may complete the paper application included in this Candidate Handbook or obtained by contacting AMP at 888-519-9901.

Incomplete applications will be returned to the candidate, along with any fee submitted less a $50 U.S. processing fee. A CPHIMS Examination application is considered complete only if all of the following conditions are met:

- Information provided is legible and accurate.
- All of the following required information is provided:
  - Personal information.
  - Examination type.
  - Application status.
  - Membership status. Eligibility for the member rate of the examination application fee requires recording the membership number, name, and address exactly as they appear in HIMSS's membership database. For information on your member record, contact HIMSS at *HIMSS Individual Member Services* at membersupport@himss.org.
  - Method of payment for the applicable fee.
  - Demographic information.
  - Signature.
- The candidate is eligible for the CPHIMS Examination and can provide evidence if requested to do so.
- Appropriate fee accompanies application (credit card, company check, cashier's check, or money order).

If *special accommodations* are required, complete and submit to AMP the Request for Special Examination Accommodations form included in this Candidate Handbook and submit with the CPHIMS Examination application and fee at least 45 days prior to the desired testing date.

Generally, within approximately two (2) weeks of receiving the paper application, AMP processes it, confirms the CPHIMS candidate's eligibility, and sends an e-mail and postcard confirmation notice with a toll-free phone number and website at which a testing appointment can be scheduled. If a confirmation notice is not received within four (4) weeks of mailing your application, candidates should contact AMP at 888-519-9901.

A candidate is allowed to take only the CPHIMS Examination for which application is made and confirmation from AMP is received. Unscheduled candidates (walk-ins) are not allowed to take the CPHIMS Examination.

## Rescheduling or Canceling a CPHIMS Examination

Although examination application fees are nonrefundable, the following options to reschedule a CPHIMS Examination are available, except in the case of special administrations conducted by HIMSS. Special administrations are nonrefundable and nontransferable to another person or another administration.

- A candidate may *reschedule the CPHIMS Examination once at no charge* by calling AMP at 888-519-9901 at least two (2) business days prior to a scheduled administration date.
- A candidate may *reschedule the CPHIMS Examination a second or additional time* by submitting to AMP a written request including their name, address, identification number, and the *$75 U.S. rescheduling fee*. A new CPHIMS Examination application is not required. The CPHIMS Examination must be rescheduled *within 90 days* of AMP confirming receipt of the original application. For payment by credit card, the credit card number and expiration date must be included.
- A candidate who reschedules a CPHIMS Examination after the 90-day period forfeits the application and all fees paid to take the CPHIMS Examination. A new, complete application and full CPHIMS Examination fee are required to reapply for the CPHIMS Examination.
- A candidate who *cancels a CPHIMS Examination after confirmation of the candidate's certification of eligibility is received* from AMP forfeits the application and all fees paid to take the CPHIMS Examination. A new, complete application and *full* examination fee are required to reapply for the CPHIMS Examination.

## On the Day of the CPHIMS Examination

### Reporting for the CPHIMS Examination

Bring with you the *confirmation notice* provided by AMP. It contains the unique identification number required to take the test and is required for admission to the testing room.

*For a computer administration*, report to the AMP Assessment Center no later than the scheduled testing time. After entering the testing location, follow the signs indicating AMP Assessment Center check-in.

For a special administration (laptop or paper and pencil), report to the designated testing room at the time indicated on the confirmation notice. The CPHIMS Examination will begin after all scheduled candidates are checked in and seated and no more than one (1) hour after the scheduled check-in begins. Follow the signs provided in the hotel/convention center to locate the testing room.

A candidate who arrives more than fifteen (15) minutes after the scheduled testing time is not admitted. A candidate who is not admitted due to late arrival must reschedule to a new date as outlined above.

## On-Site Security

HIMSS and AMP maintain examination administration and security standards that are designed to assure that all candidates are provided the same opportunity to demonstrate their abilities. The testing environment at AMP Assessment Centers is continuously monitored by audio and video surveillance equipment or examination personnel.

## Identity Verification

To gain admission to the AMP Assessment Center or a testing room, the candidate must present two (2) forms of identification. The primary form must be government issued, current, and include the candidate's name, signature, and photograph. No form of temporary identification will be accepted. The candidate will also be required to sign a roster for verification of identity.

- Examples of valid primary forms of identification are current driver's license with photograph, current identification card with photograph, current passport, or current military identification card with photograph.
- The secondary form of identification must display the candidate's name and signature for the candidate's signature verification (e.g., credit card with signature, social security care with signature, and employment/student ID card with signature).
- If the candidate's name on the registration list is different than it appears on the forms of identification, the candidate must bring proof of the name change (e.g., marriage license, divorce decree, or court order).

Candidates must have proper identification to gain admission to the Assessment Center. Failure to provide appropriate identification at the time of the examination is considered a missed appointment. There will be no refund of examination fees.

## *Use of Calculators*

Some examination questions may require calculations. Use of a silent, nonprogrammable calculator without a paper tape-printing capability or alpha keypad is permitted during testing. Use of a computer or a cellular/smartphone is not permitted. Calculators will be checked for conformance with this regulation before candidates are allowed admission to the Assessment Center or testing room. Calculators that do not comply with these specifications are not permitted in the AMP Assessment Center or testing room.

## *Inclement Weather or Emergency*

In the event of inclement weather or unforeseen emergencies on the day of examination, HIMSS, in concert with AMP, will determine whether circumstances warrant the cancelation and subsequent rescheduling of a CPHIMS Examination. If testing personnel are able to conduct business, the examination usually proceeds as scheduled.

Every attempt is made to administer a CPHIMS Examination as scheduled; however, should a CPHIMS Examination be canceled, the scheduled candidate will receive notification following the examination regarding a rescheduled examination date or reapplication procedures. In the case of cancelation, no additional fee is required to test.

For computer administrations at AMP Assessment Centers, candidates may visit AMP's website at www.goAMP.com prior to the examination to determine if any Assessment Centers have been closed.

In the event of a personal emergency on the day of examination, a candidate may request consideration of rescheduling the examination without additional fee by contacting HIMSS in writing within 30 days of the scheduled testing session. A description of the emergency and supporting documentation are required. Rescheduling without an additional fee being imposed will be considered on a case-by-case basis.

## *Failing to Report for the CPHIMS Examination*

A candidate who fails to report for a scheduled CPHIMS Examination has the option to reschedule as stated on the previous page.

## Taking the CPHIMS Examination

After identity of the CPHIMS candidate has been verified and his/her calculator has been approved, the candidate is directed to a testing carrel for a computer administration or an assigned seat for a special administration. Candidates are provided one (1) sheet of scratch paper for calculations that must be returned to the examination proctor at the completion of testing. Failure to do so will result in the test score report not being released.

For a *paper-and-pencil administration*, the CPHIMS candidate is provided oral and written instructions about the examination administration process.

For a *computer administration at an AMP Assessment Center or a laptop administration*, the CPHIMS candidate is provided instructions on-screen. First, the candidate is instructed to enter his/her unique identification number.

Then, the candidate's photograph is taken and remains on-screen throughout the CPHIMS Examination session. Prior to attempting the CPHIMS Examination, the candidate is provided a short tutorial on using the software to take the examination. Tutorial time is NOT counted as part of the two (2) hours allowed for the examination. Only after a candidate is comfortable with the software and chooses to start the examination does the examination time begin.

The *computer monitors the time spent on the examination*. The CPHIMS Examination terminates at the two (2)-hour mark. Clicking on the "Time" button in the lower right portion of the screen reveals a digital clock that indicates the time remaining. The time feature may also be turned off during the CPHIMS Examination.

*Only one CPHIMS Examination question is presented at a time.* The question number appears in the lower right portion of the screen. The entire CPHIMS Examination question appears on-screen (question and four options labeled A, B, C, and D). Select an answer either by entering the letter of the option (A, B, C, or D) or using the mouse to click on the selected option. The letter of the selected option appears in the window in the lower left portion of the screen. To change an answer, enter a different option by entering the letter of the option or by clicking on the option using the mouse. An answer may be changed multiple times.

*To move to the next question*, click on the forward arrow (>) in the lower right corner of the screen. This action allows the candidate to move forward through the CPHIMS Examination question by question. To review a question, click the backward arrow (<) or use the left arrow key to move backward through the CPHIMS Examination.

*A CPHIMS Examination question may be left unanswered for return later in the testing session.* Questions may also be bookmarked for later review by clicking in the blank square to the right of the "Time" button. Click on the hand icon to advance to the next unanswered or bookmarked question on the CPHIMS Examination. To identify all unanswered or bookmarked questions, repeatedly click on the hand icon.

When the CPHIMS Examination is completed, the number of CPHIMS Examination questions answered is reported. If fewer than 115 questions were answered and time remains, return to the CPHIMS Examination and answer the remaining questions. Be sure to answer each examination question before ending the examination. There is no penalty for guessing.

Candidates may provide comments about a test item. Comments will be reviewed, but individual responses will not be provided.

- For a *computer administration*, online comments may be provided for any CPHIMS Examination question by clicking on the button displaying an exclamation point (!) to the left of the "Time" button. This opens a dialogue box where comments may be entered.
- For a *paper-and-pencil administration*, comments may be provided on the answer sheet on the day of the CPHIMS Examination.

## Rules for CPHIMS Examination

All CPHIMS Examination candidates must comply with the following rules during the CPHIMS Examination administration:

1. No personal items (including watches, hats, and coats), valuables, or weapons should be brought into the testing room. Only keys, wallets, and items required for medical needs are permitted. Books, computers, or other reference materials are strictly prohibited. If personal items are observed or heard (e.g., cellular/smartphone or alarm) in the testing room after the examination is started, the examination administration will be forfeited. AMP is not responsible for items left in the reception area.
2. Only silent, nonprogrammable calculators without alpha keys or printing capability are permitted in the testing room. Calculator malfunction during the CPHIMS Examination does not constitute grounds for challenging examination scores or requesting additional testing time.
3. Pencils will be provided during check-in. No personal writing instruments are allowed in the testing room.
4. CPHIMS Examinations are proprietary. CPHIMS Examination questions may not be recorded or shared with any individual in any manner. No cameras, notes, tape recorders, pagers, or cellular/smartphones or other recording devices are allowed in the testing room. Possession of a cellular/smartphone or other electronic devices is strictly prohibited and will result in dismissal from the CPHIMS Examination.
5. Eating, drinking, and smoking will not be permitted in the testing room.
6. No documents or notes of any kind may be removed from the testing room. For computer administrations, candidates are provided one sheet of scratch paper for calculations that must be returned to the examination proctor at the completion of testing. Failure to do so will result in the test score report not being released.
7. No questions concerning the content of the CPHIMS Examination may be asked of anyone during the CPHIMS Examination.
8. Permission from the CPHIMS Examination proctor is required to leave the testing room during the examination. No additional time is granted to compensate for time lost.

9. No guests, visitors, or family members are allowed in the testing room or reception areas.

Candidates observed engaging in any of the following conduct during the CPHIMS Examination may be dismissed from the CPHIMS Examination session, their score on the CPHIMS Examination voided, and the CPHIMS Examination fees forfeited. Evidence of misconduct is reviewed by HIMSS to determine whether the CPHIMS candidate will be allowed to reapply for the CPHIMS Examination. If reexamination is granted, a complete CPHIMS Examination application and full CPHIMS Examination fee are required.

- Gaining unauthorized admission to the CPHIMS Examination
- Creating a disturbance or being abusive or otherwise uncooperative
- Displaying and/or using electronic communications equipment, including but not limited to pagers and cellular/smartphones
- Talking or participating in conversation with other CPHIMS Examination candidates
- Giving or receiving help or being suspected of doing so
- Leaving the AMP Assessment Center or testing room during the CPHIMS Examination
- Attempting to record CPHIMS Examination questions in any manner or making notes
- Attempting to take the CPHIMS Examination for someone else
- Having possession of personal belongings
- Using notes, books, or other aids without it being noted on the roster
- Attempting to remove CPHIMS Examination materials or notes from the AMP Assessment Center or the testing room

## *Copyrighted Examination Questions*

All CPHIMS Examination questions are the copyrighted property of HIMSS. It is forbidden under federal copyright law to copy, reproduce, record, distribute, or display these CPHIMS Examination questions by any means, in whole or in part. Doing so may result in severe civil and criminal penalties.

# Following the CPHIMS Examination

## *Score Reports*

Score reports are issued by AMP, on behalf of HIMSS. Scores are reported in written form only, in person or by U.S. mail. Scores are not reported over the telephone, by electronic mail, or by facsimile.

- A candidate who takes the examination in *paper-and-pencil format* receives his/her score report from AMP by mail approximately five (5) weeks after the examination.
- A candidate who takes the examination *on a computer at an AMP Assessment Center or on laptop* receives his/her score report before leaving the testing center, except when the examination program is in a provisional score report mode.
- A candidate who takes the examination *outside of the United States on a computer at an AMP Assessment Center will not* receive his/her score before leaving the testing center. Results will be sent via U.S. mail within two (2) business days after completion of the examination to the applicant's address of record.

The score report indicates a "pass" or "fail," which is determined by the raw score on the total CPHIMS Examination. The score report also includes raw scores for each of the major and minor categories of the CPHIMS Examination Content Outline. A raw score is the number of questions answered correctly. Responses to individual CPHIMS Examination questions will not be disclosed to a candidate. Although the CPHIMS Examination consists of 115 questions, the score is based on 100 questions. Fifteen (15) questions are "pretest" questions and do not impact the candidate's score.

Recognition of CPHIMS certification and information about CPHIMS certification renewal is issued from HIMSS in about eight (8) weeks of successfully completing the CPHIMS Examination. This package is mailed to the address provided on the CPHIMS Examination application.

## How the CPHIMS Passing Score Is Set

The methodology used to set the initial minimum passing score is the Angoff method, in which expert judges estimate the passing probability of each question on the CPHIMS Examination. These ratings are averaged to determine the preliminary minimum passing score (i.e., the number correctly answered questions required to pass the examination). This method takes into account the difficulty of the CPHIMS Examination. The preliminary minimum passing score is validated by the performance of candidates. The passing standard is applied consistently across the CPHIMS candidates who take the same form of the CPHIMS Examination.

When new forms of the CPHIMS Examination are introduced, a certain number of CPHIMS Examination questions in the various content areas are replaced by new CPHIMS Examination questions. These changes may cause one form of the CPHIMS Examination to be slightly easier or harder than another form. To adjust for these differences in difficulty, a procedure called "equating" is used. For equated CPHIMS Examinations that have different passing scores, the equating process helps ensure that the levels of CPHIMS examinee knowledge are equivalent on the various CPHIMS Examination forms.

## Passing the CPHIMS Examination

An eligible candidate who passes the CPHIMS Examination is awarded the Certified Professional in Healthcare Information and Management Systems (CPHIMS) credential. Approximately eight (8) weeks after the candidate passes the CPHIMS Examination, HIMSS mails to the candidate a certificate of recognition. Information about CPHIMS certification renewal can be found at www. himss.org. The name on the certificate and the address to which the package is mailed are based on information in the candidate's HIMSS membership record. It is the candidate's responsibility to keep this information current.

HIMSS reserves the right to recognize publicly any candidate who has successfully completed the CPHIMS Examination. Scores are never reported over the phone.

## Failing the CPHIMS Examination

If a candidate does not pass the CPHIMS Examination, the score report includes a shortened application form to apply for retaking the examination.

- To schedule a retake of the CPHIMS Examination, a candidate may apply by using the online application and scheduling feature on www.goAMP.com or by submitting the reapplication form included with the score report. To use this shortened application form, the completed application and full CPHIMS Examination fee must be submitted and a CPHIMS Examination scheduled within the 90-day period following the failed examination.
- A candidate who applies to retake the CPHIMS Examination after 90 days following the failed examination date must submit a complete application and full examination fee.

There is no limit to the number of times an individual may take the CPHIMS Examination. Every retake requires submitting a CPHIMS Examination application and full CPHIMS Examination fee.

## Scores Canceled by HIMSS

HIMSS and AMP are responsible for maintaining the integrity of the scores reported. On occasion, occurrences such as computer malfunction or misconduct by a candidate may cause a score to be suspect. HIMSS is committed to rectifying such discrepancies as expeditiously as possible. HIMSS may void CPHIMS Examination results if, upon investigation, violation of CPHIMS regulations is discovered.

## Score Confidentiality

Information about a candidate for testing or renewal of certification and examination results is considered confidential; however, HIMSS reserves the right to use information supplied by or on behalf of a candidate in the conduct of research. Studies and reports concerning candidates contain no information identifiable with any candidate, unless authorized by the candidate.

Demographic information about a candidate is shared only when beneficial to the candidate. Scores are never reported to anyone other than the candidate, unless the candidate directs such a request in writing.

## Administrative Matters

### Duplicate Score Report

A candidate may purchase additional copies of their CPHIMS score report for a fee of $25 U.S. per copy. The request must be submitted in writing to AMP, must include the candidate's name, AMP identification number, mailing address, telephone number, date of examination, and examination taken, as well as the $25 U.S. fee payable to AMP. After receipt of the request, a duplicate score report is generally mailed in about two (2) weeks.

### Name and Address Change

Candidates are responsible for keeping current all contact information. HIMSS is not responsible for communication not received due to incorrect contact information. To update any contact information, the candidate should log in to the HIMSS Member Center or contact *HIMSS Individual Member Services* at member-support@himss.org.

# Renewal of CPHIMS Certification

Achieving CPHIMS certification is an indication of mastery of a well-defined body of knowledge at a point in time. Periodic renewal of the CPHIMS certification is required to maintain certified status and to demonstrate ongoing commitment to remain current in the field. Initial certification or renewal of certification is valid for three (3) years.

Eligible candidates who successfully complete the CPHIMS Examination are provided information about CPHIMS certification renewal requirements in a certification package sent by HIMSS. A copy of the CPHIMS renewal requirements and application is also available at www.CPHIMS.org. *The CPHIMS renewal application may be submitted up to six (6) months in advance, but no later than 30 days prior to the expiration date listed on the certificate.*

HIMSS e-mails notices to candidates of their pending certification expiration. Candidates are responsible for keeping their contact information accurate. HIMSS is not responsible for communications not received due to incorrect contact information in a candidate's record.

Candidates may renew the CPHIMS credential through one (1) of the following ways:

*Successful reexamination.* To renew this way, successfully pass the CPHIMS Examination no more than six (6) months prior to expiration of your CPHIMS certification (subject to usual fees and provisions for testing). An additional CPHIMS renewal fee is not required if a candidate selects this way to renew the designation.

*Completion of 45 clock hours of continuing professional education* over the three (3)-year renewal period and payment of the renewal fee. To renew this way, submit a complete CPHIMS renewal application with the appropriate fee and report all eligible continuing professional education activities that you completed during your renewal period. Eligible activities include attending professional organization conferences, completing online courses, and attending or teaching academic courses, among other activities. There is no limitation on the maximum allowable hours. Refer to the current CPHIMS renewal requirements and application for a description of eligible activities and other provisions for renewing your certification.

CPHIMS renewal application processing requires eight (8) weeks. Candidates who meet the renewal requirements receive in the mail (at the address in their membership record) a new certificate of recognition listing the new certification expiration date, as well as information about renewing the certification. Candidates are responsible for keeping current contact information in their membership record.

### Failing to Renew

A candidate who fails to renew his/her CPHIMS certification is no longer considered certified and may not use the CPHIMS credential in professional communications, including, but not limited to, letterhead, stationery, business cards, directory listings, and signatures. To regain certification, the individual must retake and pass the CPHIMS Examination (subject to the usual fees and provisions for testing).

## Appeals

A candidate who believes he/she was unjustly denied eligibility for the CPHIMS Examination, who challenges results of a CPHIMS Examination, or who believes he/she was unjustly denied renewal of certification may request reconsideration of the decision by submitting a written appeal to the HIMSS, c/o CPHIMS

Technical Committee, 33 W. Monroe St., Suite 1700, Chicago, IL 60603 USA. The CPHIMS candidate for certification or renewal of CPHIMS certification must provide evidence satisfactory to the Appeal Board that severe disadvantage was afforded the candidate during processing of an application for the CPHIMS Examination or renewal of the CPHIMS certification or prior to or during administration of a CPHIMS Examination. The appeal must be made within 45 days of receipt of a score report or any other official correspondence related to certification or renewal of certification from the HIMSS or its agents. The written appeal must also indicate the specific relief requested. The appealing candidate is required to submit a $100 U.S. fee (payable to HIMSS) with the written appeal. The fee will be refunded to the candidate if deemed justified through action of the Appeal Board. For additional regulations related to the appeal process, contact HIMSS.

## Checklist for Becoming Certified

■ Read the CPHIMS Candidate Handbook. Use the Examination Content Outline to focus study efforts.
■ Apply for the CPHIMS Examination by one (1) of the following ways:
  – Apply online for the examination and schedule an appointment to test on computer at an AMP Assessment Center. Visit www.goAMP.com, click on "Get Started," and then follow the online instructions.
  – Mail or fax the complete CPHIMS Examination application to AMP as directed on the form. Include the examination fee, sign the application, and submit both pages of the application. When confirmation of eligibility is received from AMP, make an appointment to take the examination.
■ Appear on time for the examination on the date and at the time and location confirmed. Bring the confirmation notice, identification as described in this Candidate Handbook, and a simple calculator.

# CERTIFIED PROFESSIONAL IN HEALTHCARE INFORMATION AND MANAGEMENT SYSTEMS (CPHIMS)

## *EXAMINATION APPLICATION*

This form is to be used for exams given at established AMP Assessment Centers only.

To apply for the CPHIMS Examination, complete this application and return it with the examination fee to

Applied Measurement Professionals, Inc. • CPHIMS Examination
• 18000 W. 105th St. • Olathe, KS 66061-7543 913-895-4650

## PERSONAL INFORMATION

_____

HIMSS Member Number
☐ I am not a member of HIMSS (a unique identification number will be assigned)

_____

Name (Last or Family Name, First, Middle Initial, Former Name) (Please enter names as you wish them to appear on your certificate)

_____

Name of Company (if work address)                          Title

_____

Mailing Address (Street Address, City, State/Province, Zip/Postal Code, Country)

_____

Daytime Telephone Number with country code if outside of North America          E-Mail Address

## EXAMINATION TYPE
☐ I am applying for a computer administration at an AMP Assessment Center.

## ELIGIBILITY FOR EXAMINATION
To be eligible for the CPHIMS Examination, a candidate must fulfill one (1) of the following requirements for education and work experience. Please check one that applies from list below.

☐ Baccalaureate degree, or global equivalent, plus five (5) years of associated information and management systems experience,* three (3) of those years in healthcare.

☐ Graduate degree, or global equivalent, plus three (3) years of associated information and management systems experience,* two (2) of those years in healthcare.

\* *Associated information and management systems experience includes experience in the following functional areas: administration/management, clinical information systems, e-health, information systems, or management engineering.*

## APPLICATION STATUS
☐ I am applying as a new candidate.
☐ I am applying as a reapplicant.
☐ I am applying for renewal of certification.

## MEMBERSHIP STATUS AND EXAMINATION FEE
### Membership Status
To be eligible for the reduced CPHIMS Examination fee, a candidate must be a current member of HIMSS.

For information on joining HIMSS, visit the HIMSS website at www.himss. org. Membership must be obtained before application for examination at the reduced fee can be honored. If you have applied for membership, but have not yet received your membership number, enter NEW in the space provided for membership number.

Enter your membership no.: _____

Examination Fee

Payment may be made by credit card, company check, cashier's check, or money order made payable to AMP.

☐ HIMSS Organizational Affiliate Member . . . . . . . $270 (U.S. dollars)

☐ HIMSS National Member . . . . . . . . $300 (U.S. dollars)

☐ Nonmember. . . . . . . . . . $375 (U.S. dollars)

☐ Rescheduling Fee . . . . . . . . $75 (U.S. dollars)

If payment is made by credit card, complete the following:

☐ VISA               ☐ MasterCard
☐ American Express   ☐ Discover

_____
Credit Card Number

_____
Expiration Date

_____
Your Name as It Appears on the Card

_____
Signature

## SPECIAL ACCOMMODATIONS

Do you require special disability-related accommodations during testing? ☐ No ☐ Yes

If yes, please complete the Request for Special Examination Accommodations form included with this handbook and submit it with an application and fee at least 45 days prior to the desired testing date. Specific information about special accommodations is provided in the handbook.

## DEMOGRAPHIC INFORMATION

The following demographic information is requested.

1. How many years of experience do you have in information and management systems?
   1. 3–5 years
   2. 6–10 years
   3. 11–15 years
   4. 16–20 years
   5. More than 20

2. How many years have you worked in healthcare information and management systems?
   1. 2–5 years
   2. 6–10 years
   3. 11–15 years
   4. 16–20 years
   5. More than 20

3. What type of facility most accurately describes your primary information and management systems activities?
   1. Hospital
   2. Health Care System (corp. office)
   3. Clinical Group Practice
   4. Other Provider
   5. Payer

6. Vendor Organization
7. Health Care Consulting Firm
8. Academic
9. Law/Investment Firm
10. Government

8. Staff
9. Student
10. Consultant

4. What is your level of responsibility?
   1. CEO
   2. CFO
   3. CIO
   4. COO
   5. Director/Department Head
   6. Other Senior Management
   7. Senior Staff/Manager

5. What is your principal work focus?
   1. Administrative/Management
   2. Clinical Systems and/or Applications
   3. IT Infrastructure, Systems Implementation, and Management
   4. Management Engineering
   5. Security/Privacy
   6. Telehealth/e-Health

I am a U.S. military veteran, active duty service member, or military spouse:
☐ Yes ☐ No

SIGNATURE

I certify that I agree to abide by regulations of the CPHIMS program contained in this handbook. I believe that I comply with all admission policies for the CPHIMS Examination. I certify that the information I have submitted in this application is complete and correct to the best of my knowledge and belief. I understand that if the information I have submitted is found to be incomplete or inaccurate, my application may be rejected or my examination results may be delayed or voided.

Name (Please Print): _____

Signature: _____   Date: _____

# REQUEST FOR SPECIAL EXAMINATION ACCOMMODATIONS

If you have a disability covered by the Americans with Disabilities Act, please complete this form and the Documentation of Disability-Related Needs on the reverse side so your accommodations for testing can be processed efficiently. The information you provide and any documentation regarding your disability and your need for accommodation in testing will be treated with strict confidentiality. Please return this form to AMP within 45 days of the desired testing date.

CANDIDATE INFORMATION

_____
Name (Last or Family Name, First, Middle Initial, Former Name)

_____
Mailing Address

_____
City                     State/Province          Zip Code/Postal Code and Country

_____
Daytime Telephone Number with country code if outside of North America        E-Mail Address

---

SPECIAL ACCOMMODATIONS
I request special accommodations for the _____ examination.

Please provide (check all that apply)
_____ Reader
_____ Extended examination time (time and a half)
_____ Reduced distraction environment
_____ Large-print examination (paper-and-pencil administration only)
_____ Circle answers in examination booklet (paper-and-pencil administration only)
_____ Other special accommodations (please specify)

_____
_____
_____

Comments:_____
_____
_____

**PLEASE READ AND SIGN:**
I give my permission for my diagnosing professional to discuss with AMP staff my records and history as they relate to the requested accommodation.

Signature:_____ Date: _____

---

Return this form with your examination application and fee to Examination Services Department, AMP, 18000 W. 105th St., Olathe, KS 66061-7543. If you have questions, call the Examination Services Department at 913-895-4600.

# DOCUMENTATION OF DISABILITY-RELATED NEEDS

Please have this section completed by an appropriate professional (education professional, physician, psychologist, or psychiatrist) to ensure that AMP is able to provide the required examination accommodations.

---

PROFESSIONAL DOCUMENTATION

I have known _____ since ___ / ___ / ___ in my capacity as a
                Candidate Name               Date (month/date/year)

_____.
          Professional Title

The candidate discussed with me the nature of the examination to be administered. It is my opinion that, because of this candidate's disability described below, he/she should be accommodated by providing the special arrangements listed on the reverse side.

Description of Disability: _____

_____

_____

_____

Signed: _____ Title: _____

Printed Name:_____

Address:_____

_____

Telephone Number: _____

Date: _____ License No. (if applicable): _____

---

Return this form with your examination application and fee to Examination Services Department, AMP, 18000 W. 105th St., Olathe, KS 66061-7543. If you have questions, call the Examination Services Department at 913-895-4600.

# Index

Acceptance testing, 103–104
Access controls, 110–111
Accountable care organization (ACO), 13–14
Accounting, 111
Accreditation organizations (AOs), 18–20
ACO, *see* Accountable care organization (ACO)
Administration management
    adhering to industry best practices, 154–155
    budget risk management, 159–160
    careers in healthcare IT, 145–146
    customer relationship management
        (CRM), 160–161
    customer service functions
      problem resolution, 157–158
      request tracking, 157
      service-level management, 156
    department documentation, 155–156
    facilitating steering committee
        meetings, 153–154
    financial risk management, 158
    and in-service programs, 146
    managing projects and project
        portfolios, 149–151
    managing vendor relationships, 151–153
    operational documentation, 155
    overview, 143–144
    roles and responsibilities
      general IT, 145
      healthcare IT, 145
      senior management, 144
    staff competency
      employee development, 146
      job-related IT certifications, 146–147
      miscellaneous professional
        development, 147
      and organizational training, 146
      performance evaluation, 148–149
    system documentation, 155
Administrative and financial services, 47–48
Administrative applications, 32

ADMs, *see* Automated dispensing machines
    (ADMs)
AHIMA, *see* American Health Information
    Management Association (AHIMA)
Ambulatory/outpatient care, 8
American College of Radiology, 31
American Health Information Management
    Association (AHIMA), 33
American Medical Informatics Association
    (AMIA), 15
American Telemedicine Association (ATA), 37
AMIA, *see* American Medical Informatics
    Association (AMIA)
AOs, *see* Accreditation organizations (AOs)
Application Service Providers (ASPs), 27
As-is process, 67
ASPs, *see* Application Service Providers (ASPs)
Asynchronous transfer mode (ATM), 29
ATA, *see* American Telemedicine Association
    (ATA)
ATM, *see* Asynchronous transfer mode (ATM)
Auditing, privacy and security, 113
Authentication, 110
Automated dispensing machines (ADMs), 47

Benchmarks, and leadership, 132
Best-of-breed *versus* single-vendor solution, 75
BPM, *see* Business process management (BPM)
BPMN, *see* Business Process Model Notation
    (BPMN)
BPR, *see* Business process reengineering (BPR)
Bring your own device (BYOD), 28, 71
Budget risk management, 159–160
Budgets, and leadership, 131–132
Bureau of Vital Statistics to the American Heart
    Association, 37
Business communications, and
    leadership, 133–137
Business continuity plans, 97–98, 113
Business process management (BPM), 66–67

Business Process Model Notation (BPMN), 71
Business process reengineering (BPR), 71
Buy *versus* build decision, 74–78
BYOD, *see* Bring your own device (BYOD)

CAHs, *see* Critical access hospitals (CAHs)
California Health Care Foundation (CHCF), 34
CAP, *see* College of American Pathologists (CAP)
CBI, *see* Clinical and business intelligence (CBI)
C-CDA, *see* Consolidated-Clinical Document Architecture (C-CDA)
CDSS, *see* Clinical decision support system (CDSS)
Center for Disease Control and Prevention, 12
Centers for Medicare & Medicaid Services (CMS), 13, 33, 130
Central processing unit (CPU), 46
Certification in Health Information Management (CHIM), 15
Certified Information Systems Security Professional (CISSP®), 14
Certified in Healthcare Privacy and Security (CHPS), 15
Certified Professional in Healthcare Information and Management Systems (CPHIMS) certification, 15, 147
CFO, *see* Chief finance officer (CFO)
Change control, 105
Change management, 90
CHC, *see* Community health center (CHC)
CHCF, *see* California Health Care Foundation (CHCF)
Chief finance officer (CFO), 154
Chief health information officer (CHIO), 15
Chief information officer (CIO), 14, 144
Chief information security officer (CISO), 144
Chief medical information officer (CMIO), 15, 144, 153
Chief nursing information officer (CNIO), 15, 144
Chief operating officer (COO), 153
Chief security officer (CSO), 14
Chief technology officer (CTO), 15, 144
Children's Health Insurance Program (CHIP), 9
CHIM, *see* Certification in Health Information Management (CHIM)
CHIO, *see* Chief health information officer (CHIO)
CHIP, *see* Children's Health Insurance Program (CHIP)

CHPS, *see* Certified in Healthcare Privacy and Security (CHPS)
CIO, *see* Chief information officer (CIO)
CISO, *see* Chief information security officer (CISO)
CISSP®, *see* Certified Information Systems Security Professional (CISSP®)
CLIA, *see* Clinical Laboratory Improvement Amendments (CLIA)
Clinical and business intelligence (CBI), 37
Clinical applications, 30–32
Clinical decision support system (CDSS), 47
Clinical functions, and systems analysis, 46–47, 54–56
Clinical Laboratory Improvement Amendments (CLIA), 31
CMIO, *see* Chief medical information officer (CMIO)
CMS, *see* Centers for Medicare & Medicaid Services (CMS)
CNIO, *see* Chief nursing information officer (CNIO)
College of American Pathologists (CAP), 31
Commercial off-the-shelf (COTS), 66
Communication protocols, 30
Community health center (CHC), 8–9
Comparative analysis
    benchmarks, 132
    budgets, 131–132
    financial and nonfinancial indicators, 132
    quality indicators, 132–133
    and systems analysis, 59–60
Comprehensive care services, 11
Computed tomography (CT), 31
Computerized practitioner order entry (CPOE), 47, 75, 91, 141
Conditions of participation (CoP), 19
Confidentiality, 111
Consolidated-Clinical Document Architecture (C-CDA), 11
Consulting services, and leadership, 137–138
Consumer applications, 33–35
COO, *see* Chief operating officer (COO)
CoP, *see* Conditions of participation (CoP)
Cost-benefit analysis, 61–62
Cost optimization, and revenue, 50
COTS, *see* Commercial off-the-shelf (COTS)
CPHIMS, *see* Certified Professional in Healthcare Information and Management Systems (CPHIMS) certification
CPOE, *see* Computerized practitioner order entry (CPOE)

CPT, *see* Current procedural terminology (CPT)
CPU, *see* Central processing unit (CPU)
Critical access hospitals (CAHs), 9
CRM, *see* Customer relationship management (CRM)
CSO, *see* Chief security officer (CSO)
CT, *see* Computed tomography (CT)
CTO, *see* Chief technology officer (CTO)
Current procedural terminology (CPT), 36
Customer relationship management (CRM), 160–161
Customer service functions
  problem resolution, 157–158
  request tracking, 157
  service-level management, 156
Cybersecurity, 113

DAMA®, *see* Data Management International (DAMA®)
Data analysis, 96
Data communication protocols, 30
Data integration, 36–37
  and availability, 111
Data management, 72–73
  controls, 112–113
Data Management International (DAMA®), 72
Data storage, in healthcare IT, 27
Data warehouses, and healthcare IT, 37
Define, measure, analyze, improve, control (DMAIC), 71
Department documentation, 155–156
Diagnostic and pharmaceutical services, 9
DICOM, *see* Digital Imaging and Communications in Medicine (DICOM)
Digital Imaging and Communications in Medicine (DICOM), 35, 68
Disaster recovery, 97–98, 113
Discharged not final billed (DNFB), 132
DMAIC, *see* Define, measure, analyze, improve, control (DMAIC)
DNFB, *see* Discharged not final billed (DNFB)

Educational strategies, for IT staff, 138–139
EHRs, *see* Electronic health records (EHRs)
Electronic health records (EHRs), 15, 25, 30, 46, 67, 112, 127, 144
Electronic materials management (EMM), 47
Electronic medical records (EMRs), *see* Electronic health records (EHRs)
Electronic medication administration records (eMARs), 75

EMARs, *see* Electronic medication administration records (eMARs)
EMM, *see* Electronic materials management (EMM)
Employee development, 146
EMRs, *see* Electronic health records (EHRs)
Enterprise project portfolio management (EPPM), 149
Enterprise risk management (ERM), 158
EPPM, *see* Enterprise project portfolio management (EPPM)
ERM, *see* Enterprise risk management (ERM)
Ethical business principles, and leadership, 130–131
European Cooperation for Accreditation, 31

FDA, *see* Food and Drug Administration (FDA)
Financial and administrative services, 47–48
Financial and nonfinancial indicators, 132
Financial applications, 32–33
Financial risk management, 158
Food and Drug Administration (FDA), 17, 28
For-profit private hospitals, 7
FTEs, *see* Full-time employees (FTEs)
Full-time employees (FTEs), 145

Gantt chart, 124
GDP, *see* Gross domestic product (GDP)
General practitioners (GPs), *see* Primary care providers (PCPs)
Government-managed hospitals, 6
Government role, and healthcare, 16–17
Gray-box testing, 102
Gross domestic product (GDP), 16–17
Group discussions and meetings, 137

Hardware, in healthcare IT
  data storage, 27
  medical devices, 28–29
  mobile devices, 27–28
  servers, 26–27
  technology infrastructure, 26
HCPC, *see* Health and Care Professions Council (HCPC)
Health and Care Professions Council (HCPC), 17
Health and Human Services (HHS), 130
Health and Social Care Information Centre (HSCIC), 12
Healthcare Information and Management Systems Society (HIMSS), 70, 129
Healthcare information systems, 95–96

Healthcare Information Technology Standards
   Panel (HITSP), 56
Healthcare organizations, 4–10
   access to comprehensive care services, 11
   and accreditation organizations (AOs), 18–20
   community, 8–9
   diagnostic and pharmaceutical services, 9
   effective transfers of care, 11–12
   general portability of care, 12
   healthcare payers, 9–10
   and HIT/HIM professions, 14–16
   hospitals, 5–8
   and organizational models of care, 13–14
   outpatient or ambulatory care, 8
   and professional associations, 17–18
   public and population health
      information, 12
   and regulatory agencies, 17
   and reimbursement for quality care, 13
   role of governments, 16–17
Healthcare payers, 9–10
Healthcare regulatory agencies, 17
Health Infomration Technology for Economic
      and Clinical Health (HITECH)
      Act, 47, 108
Health information exchanges (HIEs), 12,
      35, 108
Health information management (HIM), 14
Health Information Portability and
      Accountability Act (HIPAA), 15,
      108, 129
Health information technology (HIT)
   alternative processes for, 58–59
   careers in, 145–146
   clinical and business intelligence (CBI), 37
   comparative analysis, 59–60
   data integration, 36–37
   data warehouses, 37
   deficiencies in
      industry standardization, 58
      patient support and satisfaction, 57
      prescription errors, 58
      revenue generation, 57–58
   hardware in
      data storage, 27
      medical devices, 28–29
      mobile devices, 27–28
      servers, 26–27
      technology infrastructure, 26
   health information exchanges (HIEs), 35
   implementation
      administrative and financial
         services, 47–48

   clinical functions, 46–47, 54–56
   infrastructure, 48–49
   security-related applications, 48–49
   integration status, 56–57
   interoperability and standards, 35–36
   leadership and strategic plan, 122–124
   networks in
      communications, 30
      infrastructure, 29–30
   overview, 3–4
   privacy and security, 38–39
   proposal evaluation, 60–61
   software in
      administrative applications, 32
      clinical applications, 30–32
      consumer applications, 33–35
      financial applications, 32–33
   telehealth and telemedicine, 37–38
Health Level Seven (HL7), 11, 28, 35, 67, 92
Health Resources and Services Administration
      (HRSA), 9
HHS, *see* Health and Human Services (HHS)
HIEs, *see* Health information exchanges
      (HIEs)
HIM, *see* Health information management
      (HIM)
HIMSS, *see* Healthcare Information and
      Management Systems Society (HIMSS)
HIPAA, *see* Health Information Portability and
      Accountability Act (HIPAA)
HIT, *see* Health information technology (HIT)
HITECH, *see* Health Infomration Technology
      for Economic and Clinical Health
      (HITECH) Act
HITSP, *see* Healthcare Information Technology
      Standards Panel (HITSP)
HL7, *see* Health Level Seven (HL7)
Hospitals, 5–8
HRSA, *see* Health Resources and Services
      Administration (HRSA)
HSCIC, *see* Health and Social Care Information
      Centre (HSCIC)

ICD, *see* International Statistical Classification
      of Diseases and Related Health
      Problems (ICD)
ICUs, *see* Intensive care units (ICUs)
IDS, *see* Integrated delivery system (IDS)
IEEE, *see* Institute of Electrical and Electronics
      Engineers (IEEE)
IFHIMA, *see* International Federation of Health
      Information Management Associations
      (IFHIMA)

IHE, *see* Integrating the Healthcare Enterprise (IHE)
IMIA, *see* International Medical Informatics Association (IMIA)
Industry standardization, and systems analysis, 58
Industry trends, and system design, 68
Information Systems Security Certification Consortium, Inc. (ISC2®), 14
Information Technology Infrastructure Library (ITIL), 127, 147
Infrastructure
    information, 71–72
    and systems analysis, 48–49
In-service programs, 146
Institute of Electrical and Electronics Engineers (IEEE), 68
Institute of Medicine (IOM), 141
Integrated delivery system (IDS), 13
Integrating the Healthcare Enterprise (IHE), 75
Integration testing, 103
Intensive care units (ICUs), 46
International Federation of Health Information Management Associations (IFHIMA), 129
International Medical Informatics Association (IMIA), 129
International Society for Pharmacoeconomics and Outcomes Research (ISPOR), 36
International Statistical Classification of Diseases and Related Health Problems (ICD), 35–36
Interoperability, and standards, 35–36
IOM, *see* Institute of Medicine (IOM)
ISC2®, *see* Information Systems Security Certification Consortium, Inc. (ISC2®)
ISPOR, *see* International Society for Pharmacoeconomics and Outcomes Research (ISPOR)
ITIL, *see* Information Technology Infrastructure Library (ITIL)
IT strategic plan and leadership, 122–124

JCI, *see* Joint Commission International (JCI)
Job-related IT certifications, 146–147
Joint Commission International (JCI), 19, 130

Kaizen, 128
Key performance indicators (KPIs), 57
KPIs, *see* Key performance indicators (KPIs)

LANs, *see* Local area networks (LANs)
Leadership

    and business communications, 133–137
    and comparative analysis strategies
        benchmarks, 132
        budgets, 131–132
        financial and nonfinancial indicators, 132
        quality indicators, 132–133
    educational strategies for IT staff, 138–139
    effectiveness and user satisfaction, 125–127
    and ethical business principles, 130–131
    group discussions and meetings, 137
    and in-house consulting services, 137–138
    and IT strategic plan, 122–124
    legal and regulatory standards, 129–130
    opportunities and constraints, 127–128
    organizational environment, 119–120
    organizational strategic planning
        goals, 119
        mission, 118
        values, 119
        vision, 118–119
    performance evaluation, 124–125
    and policy implementation, 128–129
    quality standards and practices, 141
    and risk management, 140
    staying current on IT technologies and trends, 139–140
    technical and information needs of organization, 120–122
Lean Six Sigma, 66, 71, 147
Legal and regulatory standards, 129–130
Leonard, Michael, 127
Local area networks (LANs), 29

Magnetic Resonance Imaging (MRI), 28
Medical devices, in healthcare IT, 28–29
MHealth (mobile app), 38
Mobile devices, in healthcare IT, 27–28
MPLS, *see* Multiprotocol label switching (MPLS)
MRI, *see* Magnetic Resonance Imaging (MRI)
Multiprotocol label switching (MPLS), 29

National Committee on Vital and Health Statistics, 33
Nationwide Health Information Network (NHIN), 12
Needs analysis, in healthcare facilities
    operational needs, 49
    patient access to services, 50–51
    patient quality of care, 50
    patient safety, 50
    prioritization, 51–52
    revenue and cost optimization, 50
    staff productivity and satisfaction, 50

Networks, in healthcare IT
    communications, 30
    infrastructure, 29–30
NHIN, *see* Nationwide Health Information
    Network (NHIN)
Nonprofit private hospitals, 7

Office of the National Coordinator
    (ONC), 56, 145
ONC, *see* Office of the National Coordinator
    (ONC)
Operational documentation, 155
Operational needs, 49
Operational testing, 102–103
Organisation for Economic Cooperation and
    Development (OECD), 4
Organizational change management, 90
Organizational environment, 119–120
Organizational models of care, 13–14
Organizational roles, privacy and
    security, 111–112
Organizational strategic planning
    goals, 119
    mission, 118
    values, 119
    vision, 118–119
Organizational training, and staff
    competency, 146
Outpatient/ambulatory care, 8

PACS, *see* Picture archiving and
    communication system (PACS)
Patient access to services, 50–51
Patient Protection and Affordable Care
    Act, 10, 13
Patient quality, of care, 50
Patient safety, 50
PCPs, *see* Primary care providers (PCPs)
Performance evaluation
    of administration management
        staff, 148–149
    leadership, 124–125
Personal health records (PHRs), 25, 30,
    33, 108
Pharmaceutical and diagnostic services, 9
PHI, *see* Protected health information (PHI);
    Protected Health Information (PHI)
PHRs, *see* Personal health records (PHRs)
Physician Quality Reporting System
    (PQRS), 13
Picture archiving and communication system
    (PACS), 28, 47
Planning postactivation activities, 94

PMBOK®, *see* Project Management Body of
    Knowledge (PMBOK®)
PMOs, *see* Project management offices
    (PMOs)
PMP®, *see* Project Management Professional
    (PMP®)
PMs, *see* Project managers (PMs)
Point objective (RPO), 69
Policies and procedures (P&Ps), 128–129,
    155–156
Policy implementation, and
    leadership, 128–129
Portability of care, 12
PPM, *see* Project portfolio management
    (PPM)
P&Ps, *see* Policies and procedures (P&Ps)
PQRS, *see* Physician Quality Reporting System
    (PQRS)
Prescription errors, and systems analysis, 58
Primary care providers (PCPs), 8
Privacy and security, of EHRs, 38–39
    auditing, 113
    business continuity plans, 113
    confidentiality, 111
    data integrity and availability, 111
    data management controls, 112–113
    definitions of, 108–109
    disaster recovery, 113
    ongoing system evaluation, 113–114
    organizational roles, 111–112
    overview, 107–108
    risk assessment, 109
    user access controls, 110–111
    vulnerability remediation, 110
Private hospitals, 6–7
Problem resolution, 157–158
Professional development, 147
Professional healthcare associations, 17–18
Project Management Body of Knowledge
    (PMBOK®), 150
Project management offices (PMOs), 138, 149
Project Management Professional (PMP®), 147
Project managers (PMs), 149
Project portfolio management (PPM), 149–151
Proposal sensitivity analysis, 61–62
Protected Health Information (PHI), 14, 28, 109

Quality indicators, and leadership, 132–133
Quality standards and practices, 141

Radio frequency identification (RFID), 47
RDBMSs, *see* Relational database management
    systems (RDBMSs)

Really simple syndication (RSS), 140
Recovery time objective (RTO), 69
Regional health information organizations
    (RHIOs), 35
Registered Health Information Administrator
    (RHIA), 15
Registered Health Information Technologist
    (RHIT), 15
Regression testing, 104
Relational database management systems
    (RDBMSs), 48
Request for information (RFI), 82, 86
    and system design, 73–78
Request for proposal (RFP), 82, 86
Request tracking, 157
Return on investment (ROI), 66, 158
Revenue and cost optimization, 50, 57–58
Review team members selection, 85–86
Revision control, *see* Version control
RFI, *see* Request for information (RFI)
RFID, *see* Radio frequency identification
    (RFID)
RFP, *see* Request for proposal (RFP)
RHIA, *see* Registered Health Information
    Administrator (RHIA)
RHIOs, *see* Regional health information
    organizations (RHIOs)
RHIT, *see* Registered Health Information
    Technologist (RHIT)
Risk assessment, 109
Risk management
    budget, 159–160
    financial, 158
    and leadership, 140
ROI, *see* Return on investment (ROI)
Role-based access, 110–111
RPO, *see* Point objective (RPO)
RSS, *see* Really simple syndication (RSS)
RTO, *see* Recovery time objective (RTO)

SBARC, *see* Situation, background, assessment,
    recommendation, and communication
    (SBARC)
Secondary Use Services (SUS), 12
Security audits, 105
Security-related applications, 48–49
Servers, in healthcare IT, 26–27
Service-level agreement (SLA), 124, 152
Service-level management, 156
Situation, background, assessment,
    recommendation, and communication
    (SBARC), 147
SLA, *see* Service-level agreement (SLA)

SMART, *see* Specific, measurable,
    attainable, relevant, and time
    bound (SMART)
SNOMED CT, *see* Systematized Nomenclature
    of Medicine - Clinical Terms
    (SNOMED CT)
Software, in healthcare IT
    administrative applications, 32
    clinical applications, 30–32
    consumer applications, 33–35
    financial applications, 32–33
Specific, measurable, attainable, relevant, and
    time bound (SMART), 119
Staff competency, administration
    educational strategies, 138–139
    employee development, 146
    job-related IT certifications, 146–147
    miscellaneous professional
        development, 147
    and organizational training, 146
    performance evaluation, 148–149
    productivity and satisfaction, 50
Standards compliance, of system design, 68
Steering committee meetings, 153–154
Strengths, weaknesses, opportunities, and
    threats (SWOT), 123
Stress testing, 103
SUS, *see* Secondary Use Services (SUS)
SWOT, *see* Strengths, weaknesses,
    opportunities, and threats (SWOT)
Systematized Nomenclature of Medicine-
    Clinical Terms (SNOMED CT), 35
System components compatibility, 67
System documentation, 155
System evaluation, of privacy and
    security, 113–114
System implementation
    process, 89–90
    solutions, 91–92
    strategies, 90–91
System integration, 92–93
Systems analysis
    and comparative analysis, 59–60
    cost–benefit analysis, 61–62
    deficiencies in healthcare IT
        industry standardization, 58
        patient support and satisfaction, 57
        prescription errors, 58
        revenue generation, 57–58
    and IT implementation
        administrative and financial
            services, 47–48
        clinical functions, 46–47, 54–56

infrastructure, 48–49
  security-related applications, 48–49
and needs analysis
  operational needs, 49
  patient access to services, 50–51
  patient quality of care, 50
  patient safety, 50
  prioritization, 51–52
  revenue and cost optimization, 50
  staff productivity and satisfaction, 50
overview, 45–46
proposal evaluation, 60–61
proposal sensitivity analysis, 61–62
work plan development
  accountability, 54
  background, 52–53
  executive summary, 52
  goals and objectives, 53
  resources, 53–54
Systems design
  business process management
    (BPM), 66–67
  buy *versus* build decision, 74–78
  and industry trends, 68
  overview, 65–66
  and request for information (RFI), 73–78
  standards compliance, 68
  system components compatibility, 67
  team structure, 68–69
  technical specifications, 69–73
    business process reengineering (BPR), 71
    data management, 72–73
    information infrastructure, 71–72
    usability, 70–71
System selection
  activities, 86–89
  criteria, 83–85
  and organizational change
    management, 90
  overview, 82–83
  of review team members, 85–86
Systems testing and evaluation
  final evaluation, 105–106
  methodologies, 100–101
  overview, 99
  purpose of, 99–101
  test controls, 104–105
  test execution, 102–104
  testing tools, 101–102

test reporting, 105
test strategy, 101
System support, 97

Technology infrastructure, 26
Telehealth, 37–38
Telemedicine, 37–38
Test controls, 104–105
Test execution, 102–104
Testing tools, 101–102
Test reporting, 105
Test strategy, 101
Transfers of care, 11–12

UMM, *see* Usability Maturity Model (UMM)
Unit testing, 103
Usability Maturity Model (UMM), 70
User access controls, 110–111
User and operational manuals and training, 93
User Experience (UX) Community, 70
User satisfaction, and leadership, 125–127
UX, *see* User Experience (UX) Community

Vendor relationships, managing, 151–153
Version control, 104
Veterans Health Administration, 73
Virtual private networks (VPNs), 29
Voice over Internet protocol (VoIP), 29, 123
VoIP, *see* Voice over Internet protocol (VoIP)
VPNs, *see* Virtual private networks (VPNs)
Vulnerability remediation, and EHRs, 110

WANs, *see* Wide area networks (WANs)
WBS, *see* Work breakdown structure (WBS)
White-box testing, 102
WHO, *see* World Health Organization (WHO)
Wide area networks (WANs), 29
Work breakdown structure (WBS), 149
Work plan development
  accountability, 54
  background, 52–53
  executive summary, 52
  goals and objectives, 53
  resources, 53–54
World Health Organization (WHO), 3, 29

XML Process Definition Language (XPDL), 71
XPDL, *see* XML Process Definition Language
    (XPDL)